THE AMERICAN DREAM IN VIETNAMESE

THE AMERICAN DREAM
IN VIETNAMESE

Nhi T. Lieu

 University of Minnesota Press

Minneapolis

London

The publication of this book has been aided by a College of Liberal Arts subvention grant awarded by the University of Texas at Austin.

An earlier version of chapter 3 was published as "Remembering 'The Nation' through Pageantry: Femininity and the Politics of Vietnamese Womanhood in the *Hoa Hau Ao Dai Contest*," *Frontiers: A Journal of Women Studies* 21, no. 1 (2000): 127–51; reprinted with permission of the University of Nebraska Press; copyright 2000 by Frontiers Editorial Collective. An earlier version of chapter 4 appeared as "Performing Culture in Diaspora: Assimilation and Hybridity in *Paris by Night* Videos and Vietnamese American Niche Media," in *Alien Encounters: Popular Culture in Asian America*, eds. Mimi Thi Nguyen and Thuy Linh Nguyen Tu, 194–220 (Durham, N.C.: Duke University Press); copyright 2007 by Duke University Press; all rights reserved; reprinted with permission.

Published by the University of Minnesota Press
111 Third Avenue South, Suite 290
Minneapolis, MN 55401-2520
http://www.upress.umn.edu

Library of Congress Cataloging-in-Publication Data
Lieu, Nhi T.
The American Dream in Vietnamese / Nhi T. Lieu.
  p. cm.
Includes bibliographical references and index.
ISBN 978-0-8166-6569-3 (hc : acid-free paper) – ISBN 978-0-8166-6570-9 (pb: acid-free paper)
1. Vietnamese Americans–Ethnic identity. 2. Vietnamese Americans–Cultural assimilation. 3. Popular culture–United States. 4. Popular culture–Vietnam. I. Title.
E184.V53L54 2011
305.895922'073–dc22
                    2010032641

Printed in the United States of America on acid-free paper
The University of Minnesota is an equal-opportunity educator and employer.
18 17 16 15 14 13 12 11   10 9 8 7 6 5 4 3 2 1

This book is dedicated to my family, the nucleus of my support system: my lifelong partner, Toan Leung; my parents, Mo Lieu and Nhung Truong; and my children, Sophie and Ethan.

Contents

Introduction   Private Desires on
Public Display

MORE THAN THREE DECADES have passed since the fall of Saigon, but the jarring words *Viet Nam* still haunt many Americans. Known as the unforgettable war lost by the United States, "Viet Nam" was not regarded by the popular media as a nation in its own right. Torn by political conflicts that unleashed massive confusion and tragedy upon its own people, the besieged country was seen as an unfathomable quagmire that divided the American nation and continues to resonate darkly in America's historical memory, especially in light of our contemporary involvement in Iraq and Afghanistan. For the Vietnamese refugees and immigrants who fled the war and their defeated nation, starting a new life elsewhere afforded them countless opportunities as well as insurmountable challenges. From these bleak circumstances, they have constructed for themselves new ways to make sense of their experiences.

Metropolitan settings and their surrounding suburbs throughout the world have become new places of resettlement for a significant number of people who fled Vietnam during and since the fall of Saigon in 1975. Vibrant ethnic neighborhoods and communities thrive in global cities, serving not only tourists, but also continuous flows of new immigrants who relocated in the aftermath of empire and colonialism. While these areas of immigrant resettlement serve as gathering places for dispersed members of the Vietnamese community, spatial anonymity in these locations has paradoxically allowed for the proliferation and public display of the most visible signs of diasporic Vietnamese cultural production. In the form of glossy airbrushed posters, hypervisible images of diasporic Vietnamese entertainers cover storefront windows of Vietnamese-owned restaurants and ethnic businesses, advertising the latest concert/entertainment variety show coming to town. The ads contain collages of singers, dancers, and performers where female artists are scantily clad or provocatively posed in form-fitting

Figure 1. A storefront window in London, England, prominently features a poster advertising *Paris by Night* 75 "Journey to the Far East." From *Paris by Night* 77 "30 Nam Vien Xu"("30 Years Abroad"), directed by Michael Watt (2005).

traditional and modern clothing, and male artists appear fashionably hip and ultra cool in flashy colored suits.

The images depicted on the posters are often so eye-catching they elicit responses of sexual curiosity and risk potential for narrow interpretation by a general public that does not understand Vietnamese culture in its contemporary form. For instance, one outlandish ad featuring young Vietnamese women in bikinis prompted a non-Vietnamese onlooker I overheard to exclaim lustfully, "What a race full of hotties!" outside a New York City Vietnamese restaurant. The prevalent use of sex to market the diasporic Vietnamese entertainment industry and the very public display of exotic, sexy Asian bodies on the posters capture the attention of people from both inside and outside the community. Nonetheless, such comments made by people unfamiliar with Vietnamese cultural productions not only misconstrue the posters' immediate functions, but also fail to recognize the cultural cues connected to the images. Because the fine print is written in Vietnamese, the signs of Vietnamese popular culture operate only at the superficial level of racial difference. The arousing images of Asian women grab the attention and heighten the sexual interest of those outside the community while engendering Orientalist assumptions.[1] Reducing cultural forms to mere sexual representations, these marketing strategies risk dangerous potential misreading by those outside the community while reinforcing self-Orientalization.

For people familiar with the activities of Vietnamese immigrant communities, however, these posters contain deeper cultural meaning beyond the hypersexualized veneers. The recurring use of sex appeal remains an effective marketing strategy to attract audiences, but the posters featuring exilic Vietnamese pop stars represent a rare opportunity for local Vietnamese communities to participate in a social gathering with their compatriots.[2] Attendance at the event itself promises to be a special experience not only of nostalgia and remembering but also of glamour and style. Members of the community attend live shows to see their favorite Vietnamese celebrities and to be seen by others. Formal clothing is usually not required, but men often dress in their fanciest suits, while women don the traditional *ao dai*, the flowing tunic symbolic of Vietnamese femininity, or an evening gown as if they were attending a Hollywood movie premiere or an awards ceremony. Treating the event with such regard, the entertainers themselves reciprocate the performance to their fans by mimicking American movie stars and music artists as well as the lure associated with the mainstream entertainment industry.

The universal appeal and overwhelming popularity of the Vietnamese musical variety shows are so striking that almost every person of Vietnamese heritage, regardless of his or her level of Vietnamese language comprehension, immediately recognizes the meanings behind the posters and the niche entertainment industry they represent. This alternative culture industry, which formed quickly after the refugees escaped from Vietnam, has produced a wide array of popular cultural forms from live music and dance shows to recorded audio-visual materials in the form of cassettes, videotapes, compact discs, karaoke laser discs, and DVDs. Whether one is an adoring fan or a critical viewer, visual media such as the posters function to attract potential Vietnamese audiences. Their public presence in urban spaces of Vietnamese settlement indicates that a marketable community is nearby; their ubiquity across national and state boundaries attests to the global circulation of Vietnamese cultural production and the transnational character of the Vietnamese diaspora.

I juxtapose the diametrically opposed images of the despondent war-torn refugees with that of the modern diasporic subjects embodied by the performers on the glossy posters because they illustrate how the first image paralyzes us if we limit ourselves to seeing the Vietnamese experience as such, while the second image has the potential to deepen and expand our cultural knowledge about these people and their desires to live their lives free from the constraints of the first image. In particular, these images point us to the vast and wide-ranging ways we can powerfully investigate the historical implications of these experiences as they are linked to the American past.

I first encountered the cultural forms I allude to above during my teen-age years growing up in the mid-1980s in Southern California. My parents enjoyed consuming popular culture created by Vietnamese immigrants because it offered them an alternative form of entertainment from main-stream American media fare. Watching video recordings of musical perfor-mances in Vietnamese allowed them to wax nostalgic over love songs they had heard in Vietnam while taking pride in the talent "our community" was able to nurture after migrating to the United States. On the other hand, my brother and I had no interest in ethnic media except when a Vietnamese performer would attempt to sing a familiar American pop tune. Growing up in the 1980s, we were loyal fans of popular American and British per-formers and bands such as Michael Jackson, Madonna, Cyndi Lauper, the Go-Gos, and Duran Duran, and we laughed whenever a Vietnamese immi-grant singer would perform an imitation of these stars in their heavily accented English. It was even more unnatural for us to see Vietnamese per-formers dancing and gyrating on stage as if they were the *Solid Gold* danc-ers. Though disgruntled by what they considered "inappropriate acts" that deviated from "proper" Vietnamese behavior, my parents used these star-tling images to instruct us how *not* to behave. Meanwhile, they still wanted us to watch these videos because the next performance might teach us something about Vietnamese culture.

My parents' ambivalence toward these variety show videos reveals a tell-ing aspect about Vietnamese diasporic cultural production and the rela-tionships viewers forge with these popular forms of culture. The experience of watching gave my parents and those in their generation a mode for remi-niscing and preserving their memories, but their discomfort and reluctance to accept the videos' sexualized imagery illustrate not only disagreement with but also uncertainty about the role cultural production would have in forming the identities of the next generation. Nevertheless, the videos remained the only source for observing some semblance of our cultural heritage at the time. Their presence in our home served as a disruption to the mainstream television programming we had voraciously consumed in our eagerness to learn English. As a viewing option that featured Vietnamese language, music, personalities, and overall entertainment, the videos offered an alternative that placed the Vietnamese experience at the center amid multiple marginalities. In some ways, my parents enjoyed the utopian forms of entertainment and believed they allowed us to connect to some sense of culture and history we would otherwise be losing. Yet, as theorist Nancy Fraser warns, "[s]ubaltern counterpublics are not always necessarily virtuous. Some of them, alas, are explicitly antidemocratic and antiegalitarian."[3] My parents were loath to wholeheartedly embrace a subaltern counterpublic that was dictated by an assimilationist project. Their hesitancy and cautious acceptance also represented a larger fear and anxiety about the role popular culture would play in shaping our identities as Vietnamese growing up in the United States.

Having now been in existence for more than twenty-five years, the low-budget productions of my childhood have since transformed into arguably the most popular cultural form in the Vietnamese diaspora today. These changes can be measured by adaptations to technology in form as well as in content. Early video productions were initially released on single VHS tapes in the 1980s. However, as the shows got longer and more elaborate, they were extended to double videos and then packaged as triple videos by the 1990s. Videos are now being phased out and replaced by DVD technology. The global circulation of Vietnamese exilic cultural production through various forms of portable electronic and digital technology in marginal spaces of "ethnic" media has created a trend that Hamid Naficy calls "decentralized global narrowcasting."[4] Similar to the televisual productions of Iranians in Los Angeles (profiled in Naficy's work), exilic Vietnamese media productions, coexisting alongside mainstream media, cater to ethnic Vietnamese in the diaspora. Placing Vietnamese bodies at the center and celebrating exilic talent with pride, the diasporic entertainment industry has created a niche media system and a market that willingly consumes what it produces. The infrastructure that makes up the industry produces videos that work in tandem with promotional traveling concerts. The live concert shows are then made available for wide distribution and mass consumption to Vietnamese throughout the diaspora and as counterfeits in Vietnam. Despite the reopening of Vietnamese borders to commerce and tourism in recent years, the vocal politics of anticommunism continues to dictate the tenor of the community's relationship to the homeland. Most Vietnamese immigrants believe that Vietnam is a repressive communist country with a corrupt government that continues to commit human rights violations against its people and this idea has only strengthened their sense of cultural nationalism. The status of exiles, especially in the early period of Vietnamese migration, has both stimulated cultural production and made the collective consumption of media, electronic technology, and videos the primary mode for the Vietnamese in diaspora to imagine themselves as a community. Cultural production in the age of electronic media and heightened technology has thus linked a people whose sense of nostalgia is girded by a fervent belief of their exile.

The American Dream in Vietnamese is the first full-length project that examines how generative sites of cultural production contribute meaningfully to the study of Vietnamese American identity formation. Drawing particular attention to undertheorized, previously neglected cultural expressions in leisure and entertainment, this book analyzes live music variety shows and videos, beauty pageants, Internet websites, and other cultural forms created by and for the Vietnamese diaspora. These sites of the "popular" are repositories for desires and fantasies that allow for investigations of simultaneously conflicting processes of assimilation, cultural preservation, and invention, alongside gendered and classed dimensions of ethnic identity.

By *Vietnamese American* I am referring to the population of people defined by Monique T. D. Truong as "Americans of Vietnamese descent: including immigrants who may have arrived prior to 1975; refugees who started arriving in 1975; those who entered the U.S. as immigrants, starting in 1979, through the Orderly Departure Program; as well as the preceding generations who have been and will be born in the United States."[5] I borrow from Truong's practical definition of the term *Vietnamese American* to connect the subjects and experiences of immigrants and refugees in my study. Moreover, I will also expand the term to include those who have settled outside of the United States that constitute the Vietnamese diaspora. There also exists a small constituency who define themselves as "exiles" from their homeland. While this definition may have been more precise in the early period of refugee resettlement, those who choose an exilic identity do so through a staunch anticommunist political stance and a self-imposition, since members of the Vietnamese diaspora are free to travel to and from Vietnam, particularly after the early 1990s.[6] When the United States lifted the trade embargo with Vietnam and reestablished diplomatic relations with the former enemy, Vietnamese Americans began returning to the former homeland and reconnecting with family members. Though these relatively liberal policies facilitate travel, many still regard familial relationships as "private" matters and continue to show contempt for state policies. Thus, as long as the Vietnamese state remains guided by communist ideology, Vietnamese immigrants desiring a free Vietnam will maintain an "exilic" relationship with their former homeland.[7]

In addition to problematizing these various incarnations of ethnic and diasporic identity, this book examines the Vietnamese immigrant experience through the lens of popular culture and serves as a critique of the discourses circulating in the mainstream media and academic institutions that often treat refugees as victims traumatized by war and devastation. To understand Vietnamese American subjectivity, it is imperative not only to delve into this community's imagination and desires for belonging, but also to view it as one formed through U.S. ideology and imperialism. Popular culture has been central to the lives of Vietnamese refugees and immigrants, yet the space of the cultural often has been neglected in studies of this population. Introduced and exposed to American democratic ideals and consumer capitalism before migrating to the imperial center, Vietnamese refugees arrived in the United States with hopes of assimilating, fitting in, and becoming free subjects in an advanced capitalist society; in essence, they wished to live the American Dream. Nowhere are these fantasies played out more vividly than in the entertainment industry that Vietnamese Americans built for themselves almost immediately after migrating to the United States. The circulation of manufactured images of transcendence through mediated technologies and sites of Vietnamese American cultural production served to produce and reproduce their immigrant desires. The public displays of these desires dramatize the community's struggle to define itself against the legacy of the refugee label that continues to pathologize their experiences in American society.

Vietnamese Americans have used popular culture to fashion their identities in complex ways—employing new technologies and marking their diasporic experiences as distinct from other racialized ethnic minorities precisely through their entangled past with the United States. In "Notes on Deconstructing the 'Popular,'" Stuart Hall emphasizes the ways capital can change people's identities by getting them to buy new products. Capital suggests novelty as a way of promoting new desires, but also ensures repetition and sameness (tradition, nostalgia, and fixed notions of culture) because corporate enterprise can easily identify market segments through these means.[8] My book's investment in Vietnamese cultural production thrives on these contradictions. Hall's seminal essay on popular culture frames this study in that the creation and reproduction of Vietnamese American cultural forms flourish on capitalist principles compatible with the American Dream. For Vietnamese refugees, who feel they were abandoned by the Americans only to lose a war to the communists, the desire to assimilate into a new environment coupled with the need to be free subjects in an advanced capitalist society necessitated both the creation of new cultural forms and the erasure of the refugee image that circulated in mainstream popular culture. Popular forms of cultural expression would in essence function simultaneously as historical archives documenting the experiences of Vietnamese migration as well as tools for expressing modern subjectivities. Moreover, they created alternative forms of leisure and entertainment that mediated the process of assimilation while providing an avenue for consumption. It is within these spaces of consumption that we are able to discern the production of desire—the desire to create new identities and to forge ways to culturally and socially pass and belong to the American nation.

Vietnamese immigrants have been particularly resourceful in adapting new technologies to advance their niche culture industry. While the use of technology may be novel, the forms of cultural invention are not necessarily new. Rather, as Fredric Jameson suggests in "Reification and Utopia in Mass Culture," popular cultural productions often thrive on genre and repetition.[9] Vietnamese diasporic cultural productions have relied upon the variety show genre because it combines song and dance elements to present a utopian vision of pleasure and free bodily movement. However, in keeping with "tradition," or the preservation of "Vietnamese culture," the performances in these shows also thrive on recycling and repeating music that invokes nostalgia and the sounds of the homeland. While Vietnamese immigrants aspire to restart their new lives, they remain tethered by the memories of their past. In her study of music in the refugee experience, Adelaida Reyes has poignantly noted that music, in the context of forced migration, functions in ways that not only trigger memories of a past life experience, but also work as an ideological tool that challenges the repressive state from which the refugees were forcibly expelled.[10] She explains that the refugees in the camps she studied preferred sad songs and love songs because the communist government prohibited these songs.[11] Responding to the restrictions of life under communist repression, Vietnamese refugees immediately exercised their newly found freedom through musical expression. Presenting a direct link to the past as well as an articulation of a possible future free from communist subjugation, these performances of nostalgia tap into what Raymond Williams calls "the structures of feeling" for this community as they connect everyone experientially through dance and song.[12]

Popular media created by the Vietnamese diaspora function on a number of levels. First, they exist as a collection of invented visual and musical culture directed against communism. Second, they serve as creative outlets expressing yearnings for a nostalgic past. Third, as cultural artifacts formed in the aftermath of migration, they may be used to study processes of assimilation, gender construction, generational conflicts, negotiations of identities, and cultural hybridity. It is in this sphere of the public that communal participation in nostalgia and cultural learning take place. Moreover, cultural production and consumption have a powerful effect on the formation of contemporary Vietnamese American identity. The variety of popular forms produced between the late 1970s and the turn of the century that I examine in this book demonstrate that public performances and niche media channels within these sites provide Vietnamese immigrants and refugees much more than pleasure and entertainment in a familiar language. They also enable new ways to literally envision Vietnamese culture in diaspora, carving out spaces for postrefugee gender, ethnic, and class identities. The formation of contemporary Vietnamese American identities, therefore, rests simultaneously on resisting the refugee image as well as constructing a middle-class ethnic identity under consumer capitalism.

For Vietnamese American consumers in search of language-specific entertainment, media forms also move into the realm of the "private" whereby leisure can be enjoyed through electronic technology particularly inexpensive and portable video.[13] Whether containing a variety show featuring Vietnamese celebrity exile performers, a beauty pageant of young women wearing ethnic dress, or actual music videos showing images of singers moving their lips alongside scenery of the Vietnamese countryside, videos are quintessential sources of entertainment for Vietnamese American immigrants and refugees. Offering something for everyone across class, region, gender, and generational lines without having to leave their household, diasporic videos exist as an alternative form of visual media available to Vietnamese viewers to consume on their own time and in the language with which they are most familiar. In theorizing the functions of video, Robert Scholes has noted that video texts not only give pleasure through narrativity but also provide cultural reinforcement that "confirm viewers in their ideological positions and reassure them of their membership in a collective cultural body."[14] The collective consumption of Vietnamese American videos has enabled Vietnamese exiles in the contemporary moment to do what Benedict Anderson argues print culture did in sixteenth-century Europe—create "imagined communities."[15] Born out of nostalgia and a deep longing for the lost homeland, overseas Vietnamese nationalism exists purely in the imagination and fantasy of exiles with no geographic space for return.

With the impressive success of this entertainment industry, Vietnamese Americans are becoming one of the fastest growing minority groups to carve their own niche in the process of cultural production in the United States. Literary scholar and theorist Lisa Lowe has argued in her notable text *Immigrant Acts* that Asian Americans have increasingly turned to culture to live out their immigrant lives because they are excluded from the American body politic: "Because culture is the contemporary repository of memory, of history, it is through culture, rather than government that alternative forms of subjectivity, collectivity, and public life are imagined."[16] Misrepresented by the mainstream media and excluded from the formal political arena, Vietnamese refugees have indeed struggled to counter the image imposed upon them as war-ravaged and state-dependent subjects. Nevertheless, Vietnamese Americans have employed culture to articulate their distinct identities–as former subjects of U.S. imperialism and as new Americans–in order to gain entrée into the political arena. It is through cultural assertions of anticommunism and citizenship that Vietnamese immigrants have begun to claim their place in the United States. Moreover, the immediate conditions of exile, particularly in the late 1970s and 1980s, further compelled Vietnamese Americans to use new technologies and electronic media to archive their experiences as well as construct and market new forms of culture built on nostalgia and what Arjun Appadurai has termed, "the work of the imagination."[17]

I write this book to address the omissions in social science literature on refugee and migration studies that often fail to consider the importance of culture, ethnic studies approaches that disregard the centrality of popular culture, and inadequate attention paid to race and ethnicity in cultural studies.[18] Investigating sites of cultural production requires close examinations of leisure, entertainment, and everyday pleasures of Vietnamese American life that others have previously dismissed as frivolous and unimportant. Despite the global circulation of Vietnamese diasporic culture, the existing published body of scholarship on Vietnamese refugees and immigrants has overwhelmingly focused on the psychological trauma of displacement, resettlement, and adaptation.[19] Guided by state department definitions and parameters, scholars studied cultural maladjustments, mental health, and other pathological aspects associated with the refugee experience.[20] Researchers tended to conduct multiple studies detailing the effects of trauma on Vietnamese refugees and fixated on their failure to acculturate into American society by citing vast differences between the American "first world" and the Vietnamese "third world." Scholars regarded Vietnamese refugees as uprooted by politics and war because the circumstances under which they arrived marked the tragic end of American involvement in a horrific and bitterly disputed war. They mourned over both the national as well as cultural displacement of these refugees, granting them no will or agency to recover their losses. Given the complex history of Vietnamese immigration and the coerced displacement of this population, emphasis on the difficulties of adaptation was important. Nevertheless, fixation on loss and psychological problems obscures and overlooks other aspects of Vietnamese immigration. Much of the existing scholarly research on Vietnamese immigrants continues to underscore the psychosocial aspects of how refugees adapt to American society, though a new generation of scholars is transforming the field.[21] I place this book in dialogue with these emerging conversations about the Vietnamese diaspora that have been increasingly concerned about culture and social aspects of migration.

My work has been shaped by cultural studies, media studies, as well as the important interventions in labor history by cultural historians and by ethnic and immigration studies scholars.[22] Most significantly, this study was influenced by the research done on leisure and entertainment revealing the cultural and political aspects of intimate relationships between men and women, parents and children, and other human desires. Understanding play in everyday life enables a fuller understanding of immigrant life and provides crucial information about class and cultural politics in the formation of identity. In fact, leisure and pleasure are significant components in the success of the exilic Vietnamese niche industry because it is only under the guise of leisure that the differential politics of the diasporic Vietnamese community are momentarily set aside or debated through acting and performance. These efforts to understand class in Vietnamese American self-representation and the complex and often contradictory ways in which they "assimilate" and "acculturate" into their respective "host" societies will lead to an exploration of the cultural terrain that Vietnamese Americans have carved for themselves through multiple forms of mediated technology.

The escape from communist Vietnam left the refugees with both the pleasures and pains of exile. Deterritorializing Vietnamese culture enables the reconceptualizion of the meanings associated with exile.

While most definitions of exile are closely linked to a "dystopic and dysphoric experience," Hamid Naficy has suggested that exile "must also be defined by its utopian and euphoric possibilities" that are "driven by wanderlust and a desire for liberation and freedom."[23] My work examines the day-to-day experiences and cultural practices of locality within a diasporic community as well as the ways in which remote Vietnamese communities are creatively linking up with one another using both electronic media and Internet technology such as websites and chat rooms to forge virtual communities in decentralized locations.

My analysis of media technology and its effects on immigrant culture challenges past studies that treat Vietnamese culture as a static set of tenets imported from the lost homeland and retained in the United States. Moreover, it undermines the essentialist notion that Vietnamese culture has remained the same despite Vietnam's multilayered history of colonialism. Such monolithic depictions abound. Paul Rutledge, for example, writes, "[t]he resilience of the Vietnamese is especially noteworthy. Historically well trained as survivors, the Vietnamese have adapted to the regimented time mentality of the Westerner."[24] Though Rutledge's study has proven useful, his analyses are tinged with Orientalist interpretations that uphold primordial ideas of Vietnamese culture. Rather than support this false sense of cultural resiliency as well as the monolithic constructions of Vietnamese culture perpetuated by misinformed scholars and even some Vietnamese Americans themselves, I argue that the formation of Vietnamese culture emerges from relentless borrowing and appropriation to meet the needs of the Vietnamese people. The community in exile invents and creates new cultural forms and practices in their new circumstances.

The complexities of Vietnamese cultural transformation cannot be simply bifurcated into a framework of "assimilation" versus "retention." Such change is a complex process involving the many different ways Vietnamese culture is invented, reinvented, remembered, and imagined though electronic and digital channels of expression.[25] Unlike previous scholars of this ethnic group, I consider not cultural "loss" but the mediation of cultural practice, particularly in an era dominated by technological advancements. I ask how, for instance, have cultural practices survived and to what extent have they transformed in the aftermath of migration and social change? Finally, because Vietnamese American uses of media representations and cultural production are not limited to the interpellation of Vietnamese American subjectivities, I also analyze how the immigrant community employs media and technology to publicly represent itself as a whole to the American nation and the rest of the world.

My methodology constitutes a creative exercise in crossing various disciplines. Using a wide range of materials, including historical and socio-logical texts, media and cultural theory, journalistic pieces, audiovisual materials, and an Internet survey, this book incorporates historical, anthropological, and sociological research on Vietnamese immigration. I perform close readings and textual/visual analyses of cultural forms and practices and an ethnographic study that incorporates oral interviews and participant-observation methods investigating cultural consumption in multiple settings. The Internet has become a useful tool to access and assess the mediated and virtual aspects of identity construction and community formation. Employing these inventive methodologies of evaluation and analysis has enabled me to piece together and reflect upon the diverse effects that technological advances in media and communications have had on the everyday lives of diasporic Vietnamese subjects. With a project that combines interdisciplinary approaches to the study of identity formation through media production and consumption, I engage with scholars in a number of fields and disciplines investigating the colliding forces of the local and the transnational as they compete in the interest of capital.

The American Dream in Vietnamese begins by taking on the discourses that surround the figure of the Vietnamese refugee in America. Within the national imaginary, the Vietnamese refugee represents a troubling, haunting presence that threatens to reignite the violent history and con-tradiction of U.S. imperialism. Tracing the history of U.S. military interven-tion and economic sponsorship of South Vietnam, chapter 1 argues that the treatment of refugees by mainstream media during and after reloca-tion served to mask the U.S. government's complicity in the Vietnam War. Consequently, the assimilation of refugees into the American landscape simultaneously served both domestic and foreign policy in promoting the United States as a democratically exceptional nation that does *not* engage in colonialism but fights for freedom.[26] The failure of the United States to attain freedom for the Vietnamese stands as a historical lesson, yet this legacy of American intervention in the fight for democracy does not deter future engagements with war in the Persian Gulf.

The ambivalent incorporation of Vietnamese American subjects into U.S. society took place in a way that fostered a double identity for refugees. They functioned both as model minority and non–model minority subjects. As model minorities, they worked diligently to further the ideals of American pluralism and contribute to the American Dream. As non-model minorities and pathological objects created by refugee discourse, they helped to perpetuate the idea that they remain in need of American assistance—an extension of the same type of assistance they required in Vietnam. Vietnamese Americans posed problems for other Asian Americans who tried to include them in conventional racial discourses about minority rights. Straddling these two conditions of perceived success and perceived neediness, Vietnamese Americans struggled for viable forms of self-representation.

The refugee narrative provides a discursive tool for Vietnamese Americans to connect with their immediate past, but as an emerging minority group, they forged a distinct identity for themselves in the United States. In chapter 2, I chart the historical and social development of Southern California's Little Saigon and explore its emergence as the cultural, political, and economic center of the Vietnamese diaspora. I contend that, though small in scale, the local experience of exile in Little Saigon is intricately linked to the global emergence of Southeast Asia, particularly in the late 1980s and early 1990s. As in Vietnam, however, the capitalist economic development of Little Saigon was not conceived by the work of ethnic Vietnamese alone. With business experience and access to capital, ethnic Chinese refugees from Vietnam played a crucial role in building Little Saigon. Through war, transnational migration, and resettlement, the uninterrupted ethnic strife that circumscribes the contested relationship between ethnic Vietnamese and ethnic Chinese refugees from Vietnam may be best understood as what I call an "overlapping diaspora." The reinstitution of pre-migration economic power relations and the anxiety over the Chinese presence in Little Saigon shaped the ways in which Vietnamese exiles carved their distinctive identity in the United States. As such, the Vietnamese American community constructed cultural institutions in the ethnic enclave to forge a public identity for themselves under the shadow of Chinese figures that held economic power. Little Saigon became a cultural battlefield where Vietnamese Americans fought to distinguish themselves from other immigrants. The insistence on Vietnam's impact on American cultural memory, the legacies of the war, along with the abundance of ethnic cultural production not only made visible but also solidified a voice for the refugee population in Southern California's Orange County. So much so that in recent years, Vietnamese Americans have begun to enter the mainstream political arena. Though polls have indicated that they tend to be independent, their gains in political power have resulted from strategic alliances forged with conservatives over the prevailing struggle against communism. Continuing the Cold War discourse of anticommunism, Vietnamese refugees embraced their new role as the ethnic "suburban warriors" who would lead the crusade against communist forces, mainly the regime currently holding power in Vietnam.[27] A development that has become even more compelling in Little Saigon is the new political negotiation Vietnamese Americans are forced to make with Latinos who also vie for power and representation. The lessons learned from these interethnic relationships serve as a strong reminder that the Vietnamese American community must delicately balance both transnational and local issues as they enter electoral politics.

In chapter 3, I discuss how a cultural critique of Vietnamese American beauty pageants deepens our understanding of the intricacies of community representations and identities. Ethnic beauty pageants can be read as civic contests of citizenship countering Asian exclusion from mainstream standards of beauty and as a display of cultural pride. However, a close reading of these community rituals reveals their reinforcement of traditional gender roles, cultural authenticity, and racial purity. In Vietnamese beauty pageants, the bodies of the contestants are adorned in ethnic dress and are used to symbolize a peaceful Vietnamese nation before foreign invasion, war, and dispersion of its population. This mythical narrative speaks to a refugee community that has shared the traumas of colonization, war, dislocation, diaspora, and resettlement. Moreover, beauty contests allow organizers, participants, and audience members to recapture aspects of their former lives, momentarily forgetting their daily lives in the United States where they have to contend with economic struggles, cultural differences, linguistic difficulties, and racial discrimination. In so doing, however, they also reestablish patriarchal ideals of enclosed nationhood and traditional gender hierarchies. Additionally, they construct a contradictory politics of representation that demands, on the one hand, that young female contestants be "ethnically authentic," yet on the other hand privilege new "hybrid" and "modern" beauty standards that may be achieved through the promotion of cosmetic surgery.

Chapter 4 focuses on the cultural and representational work of niche media and videotexts produced by and for the Vietnamese diaspora. As the VCR revolutionized home entertainment for non–English speaking households in the 1980s, Vietnamese Americans witnessed the creation of *Paris by Night* videos—a series of commercially produced videotapes of

Vietnamese variety show performances consisting of elaborate musical and dance numbers, comedy skits, and fashion shows of Vietnamese women in traditional dress. As cultural commodities, these videos had powerful ideological resonance that transformed viewer experiences through the projection of multiple possibilities for the articulation of postrefugee gender, ethnic, and cultural identities. Combining pictures and sounds, the videos, in particular, offered audiences conflicting ways of imagining themselves as part of a larger community. These inexpensive, accessible, conveniently mobile technologies became the primary communicative means for Vietnamese Americans to grapple with issues such as gender, sexuality, acculturation, assimilation, and "the generation gap." Under the guise of entertainment, Vietnamese video and niche media production used the variety show form to construct song and dance spectacles to invoke memory, nostalgia, and an idealized, utopian nationalist vision of a community advancing under capitalism. As such, I argue that Vietnamese cultural productions privilege a "new" diasporic Vietnamese subjectivity, shedding an "impoverished refugee" image for a new hybrid bourgeois ethnic identity.

The concluding chapter weaves the book together by meditating on the future of the diaspora as it relates to the homeland in the aftermath of normalized trade relations and amid the instability of global capitalism. I examine the formation of diasporic publics through the category of "audience" and explore how niche media reception by the Vietnamese diaspora is challenged by cultural production from the homeland. To investigate how audiences make meaning of diasporic cultural productions and the complex ways in which these media forms are received, interpreted, and consumed, I employed a range of research strategies including participation-observation, personal interviews, and an online survey. I argue that the popular culture of the Vietnamese diaspora has become so hegemonic that it carries meanings imbued with a politics of belonging. Knowledge of popular culture positions a Vietnamese subject as an "insider" even if he or she does not have access to language. Elaborating upon my interpretive readings of the popular cultural forms discussed in previous sections of the book, the last chapter engages in a dialogue with participants and fans of Vietnamese diasporic media and investigates the extent to which people use new digital technologies as a tool of communication. Using complementary research methodologies enabled me to see the multiple ways and various sites that diasporic Vietnamese experience leisure through media. From these approaches, I learned about individual media use and preferences as well as personal histories, migration experiences, cultural and identity issues, and political affiliations. The various spaces of media reception allowed me to hone in on how immigrants respond to cultural performances as well as their experiences of reception.

Though access remains limited, the Internet is transforming, reshaping, and altering diasporic Vietnamese subjects while enabling the constitution of the (virtual) Vietnamese nation in cyberspace. Cultural studies scholar Ella Shohat has suggested that cyberspace has allowed for a new mode of fetishizing the lost homeland whereby the act of logging on allows interactive networks of dispersed peoples to convene in a shared space to forge a virtual nation.[28] For the Vietnamese diaspora, the frontier of cyberspace may be the ideal site for the construction of a post-Habermasian public sphere whereby the anonymity of this virtual realm allows for cultural critique of hegemonic Vietnamese American self-representations and cultural productions.[29] Nevertheless, I remain cautious about embracing this potentially liberating space and the technologies that promise freedom, information, and democracy. This is because transnational flows of capital and new forms of consumption present a paradox for the diasporic community. While the blurring of borders may gesture toward efforts of resistance against dominant forms of culture, what globalization actually does to the Vietnamese diasporic community is reinvigorate the tradition of surveillance within it.

Chapter 1   Assimilation and Ambivalence: Legacies of U.S. Military Intervention

THE CONFLICT in Vietnam was one of the most brutal and destructive wars fought between Western imperial powers and the peoples of Asia, Africa, and Latin America. During the Cold War, both sides used the killing in Vietnam as an object lesson for their cause. More modern weapons technology came into use in the Southeast Asian peninsula than anywhere in the history of warfare up to that point. Toxic herbicides and chemicals poisoned water, land, and air while explosives maimed bodies and decimated local civilian populations. The war physically seared Vietnamese bodies and psychologically imprinted their minds with horror, rage, denial, and repression to an extraordinary degree. Though more than thirty years separate the events of the war from the present, these memories and wounds—be they physical or emotional—still powerfully permeate the private lives of those who survived the war and fled Vietnam. As time passes, these scars and recollections crystallize to form the raw materials used by people of the Vietnamese diaspora to construct their new identities.

This chapter traces the formation of contemporary Vietnamese American identities back to U.S. participation in the conflict in Vietnam to argue that cultural memories mediated by war shaped discourses of the refugee experience that followed. I contend that after dispersal and resettlement, Vietnamese asylees grappled directly with their refugee status and struggled to justify their social existence in response to the public discourse regarding their plight. The overwhelming focus on their trauma in many ways submerged historical memories and obfuscated the impact of American involvement in Vietnam while simultaneously creating an overdetermined construction of their identities as war victims. Vietnamese refugees and immigrants indeed shared a past circumscribed by war, but they are by no means a homogeneous group. In this chapter, I situate Vietnamese refugees at the intersection of two oppositional discourses that racialized

Figure 2. From Thuy Nga's *Paris by Night 77*. "30 Nam Vien Xu" ends its remarkable commemoration DVD by zooming in on the Vietnam Veterans Memorial in Washington, D.C., to send out a special message from the Vietnamese American community.

them as both traumatized victims and model minorities. The assimilation process required them to employ one representational strategy—that of the successful model minority—to refute the other—the haunting figure of the destitute refugee. Both representations served to erase the history of U.S. involvement while homogenizing the Vietnamese as a monolithic group. This chapter, then, highlights not only the diversity within this immigrant group, but also discusses the larger implications refugee representations have overshadowed. I argue that refugee discourse has largely pathologized Vietnamese experiences by presenting distorted images and descriptions of the treatment of refugees before, during, and after relocation. These hegemonic representations of Vietnamese as war victims not only became the source from which these immigrants projected their identities but also form the blueprint that frames future studies of this group. Furthermore, the figure of the war refugee homogenized class and ideological differences. In this chapter, I maintain that class analysis is crucial for understanding the refugee community and that the reproduction of class privilege has enabled elite voices to emerge as cultural gatekeepers of the Vietnamese diaspora.

My work critically interrogates the politics of labeling in refugee discourse by tracing the history of American imperialism, U.S. economic and military sponsorship of South Vietnam, and the eventful migration of the refugees.[1] In arguing for new scholarship that examines both imperial as well as transnational connections, anthropologist Nina Glick-Schiller writes, "the role of the United States in the world, whether as a military presence or as a major benefactor of the new economic world order, stands as an untheorized aspect of the migration processes."[2] I heed Schiller's call to theorize and interrogate U.S. power as it shaped Vietnamese patterns of migration, American memory, as well as immigrant identity formation. Deciphering the complicated politics of Vietnamese self-representation refracts the lasting implications of labeling and myth-making in the process of becoming Vietnamese American. Moreover, it reveals how a displaced population negotiates experiences and memories of war, migration, and incorporation while navigating a new terrain fraught with cultural misunderstandings. As refugee subjects entered American soil and adopted the United States as their new home, they confronted a host of different responses.

The Landscape of Refugee Reception

After Saigon fell to communist rule at the end of April 1975, U.S. participation in the Vietnam War ended bitterly and abruptly, leaving thousands of people fearful of political reprisals and desperate to begin their lives elsewhere. Perilous circumstances impelled a movement of refugees who evacuated from a politically unstable Southeast Asia between 1975 and 1977. Life-threatening conditions prompted approximately 200,000 people to leave Vietnam in the first wave, but hundreds of thousands subsequently followed throughout the late 1970s and early 1980s, often traveling through dense jungles on foot and rough waters at sea. Their mass exodus as the destitute "boat people" captured worldwide attention and prompted a number of nations, including Australia, Austria, Belgium, Canada, Denmark, France, Germany, Greece, and the Netherlands, to grant them political asylum.

The American public was uncertain what to make of the influx of refugees arriving to the United States. To a nation still divided over one of its most difficult wars, the new group of stateless individuals challenged the U.S. government after its military failure in Vietnam. America was nonetheless morally obliged to assist the evacuees in reestablishing their lives. Sociologist Paul Rutledge acknowledges, "We [Americans] had all fought alongside the Vietnamese, and had not persevered in helping them win freedom for their country. Assisting them in relocation and allowing asylum in the United States was not only an obligation, it was also a means of dealing with the national guilt."[3] Providing aid to the refugees allowed the

U.S. government to reconcile with its past and, to a certain extent, complete the task it was unable to fulfill in Vietnam.

However, this relationship of guilt and responsibility masks a complex history of U.S. imperialist intervention in Vietnam and perhaps its consequence of greatest significance—the mass exodus of refugees from the embattled nation. The existing literature on Vietnamese migration to the United States has not thoroughly investigated this multilayered historical relationship.[4] One major reason for this is because when the southern capital city of Saigon fell under communist attack, media representations of Vietnamese people transformed overnight from enemies who were largely indistinguishable from U.S. allies to asylum-seeking refugees desperately in need of a place of settlement. The dramatic process by which the refugees escaped the communist regime etched lasting impressions on the eyes of the world as the global media printed photographs of panic-stricken people dashing through the gates of the U.S. embassy, madly rushing to rooftops, and desperately clinging to helicopters. These emotionally wrenching scenes not only evocatively conveyed Southern Vietnamese panic, fear, and despondency as the war came to an abrupt close, but they profoundly affected the ways in which Vietnamese refugees would be configured and perceived in the United States.

Americanization in Vietnam

The nation of Vietnam and its people were first introduced to the American public in the early 1960s when the conflict in Vietnam became the first war to visually come through television sets in people's living rooms. Although a small number of students, language teachers, and diplomats had immigrated to the United States prior to that period, this minute population received virtually no public interest.[5] Most Americans at the time fixated their attention on the war and what was happening to the Vietnamese people *in Vietnam* and the American soldiers who were sent there. Television created an image of Vietnam as a nation that was foreign, rural, tropical, vast, and undeveloped. Literary scholar Renny Christopher recalls that Vietnamese villages were depicted "as alien, and unreal, as pictures of the moon." In the tumultuous 1960s, images of Vietnam and the moon were often shown back to back, "only separated by commercials of cars and dish detergent."[6] Depicting news footage of Vietnamese lands as distant and unfamiliar made it justifiable for the U.S. military to bomb the land (along with the civilians that inhabited it) in the service of war to contain the global spread of communism. As a nation torn by internal political strife, civil wars, and colonial rule, Vietnam appeared in need of modern American military assistance to prevent it from becoming the next domino. When the United States intervened and the war lingered for nearly a decade, the politics of the Vietnamese conflict commanded the attention of the American people, creating much confusion as to how to handle the chaos that was occurring in Southeast Asia.

U.S. military and corporate presence in Vietnam intensely complicated the process of Vietnamese migration to this country. Obfuscating America's economic interests with fears about the spread of communism, the U.S. government maintained a violent anticommunist agenda while conducting a destructive war in Vietnam. Along with military, political, and economic involvement in the war, foreign presence intensified class conflict in Vietnam. In many ways, the U.S. presence consolidated the class distinctions the French created in South Vietnamese society. With corporate America planted on Vietnamese soil, Western capitalism expanded throughout South Vietnam in the 1960s and 1970s and enabled the formation of an emerging Vietnamese bourgeoisie. Americans penetrated South Vietnamese society, forging unequal economic relationships whereby the economy of South Vietnam was almost completely dependent on American imports and the Ú.S.-sponsored Commercial Import Program served every basic need of the Vietnamese population.[7]

Along with military assistance, the United States provided Vietnam with consumer goods as well as material culture in the form of popular icons, music, art, film, and literature. Historian William Duiker observed: "Some of the most affected by U.S. influence were the so-called gilded youth of the big cities, many of whom had adopted a culture characterized by rock music, drugs, prostitution, and the individualist ethic."[8] The Americans had left such an immense cultural impression that when the communists entered the South after 1975, they alleged that the South Vietnamese had been "poisoned by the 'noxious weeds' of American bourgeois culture."[9] The new generation of Vietnamese youth that grew up with both French and American cultural influences adopted the "bourgeois" character that became part of their identity and used it as tool of resistance against communism and its rural, peasant associations. The formation of the modern Vietnamese immigrant subject can be traced to this rejection of the pastoral and impoverished, descriptors often used to describe the "backward" communists from Hanoi.

Economically, the United States maintained a hegemonic relationship with Vietnam and its people. The Vietnamese government welcomed

Americans and their commerce because U.S. imports stimulated growth and generated capital. To many, American presence symbolized modernization and progress. In particular, the middle class welcomed American products because they increased the wealth of many South Vietnamese merchants. Reflecting upon America's allure, Duong Van Mai Elliott recollects in her memoir:

> Of all the U.S. aid programs, the economic one was the most ingenious. It funded Vietnamese government expenditures while at the same time building up a middle class of civil servants, military officers, businessmen, and landowners, and supplying consumer goods to raise their standard of living. The aim was to make life so comfortable for this middle class—the most likely source of support for Diem [then President of the Republic of Vietnam who was believed to be a puppet of the American government]—that they would resist communist appeals and stay loyal to him.[10]

Serving to mask political intentions of maintaining a puppet government in Vietnam, U.S. economic and technological "assistance" programs catapulted an affluent middle class to power and introduced them to social and cultural trends from abroad.[11] Meanwhile, U.S.-established multinational corporations in Vietnam recruited several hundred thousand Vietnamese workers, and by the early 1970s, an additional 17,600 others were employed by the U.S. government.[12] The Vietnamese provided both a source of labor and a market for the consumption of American products, creating a cycle of interdependency between the two nations.

The cross-cultural and economic exchanges between the United States and South Vietnam transformed the Vietnamese citizenry and, in some respects, prepared them for life in America. However, the Americanization processes that took place in Vietnam remain largely under-researched and plagued by the amnesia of direct U.S. involvement. Scholars grounded in a tradition of immigration research concerned with assimilation often failed to recognize the previous exposure refugees had to American institutions in Vietnam. The earliest research on Vietnamese refugees consisted of sociological studies that fixated on the perceived inability of refugees to properly integrate and adjust to life in the United States.[13] Barry Stein's study, for example, reasoned that the Vietnamese would have difficulties adjusting to American society because they were "the first sizable non-European or European-culture refugees to come to the U.S. and no other large refugee group has come from a land with so low a level of development." Even though Stein studied the effects of downward mobility and occupational displacement among first-wave refugee elites, he was convinced that the "cultural differences, shocks, misunderstandings, and adjustments have been more formidable; the language harder to learn; and the disparity between occupational titles and actual skills wider for the Vietnamese than for other groups."[14] The narrow conception of the refugees' cultural awareness, combined with the author's underestimation of their abilities to adapt, contributed to the construction of the Vietnamese as unassimilable foreigners.[15] Moreover, the idea that it was "too difficult for them ever to integrate into our society" racially marked the refugees as well as further enhanced the national amnesia of U.S. cultural imperialism abroad.[16]

As scholars grappled with ways to understand the newcomers, the federal government assured that the process of forgetting and reconciliation occurred early on for the refugees.[17] This often took place before the refugees settled on U.S. soil. Gail Paradise Kelly's research on education occurring in refugee camps examines the process of acculturation through indoctrination.[18] Using interviews from social workers and agency coordinators rather than actual interviews of the immigrants themselves, Kelly observes and describes the reactions of Vietnamese subjects from evacuation, to "being processed," to undergoing crash courses in Americanization and English language training at the camps, to adjustment, and finally, to resettlement. Unveiling the errors of American attempts to teach both English and "American culture" in survival English courses, Kelly argues that the failure of survival English resulted from relief workers' unclear definitions of American culture that were often disguised as "middle class values." Covering multiple aspects of Vietnamese Americanization, Kelly's monograph remains invaluable for understanding rapid transformation of the Vietnamese from refugees to immigrants.

Gail Kelly's important study reveals the assumptions that social workers, ESL teachers, and scholars had about the lack of familiarity to American cultural forms. Yet these assumptions locate the "middle class values" only on the side of the Americans and overlook the intricate ways Americanization occurred every step of the way, particularly before migration (as discussed above). Moreover, these studies fail to take into account how Vietnamese immigrants *did* actively cope with and survive in the United States. The "first wave" of refugees from Southeast Asia was comprised of high-ranking officials of the South Vietnamese government, military leaders, and provincial politicians. Some worked closely with the Americans in Vietnam as secretaries, chauffeurs, translators, intelligence experts, and propagandists. Others were employees of U.S. corporations such as Chase Manhattan Bank, Exxon, IBM, TWA, and Pan American Airlines. Although a smaller group of lower-level officials, teachers, rank and file military personnel, petty traders, and fishermen had less direct contact with Americans, their exposure to American culture in Vietnam remains an important aspect of their adjustment.[19] The U.S. government had intended only to evacuate American citizens and their dependents and "high risk" Vietnamese officials and elites whose lives may have been endangered by the communist regime, but the extreme disorganization of the evacuation process made it impossible for this type of selection to occur.[20] Consequently, the mass exodus out of Vietnam consisted of a heterogeneous and diverse population of Vietnamese who suddenly became homogenized as "refugees."

Disciplinary Implications of Refugee Discourse

Having survived the devastation of war, the asylum seekers who escaped Vietnam endured tremendous stress and psychological trauma. Despite the mental and physical duress, the refugees were still subject to a strenuous screening process through which they were disciplined and managed. The federal government's temporary plans for refugee selection proved adequate when applied to the first group, but as unprecedented numbers of subsequent waves of refugees fled the shores of Vietnam by the late 1970s and early 1980s, a crisis emerged for which the United States was unprepared. Anthropologist Paul Rutledge explains that the first and second waves of refugees contained perceived "friends" of America, but "subsequent waves of Vietnamese refugees would be looked on with disdain as fortune hunters, persons who were fleeing economic depression."[21] While these distinctions are analytically significant, it cannot be denied that the government treated *all* refugees as anomalous cases. In her study of refugee discourse, Liisa Malkki observes that displaced populations "are not ordinary people, but represent, rather, an anomaly requiring specialized correctives and therapeutic interventions."[22] The refugees understood the political ploys of which they were a part, fully aware that any sign of pathology would pose a danger and threaten their chances of admission to a new nation. They knew they had to present themselves as healthy minds and bodies capable of discipline even at the cost of remaining silent and concealing pain from ailments, disorders, or illness.[23]

Refugees eagerly performed the role of healthy subjects but were often betrayed by medical professionals, social scientists, and policy researchers who studied them. While some refugees may have suffered serious mental illnesses and posttraumatic stress disorder, health professionals often exposed these problems and even invented pathologies they assumed were associated with the refugee experience. Once again, in her critique of refugee studies, Liisa Malkki explains that relief workers and researchers had a tendency to "locate 'the problem' not in the political conditions or processes that produce massive territorial displacements of people but rather, within the bodies and minds (and even souls) of people categorized as refugees."[24] Referring to the abundant research and scholarship on refugees that emerged between the late 1970s and 1980s, Malkki's observations help us to understand why so much research was conducted on the Vietnamese refugees in fields of social science, and especially, psychology.

Social scientists applied psychological and medical theories to rationalize the severe conditions the refugees experienced rather than attempt to understand the challenges of their plight.[25] For example, when sociologists William Liu, Maryanne Lamanna, and Alice Murata were permitted to enter refugee camps to conduct interviews and questionnaires, they did so to "monitor" refugee adjustments in support of the Asian American Mental Health Research Center's National Community Advisory Board.[26] Similar studies carried out by policy scholars based on such interviews and surveys made it a priority to study social behavior, mental health, and other traumas associated with forced migration.[27] While these psychological surveys provided rich and important information on how Vietnamese immigrants adjusted to the United States, they inevitably placed the minds and bodies of refugees on trial, making issues of trust and mistrust integral to the study of refugees.[28] This body of literature not only pathologized the resettlement process and assumed that Vietnamese refugees had always been alienated from American cultural forms, but also set the framework for future studies of this population. It is not until recently that these frameworks have been challenged, mainly by an emerging group of Vietnamese American scholars trained in academic institutions in the United States.[29] I consider my study to be part of these shifting perspectives on Vietnamese Americans that seek to challenge such misconceptions and propose new approaches to studying Vietnamese diasporic experiences.

Racial Politics of Humanitarianism and Debates over Resettlement

Cultural misunderstandings existed not only in early academic scholarship but also in refugee policy. The federal government expressed much anxiety about refugee social and cultural adjustment. Its ad hoc plans for refugee resettlement reveal the conditions of unpreparedness the United States was in for the arrival of the refugees.[30] The recession of the early 1970s and the depressed state of the U.S. economy made it difficult for the American public to accept incoming Vietnamese refugees. Some people expressed overt hostility toward the prospect of the refugees' arrival onto U.S. soil. One woman from Arkansas reportedly responded to the potential influx of the new immigrants by stating, "They say it's a lot colder here than in Vietnam. With a little luck, maybe all those Vietnamese will get pneumonia and die."[31] Others, such as Senator George McGovern of South Dakota, favored the application of stringent and selective immigration policies supporting only a few Vietnamese elites. He declared, "90% of the Vietnamese would be better off going back to their own land" justifying that only "a handful of government leaders were in real danger of reprisals."[32] While U.S. government officials agreed upon assisting a small number of privileged refugees, most Americans feared that the massive influx of new immigrants would create situations where refugees would be competing with Americans over limited resources. For example, before any refugee ever settled in California, Robert Gnaizda, the deputy secretary of the state Health and Welfare Agency, expressed concerns regarding the potential for change in California's economy pending the arrival of the refugees. Gnaizda asserted, "If we get a small number, we are going to take care of them in the best tradition of California—whose history of racial-ethnic mixing we are proud of, but no American would welcome Vietnamese if in fact they are going to disrupt the economy and the housing market."[33] Americans further expressed their antirefugee sentiment in a Gallup Poll taken in May of 1975 indicating that 54 percent of all Americans were opposed to admitting Vietnamese refugees to live in the United States while only 36 percent were in favor.[34] With a depressed state of the economy, historical amnesia, and xenophobia, nativist sentiment was not only common but unsurprising given the history of U.S. immigration policy, particularly toward Asian immigrants throughout the late nineteenth and most of the twentieth centuries.[35] Moreover, resistance against the refugees also reveals that the nation remained unresolved, unhealed, and divided over its involvement in Vietnam.

Although anti-immigrant sentiment expressed against the refugees carried racial overtones, the rhetoric used to convince Americans to assist the refugees made no mention of their race. To tone down the menacing image of war refugees flooding the shores of the United States, politicians such as President Gerald Ford employed the colorblind language of humanitarianism to garner public support for resettlement. Referring to America's "humanitarian" record that undergirded Cold War ideology, Ford insisted that the United States welcome the refugees in their efforts to escape the shackles of communism. He angrily exclaimed, "We didn't do it to the Hungarians. We didn't do it to the Cubans. And damn it, we're not going to do it now."[36] Urging Americans to support refugee resettlement, Ford ended his plea by calling on Americans to "welcome the refugees and Congress to appropriate $507 million to settle them."[37] With great reluctance, Congress allotted "several million dollars in aid for the refugees, and a growing army of organizations and individuals signed on to help the newcomers plunge into the American melting pot."[38] Despite national reaction against the refugees, the U.S. government eagerly came to the aid of the people they were unable to assist in winning a long, drawn-out war because they were convinced that it was now their responsibility to aid these displaced émigrés.

The rhetoric of humanitarianism not only evaded racial issues, it also concealed and disavowed the political nature of how the refugees were racialized, processed, resettled, and studied. Similar to other subjects of U.S. imperialism such as Filipinos, Koreans, Puerto Ricans, and Cubans, the refugees from Vietnam experienced racism prior to setting foot on American soil. Reexamining this tangled history of racial formation, especially before migration took place, exposes the racial politics embroiled in the conflict. Race consistently dictated the rules of war in Southeast Asia. Although men of color disproportionately represented the U.S. military, the overwhelming presence of white working-class American men fighting against Asians in Vietnam places race as a central ideology shaping the war.[39] Additionally, popular representations reflected and dramatized the racial tensions on the battlefield. In his study of cultural productions reflecting the Vietnam War experience, David Desser writes about the homogenization of the Vietnamese people:

> This is the simple but painful refrain heard time and again from veterans, in novels, and in films: that they could not distinguish ally from enemy, friend from foe. The Occidental, racist cavil that all Orientals look alike became painfully all too true in Vietnam.[40]

While the stories of individual soldiers reveal a problematic situation of racial tension on the battlefield, historian Michael Hunt offers more insight into America's foreign policy toward the Vietnamese as he observes:

> We dehumanized the Vietnamese by the everyday language applied to them. We called them "gooks" or "slopes" (just as we had earlier derided other unruly people as "gu-gus" and "niggers"). Reflecting our diminished sense of their humanity, we made massive and indiscriminate use of firepower and herbicides, killing noncombatants as well as combatants and poisoning the land. At the same time, we promoted a pattern of national development informed by the American experience, taught the Vietnamese how to fight and govern, and when necessary both fought and governed for them. The resulting devastation, dislocation, and subordination was the price the Vietnamese paid for our self-assigned crusade to stop communism, save a people we regarded as backward, and revitalize an outmoded culture.[41]

I quote Hunt's explication at length because it exposes the racial logic of U.S. imperialism and its greater implications in America's decision to fight the war in Vietnam. The United States acted in self-interest, allowing their military machine to ravage the Vietnamese landscape, poisoning it with defoliants such as Agent Orange and indiscriminately destroying human life in the process. Such devastation contributed to making life in Vietnam unbearable. The refugees who ultimately fled Vietnam did not leave merely because Saigon fell into the hands of the communist rulers. The effects of the war made it very difficult to sustain life in such a toxic devastated environment.

As the war persisted, American soldiers who went to Vietnam complained about the difficulties of distinguishing "good" Vietnamese from "bad" Vietnamese. This inability to distinguish enemy from civilian and friend from foe prompted American soldiers of Asian descent to charge that they should not have to fight against their "Asian brothers and sisters," whom they believed were liberating themselves from colonial domination.[42] Mobilizing the language of race and rights, veterans and activists of Asian descent made similar observations on the home front, declaring that the war in Vietnam was a "racist war."[43] Antiwar activists rallied to end the war, reasoning that the loss of Vietnamese lives by the hands of Americans in combat resulted from a racist ideology that had been imported from the United States to Vietnam. General William Westmoreland's racist remark claiming "the Oriental doesn't put the same high price on life as the Westerner," exacerbated the situation and made it all too clear that U.S. participation in the war in Vietnam was an exercise of American racial and ideological imperialism.[44] In its self-appointed efforts to "save" Vietnam from falling prey to communism, the United States also destroyed Vietnamese land as well as the nation's citizenry. Failing to account for the events that consequently led to the fall of Saigon distorts the historical record and places full responsibility on the refugees from Southeast Asia for their exodus from communism.

Expressions of racism toward the refugees were most prevalent in the military, which was appointed to oversee refugee relocation. Under military administration, the refugees were processed and placed in makeshift refugee camps on the U.S. mainland that were modeled after barracks and arranged into what anthropologist Liisa Malkki calls "disciplinary, supervisable spaces."[45] Only a limited number of individuals were conferred legal residency status because they were fortunate enough to possess occupational levels and skills needed in the U.S. economy.[46] The rest of the asylum seekers were admitted as parolees.[47] This status allowed them to work in the United States until they could obtain legal residency. However, because the majority of the refugees did not possess transferable skills, they were held in camps until they were ready to be sponsored out into American society to find low-wage work.

In accordance with the efforts to downplay the residual politics of the war, the federal government treated the management of refugees as, according to scholar Gail Kelly, "a nonissue."[48] This move to depoliticize the history of refugee movements created situations where they could be considered charity cases. Liisa Malkki fittingly notes, "too often refugees are perceived as a matter of international charity organizations, and not as a political and security problem. Yet refugee problems are in fact intensely political: mass migrations create domestic instability, generate interstate tension and threaten international security."[49] Masking refugee assistance with humanitarian reasons for their resettlement allowed the federal government to obscure not only political intentions, but also past mistakes of intervening in Vietnamese political governance and warfare.

The strategies policymakers used to mobilize public sentiment and justify legislation simultaneously placed Vietnamese refugees in a conservative Cold War political discourse of anticommunism and excluded them from the contemporaneous intense discourse of race and civil rights in U.S. society. This discursive moment provided the framework by which Vietnamese immigrants constructed their identities as Americans and significantly shaped how community politics would be formed after resettlement. The double position of being racialized minority subjects and refugees escaping from a repressive communist regime allowed the Vietnamese to articulate a politics that would benefit their vision of American acceptance. For some, aligning themselves with other ethnic minorities enabled ways to address racial discrimination, while others saw that fashioning a politically conservative ideology similar to that of Cuban Americans and other refugees who escaped communist regimes would be strategically advantageous. In chapter 2, I will explore the ways in which these strategies and tensions played out, but for now, I will closely examine the greater implications of class relations on Vietnamese identity formation *during* migration, which profoundly shaped social relations *after* resettlement.

Recovering "Immigrant" Bodies among Refugees: Complexities of Class Analysis

Academic research on various waves of Vietnamese migration has pointed out economic differences in occupational and class status among the refugees. Nevertheless, the tenuous relationship between those of the first wave and subsequent waves of refugees has often been overshadowed by the overwhelming focus on acculturation, assimilation, and transformations in gender relations.[50] In other words, previous studies of Vietnamese refugees prioritized their adjustment to life in the United States rather than interrogate how refugees navigated social systems they already understood in the process of migration.

For the most part, migration was an indiscriminating, leveling process that disrupted and blurred class and, to some extent, ethnic distinctions. Being classified as "refugees," a monolithic category used to describe displaced persons, erased previous identities people had in their former nation and in some ways obliterated the various categories of social distinction. Despite these homogenizing tendencies of classification, the refugees adamantly resisted the labels imposed on them. In fact, the news media that covered them often distinguished the different classes of refugees who arrived noting that the majority of "first wave" émigrés tended to be "better educated," "more privileged," and "urban," while the "boat people" of subsequent waves had much more difficulty adjusting to American society.[51]

I draw attention to both class and ethnicity not only because ethnic Chinese from Vietnam figure prominently in this immigration story, but also because these categories of cultural and social analyses profoundly mediated the ways in which the refugees themselves understood their displacement. Additionally, class and ethnicity also affected how the refugees constituted new identities after resettlement. For example, anthropologist Aihwa Ong pointed out in her research that social scientists who worked with refugee populations "provided ethno-racial classifications" for social workers and ESL teachers in a practice called "surveillance-correction," which reclassified refugees based on essential cultural and national characteristics. Ong concluded that the overly simplistic links made between "purported cultural features" and the refugees' potential abilities to work in the U.S. labor market explicitly differentiated ethnic groups "even though Vietnamese and Cambodian refugees came out of the same set of conflicts based on American intervention in Southeast Asia."[52] In effect, these artificial distinctions not only disregarded the decades of war, social upheaval, and camp conditions through which the refugees had recently lived, but they also assigned racial meaning to some refugees over others. Inevitably, the recasting of Southeast Asian refugees through ethnic classifications also consolidated class standings, leaving Vietnamese the "more assimilable" immigrant group, followed by ethnic Chinese, and then Cambodians, who would become the anti–model minority and new Asian underclass.[53]

The Vietnamese quickly understood their social standing among the other Southeast Asian refugees, and they consciously set themselves apart from those they deemed "less deserving" particularly their own co-ethnics. Reflecting upon the inevitable blurring of class boundaries during the transitional process of migration, one refugee declared, "It doesn't matter now if one is the wife of a Cabinet minister or even a Cabinet minister himself. We are all the same now."[54] Nevertheless, the realities of life in the refugee camps in Guam and the Philippines showed that class remained salient to the Vietnamese despite the social upheaval of migration. Conflict over class differences and status brewed among Vietnamese compatriots as they lived in close proximity to one another in the camps.[55] *Time* magazine reported that a member of the former Vietnamese elite complained about the liability his fellow Vietnamese fishermen and farmers created for the rest of the refugees: "You can tell by their accents that they are only peasants," he said. "They are the wrong people. They should never have come. They will only make it more difficult for the rest of the Vietnamese." In another refugee camp, reporter Terry Rambo assessed that "[m]any of the upper and middle class refugees are particularly concerned about the presence of prostitutes and others whom they consider undesirable elements."[56] Although most of the refugees represented a diverse segment of the populace who got lost in the evacuation process, not all refugees were haughty upper class elites, prostitutes, thieves, and prejudiced individuals as highlighted by American news media. Journalistic representations of the clashing of classes in the refugee camps and the insistence on class distinctions by the Vietnamese, however, underscore the social realities and continued significance of class status to members within the community. Fearing that Americans would misinterpret Vietnamese social behavior based on a few "undesirable elements" among the refugees, elites distanced themselves from the "lower classes" and steadfastly maintained differences among them, consistent with their former social positions in Vietnamese society.

The Vietnamese penchant to preserve class difference reveals both an attempt by the elites to hold on to a sense of identity that was being threatened by the immigration process and a keen awareness of U.S. immigration policy to which all Vietnamese were now subject. To many refugees, the decision to flee Vietnam meant that they would risk losing their lives and the social status they once held in South Vietnamese society. They also understood that they had to comply with what Americans expected them to become—grateful and respectable new immigrant subjects. Without transferable job skills, they would have to at least be "presentable," or healthy and able bodies, worthy of asylum. Because the U.S. government granted preference to Vietnamese elites and professionals whom they considered "more Westernized" and "well-educated," those who did not fit in this category had to demonstrate that they too would "not become a burden to the government."[57] The self-discipline required of refugee subjects to prove their "worth" to the government and to the American public circumscribed refugee subjectivity and engendered resentment toward those who fell below the "moral" requirements of rescue.[58] This placed tremendous burdens on the refugee subject to fashion an identity that would fit into the mold of a model minority subject. Moreover, it fails to account for those who had the social, cultural, and class advantage to pass due to their previous knowledge and interactions with Americans.

The intense focus on refugee bodies and minds in the mainstream press and in academic literature not only casts a shadow on the Vietnamese American community that had already settled in the United States, but also overlooks the classed experiences of the few Vietnamese refugees who silently integrated into American society due to their abilities to overcome financial requirements. While it is entirely possible to classify this category of people as "economic" refugees, I hesitate to do so because it fails to account for the repercussions they would face had they remained in Vietnam.[59] Nevertheless, according to Gail Paradise Kelly, "between 8,000–10,000 immigrants resettled without sponsors. These were persons who had over $4,000 per family member in liquid assets upon arrival in the United States or who were resettled directly by their employers from Vietnam."[60] The report to Congress on March 15, 1976, by the HEW Task Force for Indochinese

Refugees could not account for their whereabouts in the United States. Classified as "unknown," this group of asylees probably entered the U.S. as "immigrants" rather than "refugees" under the Immigration Act of 1965. With enough capital and continued employment or access to employment opportunities, they settled without state assistance and seemingly assimilated into American society with relative ease. The glaring void that leaves this group nearly unaccounted for serves as a telling reminder that refugee management, as well as the documentation of their experiences, was uneven and inconsistent.

I point to these gaps to illustrate the federal government's ineffective efforts to control corporate interests as well as the actual labor, embodied by the refugees, upon which these companies relied. Moreover, I argue that these cases illustrate the inability of previous scholars and researchers to recognize the United States as a colonial power that penetrated into the territories it vowed to "protect."[61] American forces did not enter Vietnam solely for military and political purposes. As mentioned previously, the United States existed as an economic power upon which the Vietnamese continually depended. When the Americans left Vietnam, many brought their employees with them.[62] The business and finance section of *Newsweek* reported that companies such as IBM, Chase Manhattan Bank, and other multinational corporate entities sent representatives to Camp Pendleton in search of former employees. A number of companies extended some form of economic assistance to the refugees, while others rehired them. Most fortunate were the approximately "46 Pan-American World Airways employees [who] never saw the inside of a refugee camp at all, except to work there as translators. Pan Am put them and 266 dependents up in hotels and private homes."[63] Acting either in self-interest or for humanitarian reasons, U.S. corporations assisted Vietnamese refugees in granting them gainful employment, oftentimes resuming the relationship they had in Vietnam. The generous response to aid former employees by major corporations reveals that corporate investment in Vietnamese labor during the war coincided with that of the federal government's military involvement in Vietnam. Because the biggest employer of the Vietnamese refugees was the U.S. government, it was not possible for the majority of the refugees to regain their jobs. Furthermore, civil service regulations at the time barred refugees from applying due to their "alien" status.[64]

While the mainstream press covered stories of refugees who worked for American corporations, academic research has not fully investigated the experiences of the few financially independent Vietnamese who had truncated stays at the camps and were given their jobs back by American corporations that sponsored them. The lacuna in this history suggests the following: (1) money not only permitted former American corporate employees from Vietnam to bypass processing in refugee camps, it also gave them "immigrant" status; (2) scholarship on refugees was restricted within the confines of refugee camps—anything beyond those borders was not a concern; and (3) the federal government selectively erased the histories of corporate colonial enterprise. The U.S. government, the largest employer of Vietnamese civilians, bore the greatest responsibility to the asylum-seekers. Rather than force many of the refugees and other high-ranking officials into poverty, the government conferred upon them jobs as counselors and mediators of adaptation and resettlement.[65] This enabled many former Vietnamese elites to regain their social status in the United States. Though many of these stories remain undocumented, I suggest that we consider the omissions of this history because the upper-class elites, along with their cultural familiarity with American social mores, would later reclaim their former social standing and become key players in the ideological governing of the Vietnamese American community. It is through their social and cultural capital that the enclave communities are built. I explore the full implications of the convergence of these histories in the following chapter, but before I do so I want to discuss how Vietnamese subjects entered public discourse in the 1980s and explain the complexities of their racial representations.

The Significance of Race and Geopolitics in Model Minority Discourse

The universal language of humanitarianism along with the Cold War anti-communist rhetoric used by politicians that dictated refugee policy served three practical functions: (1) convince the American people that the federal government made the morally justifiable choice of accepting and assisting refugees, (2) obscure class and ethnic differences among the émigrés, and most important, (3) leave Southeast Asians out of the controversial Civil Rights discourse on race. However, by the 1980s, merely five years after the "first wave" of refugees resettled, it became clear that refugees from Southeast Asia no longer occupied an exceptional space in the spectrum of race relations in the United States. The mainstream media began praising Vietnamese immigrants—and especially young children who excelled academically—as "America's success story" and new "model minority."[66] This new status as "model minorities," a stereotype shared by other Asian Americans, symbolized the incorporation of Vietnamese refugees into the

U.S. multicultural discourses on race. Having come from the middle and upper echelons of Vietnamese society, a majority of the "first wave" refugees adjusted to life in the United States with relative ease despite the dire circumstances under which they came.[67] The arrival of later waves from less privileged socioeconomic backgrounds, however, disrupted their transition into American society. Further encumbering the process of assimilation at the time were haunting images of "boat people" leaving the shores of communist Vietnam in search of freedom. These powerful renderings of distraught "boat people" competed with human-interest stories that praised the settled refugees for their hard work, sacrifice, and struggle for the American Dream. Such tales of immigrant success contradicted representations of Vietnamese as helpless victims draining the resources of American tax-paying citizens and the reports of Vietnamese refugees as welfare dependents and nefarious gang members that had begun to proliferate in the media.[68] The bifurcated images of Vietnamese Americans reflect the deeply fraught process of Vietnamese emigration which is made more complicated by subsequent waves and classes of migrants.

These extreme class representations that dichotomized and caricatured their experiences led Vietnamese Americans to create self-representations that rejected images of the welfare-dependent refugee. Instead, they began to cautiously accept the model minority stereotype to characterize their identity as new Americans. While this was done at the expense of alienating other minorities and negating any potential for coalition building, Vietnamese refugees and immigrants were eager to erase the negative label attached to them. Moreover, they embraced the model minority myth and publicly adopted the affirming representations of upward mobility to be their new roles in American society as a way to justify their presence within it. To a group of people that had been classified as homeless and geographically uprooted, the model minority label denoted "positive" acceptance and assimilation into America's multicultural milieu. At the root of its implications, the model minority myth was and is premised upon the idea of individual responsibility. Vietnamese refugees desired to project a trajectory of self-sufficiency that they believed led to progress and to some semblance of normalcy. Nevertheless, the simplistic alignment of Vietnamese Americans with the image of the model minority belies their overall historical experiences and problematically fails to consider the discursive dynamics of how they, as newly incorporated subjects of the American nation, functioned as model minorities and non–model minorities, and most powerfully, as refugees for varied ideological purposes.

As I argued above, the American public expressed much ambivalence toward the newcomers, particularly at a time of national economic crisis in the 1970s. Moreover, when the refugees continued coming, not only from Asia but from places like Africa, Latin America, and the Caribbean, the public's perception of these newcomers as freedom fighters against the global war on communism began to wane and even become suspect. Aihwa Ong argues that "floods of refugees—both legal and illegal—escaping from natural disasters, civil wars, ethnic wars, and adverse conditions in poor countries" instigated "compassion fatigue" and "a climate of antagonism" that greeted the "refugees *of color* (emphasis mine)."[69] As the language of race entered the discourse on refugee rescue, public sentiment became increasingly hostile toward those in need of asylum.

In response to the changes in policy and public resentment, academic studies on Vietnamese refugees began aligning them with other immigrants from Asia such as the Chinese and Japanese.[70] To ethnic studies scholars, refugees from war-torn Southeast Asia exemplified the antithesis of the "model minority," a racialized construct solidified by the mainstream media that set Asian Americans apart from other minorities in the late 1960s. Against the backdrop of the civil rights movement, in which racial minorities, mainly African Americans and Latinos, openly and vociferously challenged racist hierarchies in the United States, journalistic reports depicted Japanese and Chinese Americans as exemplary Asian minorities demanding no change of the status quo.[71] Eliding persistent structural problems that governed race relations in American society, the press cited Asian "cultural values" and "strong work ethics" as reasons for the successful achievements of these ethnic groups. Soon after, other Asian American groups received similar praise. The racial formation of Asians as the "model minority" pitted them against other minorities of color and excused white racism, while it simultaneously concealed the various problems that working-class Asian immigrants and refugees faced.

While the privileges that Asian Americans had over other minorities in areas such as income, education, and occupational status cannot be denied, one major concern in the discipline of Asian American studies has involved resisting and challenging the model minority myth.[72] When the influx of Southeast Asian refugees entered the United States, their state-dependent status and initial inability, or perceived inability, to successfully integrate into the American economic structure rendered them a special case of Asian immigrants that would demystify the model minority myth. Moreover, as political asylees from an American war in Southeast Asia, the refugees essentially fulfilled the role of a "new underclass" that would debunk the model minority thesis. As an illustration of the racial inequalities that still persisted in the United States, the otherness of the refugees enabled an apparent but uneasy alliance with racialized communities in the fight for social and economic justice. This critique of the model minority construct, according to anthropologist Sylvia Yanagisako, became "an integral practice of Asian American studies because the myth calls into question the solidarity of Asian Americans with other people of color in the United States."[73] Refugees from Southeast Asia did indeed function as the anti–model minority. It cannot be denied that a majority of Vietnamese immigrants did require the financial assistance of the federal government. Their immigration status as asylum seekers forced them to be in a periodic state of financial dependence on the government—as a non–model minority.

Despite the complex history I discuss above, the ethnic and class diversity of the refugee population, and the demographic changes resulting from various waves of immigration from the 1970s to the 1990s, this practice still persists. Southeast Asians continue to function as the representative challenge to the model minority myth as they are the "other" in Asian America.[74] Rendering the experiences of Southeast Asian immigrants as victims and exemplary non–model minorities created hypervisible images of the state-dependent refugee that limited their representations. This move to cast the refugees as Asian American "others" not only overlooks significant class and ethnic distinctions but also forgets America's imperialist past and the discursive powers of the refugee narrative as it collides with the model minority myth.

Most important, it is problematic to homogenize Southeast Asian immigrants as representing the "other Asian America." In her study of refugees and citizenship, Aihwa Ong argues that during the migration process, an "ideological whitening of Vietnamese and ethnic Chinese immigrants (the stereotyped entrepreneurial self starters)" occurred compared to the "blackening" of refugees from Cambodia and Laos.[75] This conceptual and spatial distancing between ethnic groups created racial, cultural, and social hierarchies that classified certain ethnic groups as more assimilable than others even though they came from similar historical circumstances. Ong concluded that "regardless of the actual, lived experiences and cultural beliefs of Cambodians—social workers, policymakers, and the media clearly demarcated the form and content of their citizenship as low in human-capital potential and in economic productivity, a position detrimental to the normal biopolitical standards of American citizenship."[76] This casting of

Cambodians as the new American working and underclass configured both Vietnamese and ethnic Chinese as more "assimilable" immigrants capable of transcending their disposition as refugees.

Along these lines, Vietnamese immigrants were and continue to be particularly invested in their own stories, particularly those that deal with overcoming adversity through war, reconciliation, and assimilation.[77] Writing to dispel assumptions about their loyalty to the United States and to share their plight as war refugees, Vietnamese personal narratives, particularly in the form of humanist testimonials, flourished throughout the late 1980s and early 1990s.[78] Vietnamese refugees made their escape narratives available for American consumption to serve a number of purposes.[79] The quintessential refugee narratives were often translated and compiled by anthropologists and sociologists that did fieldwork in Vietnamese American communities. Anthropologist James Freeman's *Hearts of Sorrow*, for example, painted a portrait of Vietnamese America through a series of personal narratives. Claiming that his book is a corrective to the misconceptions and assumptions people had about Vietnamese Americans as "welfare abusers, undeserved receivers of special governmental treatment, and takers of jobs away from other Americans," Freeman reconstructed the experiences of Vietnamese Americans through oral history and translation.[80] Yet in his work, Freeman depicts Vietnamese Americans as model minorities and reformable immigrants and citizens to replace negative stereotypes. These refugee stories not only justified the actions of the government, but also portrayed the protagonists as the emerging "model minority." Given the seemingly positive portrayal, Vietnamese Americans began adopting these strategies. Constructing themselves as the new "model minority" and rejecting the image of what Viet Thanh Nguyen calls "bad subjects" enabled Vietnamese refugees to enter America's discourse on race on their own terms.[81] The historical circumstances and the specific conditions of the Vietnamese experience molded them into the "good subjects" who embraced not only the ideals of capitalism but also the ideology of self-responsibility espoused during the political climate of the Reagan era.

Incorporation and the Rhetoric of Individual Responsibility in Identity Politics

Although the state interpellation of the refugees during the war left lasting impressions on their identity, the tenuous relationship forged between the refugees, the U.S. military, and the federal government after their arrival provided a guiding force that would determine the future of Vietnamese identity politics. The conservative climate of the 1980s on one hand received the refugees escaping communism with open arms of freedom, but on the other hand, it reconditioned them to become grateful subjects needing to pay their debt to America. As Yen Espiritu astutely points out, "Vietnamese could only be incorporated into modern subject-hood as *refugees*; that is, only when they reject the purported antidemocratic, anticapitalist, (and thus antifree) communist Vietnam and embrace the free world."[82] She goes on to explain that the privileging of stories of extreme tragedy and success "naturalizes Vietnam's neediness and America's riches and produces a powerful narrative of Americ(ans) rescuing and caring for Vietnam's 'runaways' that erases the role the U.S. interventionist foreign policy and war played in inducing this forced migration in the first place."[83] Ways of forgetting, practiced by both the United States and the refugees themselves, infuse the process of identity construction for the refugees. Moreover, the tremendous sense of personal responsibility and desire to become good subjects also shaped how the refugees perceived themselves, setting their political agenda as future citizens of the United States.

Many scholars have had difficulty understanding the complicated politics of the Vietnamese American experience. Ethnic studies approaches, in particular, continue to grapple with the contradictions presented to them by refugee subjects. Emerging from the activism of the left, Asian American studies as a discipline grew from minority discourses that were concerned with race and class inequalities in the United States. Arguments that Asian Americans made against U.S. participation in the war reflected the politics of the Third World Movement in the United States, *not* in Vietnam. Vietnamese American political leanings do not neatly align with other Asian American groups either. In terms of traditional politics, they deviate from other racialized immigrant groups because of their staunch support for the Republican Party and the U.S. military. Recalling the prowar actions of Republican leaders in the war in Vietnam and their firm anticommunist stance throughout the Cold War, many Vietnamese Americans continue to associate anticommunism with conservatism. Hence, the progressive politics of Asian American scholars oftentimes pose an affront to the conservative, anticommunist politics of the most vocal of Vietnamese Americans. Because these politics create a crisis in representation that clashes with assumptions about race, I argue that it is imperative to consider the historical context in which the refugees became incorporated.

The racial formation of Southeast Asian refugees and immigrants occurred during a time when the United States was undergoing an ideological shift toward the right. Aihwa Ong's meditation on neoliberal discourse in the postrefugee period both problematizes the inadequacies of the ethnic studies framework and demonstrates the need to reconsider the language of individual rights and morality during the period of refugee incorporation.[84] In her ethnographic study of Cambodian refugees, Ong characterizes Asian Americanist discourse as "a strategy to seek moral justice and redress for past adversity, even when recent foreign-born newcomers had no part in that history." She explains: "The point is not that individual Asian Americans may not have been discriminated against, but rather that Asian Americans must be constituted as a community of shared racial oppression in order to gain the moral capital to be considered equal citizens."[85] Ong essentially points out that the *differences* in Asian migration experiences pose many obstacles for imagining a shared coalition within this group. Thus, the strategic construction of refugees and other newcomers into the Asian American category inadvertently homogenizes them through racialization while promoting a morality-based path toward citizenship.

Since the 1980s, the global political theater has witnessed the merging of conservative and neoliberal ideologies, making individualism and self-reliance important values in the national discourses of citizenship. In the age of transnational migration and globalization, according to Aihwa Ong, "the neoliberal logic requires populations to be free, self-managing, and self-enterprising individuals in different spheres of everyday life . . . the neoliberal subject is therefore not a citizen with claims to the state but a self-enterprising citizen-subject who is obligated to become an 'entrepreneur' of himself or herself."[86] As Vietnamese subjects become incorporated into the citizenry through discourses of race and multiculturalism, they have also stressed their own focus on individual responsibility, despite their reliance on the state. Nevertheless, Vietnamese American communities are undergoing dramatic transformations in the beginning of the twenty-first century, as interests in social welfare, healthcare, immigrant rights, and other U.S. domestic concerns are becoming more pertinent to their lives. In a study of Vietnamese American political participation in Southern California, political scientist Christian Collet found: "More than half of Vietnamese Americans do not identify with a political party. Those that do identify are divided equally between the Republican and Democratic parties."[87] Although Republicans show a greater tendency to participate in politics and vote, issues relating to life in America as opposed to Vietnam mobilize Democrats, who are generally younger. It remains to be seen how the identities of this group of refugees and immigrants form as we move toward an increasingly flexible political economy.

Conclusion

The disturbing image of the refugee, especially that of the "boat person," threatens to reignite a powerful history of U.S. imperialist participation in the war in Vietnam. While the federal government has used this image, in the name of humanitarianism, to selectively disavow its history of colonial intervention, the legacy of the refugee label has shaped both public discourse and scholarship that has been produced about Vietnamese Americans. The unproblematic classification of "refugee" assigned to the Vietnamese who arrived in the United States in public policy studies and social science research created limitations in the historiography, confining it to only topics dealing with cultural and psychological adjustments, resettlement, and occupational or economic adaptation. These narrow conceptions of Vietnamese American lives have not only influenced their representation in social policy, academic research, and the mass media, but also in Vietnamese American historical and self-representation. The countless misrepresentations of Vietnamese refugees, their histories, and their actions indicate a persistent misunderstanding of Vietnamese cultural categories.

Taking the words of their informants at face value, many scholars who worked intimately with Vietnamese immigrants misinterpreted Vietnamese culture and created monolithic images of the refugees. In their research, anthropologists, sociologists, and historians neither considered the historical context and the politics of the Vietnam conflict nor attempted to reflect critically upon the discursive implications of the refugee category. While the refugee category enclosed Vietnamese Americans to "sendentarist assumptions" that tended to examine the pathological aspects of their migration, their minority status was also a subject of contentious debate. Racially, Vietnamese refugees and immigrants were grouped with other Asian Americans, yet their situation could also be placed outside the framework of civil rights discourse because the U.S. government considered their resettlement a "humanitarian" case. Additionally, their political conservatism aligns them not with other Asian Americans but with refugee groups such as Cuban Americans, who similarly had escaped communism.

Nevertheless, Vietnamese Americans desired a separate identity in the United States. Their struggle to form a uniquely Vietnamese American identity can be located in the history of the formation of Little Saigon, California.

While still maintaining their alliances with other Asian ethnic groups, such as the Chinese, the Vietnamese immigrant community struggled to forge its own ethnic identity. In the next chapter, I will explore why Vietnamese Americans opposed the mainstreaming of their business district. Blocking it from becoming "Asian American," Vietnamese Americans fought to recreate their own "Little Saigon." This desire to carve a geopolitical, social, and cultural space that is distinct from other Asians, specifically the Chinese and Japanese, shows not only new resistance on different ground, but also a need to become recognized as a separate Asian group with a profound historical connection to the United States.

Race and ethnicity are undeniably significant to the experiences of Vietnamese Americans; nevertheless, it must be recognized that these experiences are also characterized by heterogeneity and class difference. Socioeconomic status and occupation played essential roles in shaping Vietnamese migration even before the fall of Saigon, and these categories also determined the fate of some refugees and the eventual migration of others. Within categories of class are cultural meanings. In the next chapter, I will further investigate the economic and cultural significance of class as well as the transnational movement of capital as the Vietnamese American community resettles in Little Saigon.

Chapter 2   **Vietnamese by Other Means:**
           The Overlapping Diasporas
           of Little Saigon

WHEN AMERICAN TROOPS withdrew from Vietnam and surrendered the capital city of Saigon to communist forces on April 30, 1975, the defeat of the U.S.-backed South Vietnamese government left an indelible mark on the Vietnamese people who subsequently had to flee their fallen homeland. Losing their nation to enemies they had fought fiercely against was a haunting experience that prompted a collective search for alternative visions that could mitigate their tremendous losses. Upon arriving in the United States and in other asylum-granting countries, the Vietnamese refugees sought ways to negotiate their discontent and displacement. From nostalgia and a deep sense of longing, they reconstituted communities in exile and rebuilt infrastructures in the image of their lost nation. Their collective goals were twofold: to defy the communists through success in capitalist enterprise overseas and to garner enough political power throughout the Vietnamese diaspora so that one day it would be possible to bring democracy back to Vietnam.

While the latter appears to be a fantasy remote from realization, Vietnamese émigrés have proven extremely successful in rebuilding many "Little Saigons," or informal commercial and social districts resembling the former Saigon, throughout the world.[1] The most renowned and only officially recognized Little Saigon is located in Orange County, California, amid a cluster of burgeoning suburbs about seventy-five miles southwest of Los Angeles. In the heart of Westminster, this particular Little Saigon has emerged as the hub of political, social, and cultural life for Vietnamese in the diaspora. It has also become home to approximately 200,000 Vietnamese Americans, the largest population of ethnic Vietnamese outside the nation of Vietnam. With ethnic businesses and shops at its epicenter, Little Saigon spans over two miles and functions as a physical space for Vietnamese American commercial, cultural, and political activities.

Figure 3. The official "Little Saigon" sign designates the concentrated area of Vietnamese commercial development in Westminster, California, as a business district and tourist attraction. From *Paris by Night 77*, "30 Nam Vien Xu."

Vietnamese American commerce expanded from a handful of businesses in the late 1970s to nearly 2,000 commercial establishments in the 1990s. Ethnic businesses such as supermarkets, restaurants, karaoke bars, nightclubs, bakeries, noodle shops, sandwich shops, music and video stores, jewelry stores, fabric shops, medical and dental offices, cosmetic surgery clinics, beauty salons, and much more proliferate in Little Saigon. During holidays such as Tet (the Lunar New Year) and special days of commemoration such as the anniversary of the fall of Saigon, Orange County's Little Saigon attracts thousands of Vietnamese and non-Vietnamese tourists worldwide as the community publicly celebrates Vietnamese cultural heritage. Vietnamese people from all over Southern California and the diaspora come to Little Saigon to relive the past and to affirm their ethnic identity through cultural consumption and social interaction with other Vietnamese. To many Vietnamese immigrants, Little Saigon exists as a special domain in American society, for there a Vietnamese person can function without having to acquire a different language. The sheer number of Vietnamese people settling in Orange County has created a critical mass that makes the return to (or at least the lobbying for) a democratic Vietnam a genuine possibility.

This chapter explores the cultural, social, and political dimensions of Southern California's Little Saigon and the strategic ways in which

Vietnamese Americans construct ethnic identity amid Orange County's multicultural and politically conservative environment. I contend that cultural and economic institutions established by the Vietnamese immigrants in Little Saigon do more than just consolidate ethnic identity in the United States. These institutions symbolize the triumph of what South Vietnam *could have been* while they simultaneously create a market that produces and augments the desire for ethnicity. This process of creating and marketing ethnicity has both local and global implications due to the ambiguous position Vietnamese émigrés hold in the United States and the antagonistic public relationship they have with their former homeland. At the local level, the groundwork of diasporic cultural production opened doors for civic engagement whereby the infrastructure and the critical mass of Vietnamese residents inspired a sense of political participation. Yet the rallying point of that involvement surrounds issues of anticommunism, free market enterprise, and global capitalism. As a result, the productive tensions at the local level worked in tandem with the transnational markets of the Pacific Rim, particularly in the early 1990s, to allow for the flourishing of economic and political activities in Little Saigon. Extending beyond my analysis of discursive representations of Vietnamese refugees in the first chapter, I will zero in on the local experiences of cultural and social acculturation in Little Saigon and explore how Vietnamese Americans articulated citizenship that enabled their entrance into mainstream politics.

Local/Transnational Extensions and Interconnections

The ascendancy of Orange County's Little Saigon as the center of the diaspora did not occur in isolation or without conflict. Booming with cheap real estate, jobs in the nearby defense industry, and small entrepreneurial opportunities, the city of Westminster attracted people from all over the country. By the early 1980s, Orange County's white, conservative, suburban community had transformed into a heterogeneous one with a growing number of refugees from Southeast Asia. Lisa McGirr's compelling study of politics in suburban Orange County indicates that by this time, the new right had learned to manage multiculturalism while anticommunism receded into the background as "moral" issues, represented by pro-life and "pro-family" organizations, began to shape conservative politics.[2] While I concur that matters of morality began to take precedence over anticommunism during the waning years of the Cold War, I argue that the refugees from Southeast Asia actively positioned themselves as the new crusaders against communism, creating a resurgence in the movement that uses the language of morality to justify their cause.[3] In effect, knowing that the foreignness that marked them posed challenges to their adjustment, the newly arrived refugees exhibited a conservatism that made them politically acceptable in such an environment.

Although anticommunist ideology provided an important point of identification for all refugees from Southeast Asia, the ethnic Vietnamese immigrants as a community faced an additional challenge: to forge a cultural identity apart from the ethnic Chinese from Vietnam, who shared a similar migratory path and lived and worked in the area. Scholars and journalists alike have acknowledged the presence of ethnic Chinese in Little Saigon, but few scholars have analyzed the direct and indirect ways in which ethnic Chinese influenced the construction and arbitration of Vietnamese American identity. In my research, I discovered that the capitalist economic development and expansion of Little Saigon could not be separated from the history of Chinese emigration from Vietnam. The entangled histories between ethnic Chinese and ethnic Vietnamese must be traced back to Vietnam, where tensions between the two groups have extended through migration to the United States. With business acumen and access to capital from either the pooling of resources or from connections overseas, ethnic Chinese refugees from Vietnam figured prominently in the building of Little Saigon. Their entrepreneurial contributions to the enclave economy were so notable that their presence in Little Saigon constantly disrupted meanings of ethnic identity, cultural nationalism, and anticommunist politics in a community dominated by ethnic Vietnamese immigrants and refugees. Through war, transnational migration, and resettlement, the uninterrupted ethnic strife that circumscribes the contested relationship between ethnic Vietnamese and ethnic Chinese refugees from Vietnam may best be understood as what I call "overlapping diasporas."[4] The reinstitution of premigration economic power relations and anxieties over Chinese presence in Little Saigon not only shaped the ways in which Vietnamese exiles carved their distinctive identities in the United States but also enhanced how the two groups express their diasporic identities.

In what follows, I contend that ethnicity becomes powerfully salient in the overlapping diasporas for both ethnic Chinese and ethnic Vietnamese. Stuart Hall has argued that cultural identities are not only "strategic" but are also discontinuous points of identification that engage with power, culture, and history.[5] Mapping these ideas onto the overlapping diasporas, I suggest that the dynamics of ethnicity become flexible, shifting, and strategic while the *historical* experiences retain their resonance. As such, the concept of the overlapping diasporas does not preclude ethnic Chinese from their past as immigrants and refugees from Vietnam. Nevertheless, because ethnicity is deployed strategically in an overlapping context, the politics of affiliating through ethnic and cultural identification takes precedence over shared historical experiences. Consequently, the overlapping diasporas diverge at the point of ethnicity whereby emigration from Vietnam enables a different imagining of identity for both ethnic Chinese and Vietnamese subjects.

The series of negotiations with ethnic Chinese in Little Saigon provided a stage for ethnic Vietnamese immigrants to rehearse their potential in a local setting and to test their disposition as a conservative racial ethnic group in the political waters of Orange County. These interactions at the local level not only reaffirmed Vietnamese cultural identity but also enabled American citizens of Vietnamese descent to articulate a civic citizenship that would earn them public office. In recent years, a number of Vietnamese Americans have successfully entered mainstream politics by collaborating with Latinos and white, middle-class conservatives to engage in a new form of civic participation based on older conservative values of anticommunism and free-market enterprise. Running on issues that have traditionally been significant to the local community in Orange County, Vietnamese American politicians have garnered support from Vietnamese and non-Vietnamese voters alike. The effectiveness of their leadership in promoting community involvement with electoral politics has generated a reliable source to represent conservative, right-wing issues for the Republican Party. As one of many new multicultural symbols of the Republican Party, Vietnamese Americans sought to follow the path that Cuban Americans had paved in politics to challenge the government of their homeland. This path toward political ascension, however, required infrastructural as well as economic support from the ground.

Developing the Land for Capitalist Enterprise

Timothy Bui's popular film *Green Dragon* (2001) chronicles the experiences of first wave refugees and their arrival to the United States in 1975.[6] In one scene, a young Vietnamese man dreams about one day building a "Little Saigon" in America. Contrary to this Hollywood vision conjured by a second-generation Vietnamese American filmmaker, Vietnamese émigrés did not consciously plan to rebuild Saigon in Southern California. The undeveloped landscape of Westminster, however, provided a lucrative foundation for Vietnamese capitalist enterprise to burgeon in place of the nation the refugees had lost. Believing that rebuilding a new Saigon would be both an affront to the communist takeover of their fallen capital city as well as a recuperation of power for the former Republic, Vietnamese immigrants collectively worked to build "Little Saigon." This space would stand as the global center for all Vietnamese people displaced around the world. It would also be a safe haven where the exiles could fly the South Vietnamese flag, creating possibilities for imagining community and resurrecting the old capital in a new space complete with cultural institutions to foster that sense of community.[7]

It is difficult to imagine that the district now officially known as "Little Saigon" consisted of empty lots, orange groves, and strawberry and bean fields prior to being transformed by the refugees and immigrants from Vietnam. Bolsa Avenue, the main thoroughfare running through the heart of Westminster, had only a handful of small commercial establishments owned by Anglo-Americans who also had farmland in the area. Longtime developer Randy Russell of Orange County recalls, "Back in the '50s and '60s this area was just small roads." But, as Russell continues, the settlement of Vietnamese immigrants caused the area to undergo "the biggest changes" in the 1970s, "with farms being converted to housing tracts and commercial shopping centers."[8] The resettlement policy adopted by the U.S. government required the refugees to disperse across the country to ensure their financial self-sufficiency and prevent their overwhelming concentration in one community. The refugees' efforts to build concentrated ethnic communities, however, counteracted this policy. As sociologist Linda Trinh Võ explains, the Federal Resettlement Program failed to consider the important role that ethnic networks played in assisting refugees to adjust to their new environment.[9] Scattering the refugees, therefore, only delayed community formation. Many Vietnamese refugees gravitated toward places where their co-ethnics resided and moved to warmer climates reminiscent of their homeland.

Southern California became a popular destination for secondary migration, and Orange County provided an ideal environment for the new immigrants for numerous reasons. First, it offered relatively affordable housing and cheap real estate. Second, Vietnamese immigrants chose the area because of its good climate and possible job opportunities in the nearby technology and defense industries that were set up during the height of the Cold War.[10] Finally, Orange County was desirable because of its close proximity to Camp Pendleton, the Marine base where 50,000 Vietnamese refugees were processed and detained in makeshift camps while awaiting sponsorship. The refugees chose to remain close to Camp Pendleton so that they could be reunited with other family members from whom they had been separated during the process of evacuation.

The settlement of the first wave of refugees, mainly "academics, high-ranking military officers and people connected with the American embassy" facilitated the quick development of Little Saigon.[11] Many found highly skilled jobs in the booming computer, military defense, and aerospace industries that thrived throughout the 1980s.[12] Others, however, worked in jobs not commensurate with their previous professions but were able to gain self-sufficiency due to their previous exposure to American culture. As Vietnamese Americans collectively realized their potential to firmly establish a foothold in the community with their accumulated assets, they pursued what they perceived to be the American Dream by opening their own businesses.

The experiences of first wave refugees can be compared to that of other Asian immigrants who migrated to the United States in the post-1965 period.[13] Unable to find jobs corresponding to their skills, they relied on small family business entrepreneurship for upward mobility. Oftentimes, however, this depended on the unpaid or minimally paid labor of spouses, children, and relatives. Working long hours at marginal profits, few Asian American business owners managed to achieve the desired success of which they dreamed and a majority of businesses ran a high risk of failure. Still, Vietnamese immigrants and refugees believed that free enterprise paved the simplest path to financial freedom, even at the expense of requiring all family members, including young children, to work. Using family labor enabled small businesses to gain higher profits with low wages or no compensation. Former math teacher and computer store owner in Little Saigon Nguyen Huu Gi explains:

> Americans make big investment, hire manager, technicians. Vietnamese cannot afford that, but wife and children will work hard. At first I keep old job while wife and friend take care of store; later I quit to run business full time. Until last year we are here seven days a week, sometimes until 2 in the morning. Now we're doing OK, so we take Sunday off.[14]

But most people do not take weekends and holidays off, as these are the busiest days in Little Saigon. To meet the consumer demands of the successive waves of co-ethnics who arrived between the late 1980s and mid-1990s, Vietnamese shopkeepers needed to accommodate to their special needs, seven days a week, often working ten-hour days.

Vietnamese immigrants and refugees worked toward business ownership because they believed this generated opportunities for prosperity in capitalist America. Rather than struggle in the mainstream corporate system, where discrimination persisted and glass ceilings remained prevalent for ethnic minorities, Vietnamese American entrepreneurs preferred to start up businesses in the enclave economy. As more and more opened their own shops, restaurants, stores, and establishments of all sorts (including entertainment venues catering to the everyday lives of the community), a niche market that focused on the selling of ethnicity began to mushroom in Little Saigon. The enclave also enabled former business owners to reestablish what they had owned prior to fleeing from communism. Reminiscent of the lost homeland, business establishments often reclaimed their former fame by carrying the same names they once had in Vietnam. The idea inspired customers to be instantly whisked away by nostalgia as memories of their former lives in the homeland came rushing through their senses. This became a proven strategy that attracted customers in search of specialty foods and products they once had before migration.

Early Resistance to Community Formation

In order to understand the Vietnamese American community of the present, it is imperative to trace its role in Orange County's relatively recent past which began with refugee resettlement in the late 1970s. Southern California experienced a population explosion of Vietnamese refugees from both the increasing number of newcomers as well as from those who had migrated from other parts of the country, having been settled by the U.S. government in colder climates and far away from their co-ethnics. The growth of the Vietnamese immigrant and refugee community did not go unnoticed. Its rapid expansion alarmed many longtime native residents of conservative Orange County who sought ways to curb its development throughout the late 1970s and early 1980s. These efforts included passing a "citizen's petition" to stop the city from granting Vietnamese immigrants business licenses, illegal real estate redlining, and white flight.

The influx of Vietnamese immigrants and refugees instilled much anxiety among white American residents of Orange County who felt their quiet "bedroom community" was being "taken over" by foreigners.[15] Though the Vietnamese people were initially welcomed as "refugees from communism" by supporters of U.S. involvement in Southeast Asia, the influx of refugees into the conservative bastion of "lily white" Orange County caused great discomfort among existing residents.[16] This uneasiness was further exacerbated by the perceived belief that the new immigrants benefited from welfare and interest-free government loans.[17] Vietnamese immigrants actually never received such loans; rather, they tended to informally pool money together as a way to participate in business enterprise. Initially, the refugees did not pose a threat, but when their businesses began to expand in the city of Westminster in 1981, a group of local residents circulated a petition declaring "a moratorium on the issuance of business licenses to any person of Vietnamese origin."[18] Though it gathered a few hundred signatures, the city council and then Mayor Kathy Buchoz voted against it. Buchoz's strong dedication to growing the immigrant community and advocacy for economic development in Westminster never ceased. Her experience in real estate combined with the "positive relationships" she built with the refugees made her a valuable ally who would later play an important role in the Vietnamese American community.[19] In 1988, years after her service as Mayor of Westminster, Buchoz went on to work for Frank Jao, a controversial yet prominent commercial real estate developer whom I will discuss later. Jao handpicked her to work as vice president of his Bridgecreek Realty and Development Company, the largest Vietnamese American commercial developer of the area.

The petition that Buchoz defeated exists as one of many racially motivated actions against Vietnamese resettlement in the community. Other incidents showing disapproval of Little Saigon's growth and prosperity recurred through the defacement of the "Little Saigon" signs that were placed on the San Diego and Garden Grove Freeways. The *Los Angeles Times* reported that the signs were "subjected to vandalism daily by zealous patriots who viewed it as the gradual corrosion of America into pockets of ethnic communities."[20] Despite these overt acts of racial violence, Vietnamese Americans remained steadfast in making their presence more pronounced than ever in Orange County. They believed, as business professional Luu Tran Kiem did, that "the best way for [the Vietnamese immigrants] to be accepted by the American people is to establish [their] own economic self-sufficiency."[21] Committed to making their community visible, Vietnamese Americans worked diligently to establish a local presence.

As Vietnamese-owned businesses began to boom in Westminster, white residents fled to the more affluent coastal regions of Orange County such as Newport Beach and Laguna Beach, while the growing wealth of the inland communities of refugees began to confront hostility from within. A reign of gang violence plagued Little Saigon and perpetuated anti-Vietnamese sentiment throughout the 1980s. Part of the whirlwind of change that swept through the region came with the arrival of the second wave of Vietnamese refugees. The influx of "boat people" into Orange County shifted the demographics of the Vietnamese community, diversifying and creating socioeconomic, ethnic, and regional distinctions within the immigrant group. Unlike the first wave of elite immigrants who generally came from Vietnam's metropolitan cities, the second wave of refugees consisted of ethnic Chinese who lived in Southeast Asia and working-class Vietnamese from rural areas who had little or no exposure to American culture. Experiencing difficulty adjusting to American society, youth members of subsequent waves of Vietnamese refugees formed gangs that threatened their wealthier, more assimilated compatriots. News coverage of gang activity in Vietnamese immigrant neighborhoods alleged that "various criminal activities such as extortion, street crimes, and 'home invasion' robberies" often became part of life in Little Saigon.[22] Gang activities however often went unreported in Little Saigon for two reasons: first, residents would live in fear of retaliation if they went to the authorities; and second, Vietnamese immigrants did not want to draw negative attention to their community, especially as they tried to gain acceptance from the dominant culture. As a result, they continued to live under the threat of terror as they did in their war-torn society.

Gangs were not the only threat of violence in Little Saigon. The need to articulate a firm stance against communism also kept the Vietnamese community on guard. Anthropologist Aihwa Ong and others have documented the ways in which refugees lived under constant surveillance, particularly from the state.[23] Drawing from Foucault, Ong's work on governmentality demonstrates that the state structures of surveillance have regulated and circumscribed citizenship for Southeast Asian refugees. While the state remains present in the lives of Vietnamese refugees, the threat of additional surveillance among co-ethnics serves as a powerful reminder that "freedom," particularly for those who resided in dense communities with other Vietnamese, remains illusory. The moral imperative to construct the Vietnamese American community as a vehemently anticommunist one has resulted in new forms of surveillance imposed from within. In the years immediately after the communist takeover, the Vietnamese community made it a priority to sever ties with the Socialist Republic of Vietnam. They believed that depriving the Vietnamese communist government through economic isolation would choke the nation, leaving it desperate for assistance from Western democratic powers. Despite the strong conviction toward isolation, many immigrants and refugees had family members who remained in Vietnam. Maintaining personal familial ties to the homeland was a filial duty expected of those who left; they felt they had, in some ways, abandoned loved ones. Moreover, it was common practice to send remittances to family and relatives back in Vietnam, yet any positive expression toward normalizing economic relations or doing business with the Vietnamese government at the time was subject to death threats. Anticommunism functioned in multivalent ways: it served as a political rallying point for Vietnamese immigrants to maintain their commitment to the ideologies of the Cold War, and it simultaneously kept their community distinct from other Asian communities, particularly the Chinese, who did not have a very strong investment in maintaining an anticommunist agenda. Rather, ethnic Chinese Vietnamese tended to affiliate with other overseas Chinese and often deployed their identities strategically. Friction between Vietnamese and ethnic Chinese refugees from Vietnam perpetuated issues carried through the migration process, but it created a productive tension. The presence of ethnic Chinese from Vietnam disrupted and inadvertently contributed to the forging of a Vietnamese American community in Little Saigon.

Envisioning Little Saigon—Not Another Chinatown

It is significant that Little Saigon developed in a suburban community where changes to the landscape reflected both geographic and demographic transformations in the region. This former bastion of white, middle-class conservatism may have initially resisted Vietnamese settlement, but longtime residents began to incorporate the immigrants and refugees from Southeast Asia when they saw in the newcomers an eagerness to build on the land and their potential to increase revenue flow into the fledgling economy, particularly amid the downturn of the 1970s. Little Saigon expanded out of a collective yearning for basic social and cultural needs that the Vietnamese population lacked in their new place of residence. The immigrants and refugees were able to find employment and affordable housing in Orange County, but the region lacked the amenities that an ethnic enclave offered. In the mid-1970s and early 1980s, metropolitan Los Angeles and the city's Chinatown were the only outposts in Southern California where Asian immigrants could go to purchase specialty goods, groceries, foodstuffs, and other ethnic and cultural sundries such as teas, spices, sauces, and noodles unavailable in mainstream American grocery stores. For Asian residents of Orange County, however, Chinatown could only be accessible by car, which often required a day trip for many families. The long distance also posed a problem for those who did not have access to transportation.

Little Saigon emerged as a result of the collective effort of Vietnamese Americans, but the public lore surrounding this enclave often credits one person for his role in its growth and expansion: Frank Jao, an ethnic Chinese refugee from Vietnam who had the vision of building another Chinatown in Orange County.[24] A "first wave" immigrant who came to the United States in 1975, Jao was a former employee of an American corporate enterprise in Vietnam. He claims to have arrived with modest means. Jao's personal narrative, mostly recounted in print media, tells the story of a man who successfully achieved the American Dream through "hard work." He began in this country taking odd jobs such as a door-to-door vacuum salesman. As his knowledge of American business improved and his diligent work ethic became sharpened by financial opportunities, Jao became one of the most successful land developers in Westminster. Jao's visionary goals compounded with his belief in the rewards of real estate investments made him a shrewd and savvy businessman.

Jao's early vision for developing the business district has been documented widely in news media covering Little Saigon's economic growth. Jao reportedly came to the realization that a Chinatown was greatly needed in Orange County's Asian immigrant community after one of his weekend trips to Los Angeles' Chinatown. As early as 1978, Jao and several others conceived of a plan to bring the products and services to the people rather than having them drive all the way to Los Angeles. As he affirmed in an interview, "Move the business to the population, not the other way around. That's the way you make money."[25] Throughout the 1980s, Jao fronted the most significant development of the area, transforming the landscape of Westminster into what is now known as Little Saigon. Through syndication, a process by which capital for development projects is accumulated through investments, Jao, along with friends and business partners, converted empty farmland into a commercial district and ethnic enclave that catered to the needs of immigrants not only from Vietnam, but Southeast Asia more generally.[26]

Though Little Saigon would eventually receive official recognition and its own sign on the freeways of Southern California nearly a decade later, the fight to gain formal recognition for Little Saigon was a battle not only between Vietnamese Americans and the residents of Orange County. Ongoing ethnic struggles between the Chinese and Vietnamese residents that carried over from old Saigon into Little Saigon also existed throughout its various stages of development between the late 1970s to the mid-1990s. In his sociological study of Monterey Park, California, Timothy Fong argues that the money from Chinese immigrants that went into developing the area "did not so much 'whiten' as heighten racial and ethnic tensions."[27] Consequently, anti-Chinese and anti-immigrant sentiment brewed as a result of class and ethnic cleavages that formed in the "first suburban Chinatown." Likewise, Little Saigon benefited from Chinese money; however, the overlapping diasporas mitigated overt anti-Chinese sentiment creating dynamic tensions between the ethnic groups.

Forging Identity amid Overlapping Diasporas

As a result of China's former colonial control in Vietnam, people of ethnic Chinese descent were significantly present in the economic development of modern Vietnam. Research scholar Ramses Amer observed that the ethnic Chinese comprised the largest group of foreign laborers in Vietnam.[28] His study of enterprise in modern Vietnam documented that the Chinese dominated a number of industries including trade, fishing, and rice farming. Chinese merchants controlled various business sectors and had excess capital to act as moneylenders. With such economic predominance in Vietnam, the government of the former Republic could not successfully curb the activities of the Chinese population. This allowed them to strategically incorporate themselves into Vietnamese society by becoming citizens and earning the rights of Vietnamese citizenship to freely expand their business enterprises. As in numerous urban spaces through out the world, Chinese entrepreneurs carved enclave communities in Vietnam. The largest concentration of ethnic Chinese lived and worked in Cho Lon in the center of Vietnam's former capital, Saigon. This community was so insular that some of the Chinese did not learn how to speak Vietnamese at all.

During the American occupation, as Ramses Amer argues, "ethnic Chinese capitalists not only exploited the hardworking Vietnamese people but also collaborated with the Americans and the Republic of Vietnam authorities in order to make economic gains."[29] After the fall of Saigon, the communist government persecuted the Chinese, particularly the merchant class, and forcibly expelled or repatriated them back to China. The historian Sucheng Chan recounts that "the new rulers of Vietnam set their priorities on ridding their country of 'bourgeois' elements, foremost among whom were thousands of Chinese petty traders whose families had lived in Vietnam for centuries."[30] In doing so, the government closed Chinese businesses, confiscated their assets, removed them from civil service, and rationed their food. As living conditions deteriorated and discrimination intensified, an overwhelming number of ethnic Chinese fled Vietnam to become part of the cohort known as the "boat people."

Though the ethnic Chinese consisted of only 3 percent of Vietnam's population at the end of the war in 1975, they make up one-quarter of the émigrés in California and reportedly own "a disproportionate share of 'Vietnamese businesses'" in the United States.[31] A Vietnamese immigrant of Chinese descent, Frank Jao is a figure that has become a source of multiple rifts within the community, forcing it to define itself amid contested grounds. Having developed more than half of the properties in the Little Saigon district, including eleven mini-malls and two large indoor shopping centers, Jao's wealth and power can be perceived as a threat to Vietnamese identity, despite his emigration from Vietnam.

In the early 1980s, Jao caused great anxiety to the community's public image by suggesting that it would be more profitable to make the commercial district into a "pan-Asian" commercial and cultural center rather than cater solely to the Vietnamese community. Jao led this movement by naming his two largest shopping centers, "Asian Garden" and "Asian Village." In 1986, before Little Saigon received formal recognition by the state of California, he lobbied arduously to name the business district he helped build. According to *Los Angeles Times* reporter, Lily Dizon, Jao "spearheaded a movement to have the district be named 'Asiantown,'... reasoning that it would draw a more diverse group of visitors."[32] Jao believed that expanding the businesses to cater to Asian Americans, such as Koreans, Taiwanese, Cambodians, Thai, and Chinese who lived in neighboring counties, would generate more revenue even though three-quarters of the population is Vietnamese.[33]

Though Jao's plans were defeated, he was not the only one who had a pan-Asian vision. Tony Lam, another prominent member of the Vietnamese American community, who would later become the first city-elected official of Vietnamese descent, also supported Jao's vision. In 1987, Lam asserted, "We want to call our community Asiantown—not 'Little Saigon' which is too negative and reminds [American] people of the bad experiences from the war (in Vietnam)."[34] Like Jao, Lam believed that the mainstreaming of "ethnic" cultures was much more profitable and less invasive than unearthing memories of an unpopular war. In the end, the state of California submitted to grassroots activism and pressure from ethnic Vietnamese Americans who fought to designate the Little Saigon business district a special tourist zone. Insisting on cultural difference, their victory claimed the space for Vietnamese Americans and allowed for commercial enterprises to flourish in the area.

The struggle to forge the geographic space of Little Saigon reveals telling ways in which Vietnamese and Chinese Vietnamese perform strategic ethnicity in the overlapping diaspora. As an ethnic Chinese from Vietnam,

Frank Jao had the flexibility to position himself as an Asian American. Jao's Chinese identity allows him to align himself with other Chinese Americans as well as to argue for pan-Asianism without inciting resentment from the Vietnamese community. For ethnic Vietnamese Americans like Tony Lam, however, favoring pan-Asian identity over a distinctive Vietnamese identity had grave political consequences. Vietnamese immigrants remember the war with great intensity, and the misgivings still remain. On the one hand, the Vietnamese American community expresses a great desire to be included in the American body politic and to be acknowledged for the contributions its members have made in their newly adopted home. On the other hand, the refugee community continues to be perceived as a post-colonial legacy that reminds Americans of their government's failure in a senseless war. Stigmatized as a burden in American society, Vietnamese Americans are sometimes forced to negate their historical connection to the war in order to blend in. The ambivalence expressed by community leaders such as Tony Lam reflects the complicated position with which the Vietnamese American community must contend.

Not everyone in the community believed that disavowing its history served to protect Vietnamese American interests. In fact, a number of activists fought for the formal recognition of Little Saigon.[35] Part of their strategy to place Little Saigon on the map displayed both a need to increase the visibility of Vietnamese Americans and a critical reminder of the historical connection between Vietnam and the United States. When Little Saigon finally received official name recognition and designation as a tourist zone, these formalities renewed the spirits of the refugees and marked a great revival of the lost nation. More important, it ushered a resurgence of Vietnamese cultural and social life in Little Saigon unlike before.

Little Saigon's Epicenter: the Asian Garden Mall, or *Phuoc, Loc, Tho*

Ironically, no other place in Little Saigon exhibits more Vietnamese ethnic pride and cultural tenacity than the famed retail outlet owned by ethnic Chinese Frank Jao, the Asian Garden Mall. A two-story, 150,000-square-foot shopping plaza Jao and his partners built for $15 million in 1986, the Asian Garden Mall houses an array of shops selling all kinds of goods and services, including food, clothes, small gifts, toys, leather goods, shoes, designer watches, eyeglasses, accessories, books, music, and other miscellaneous items.

Customers can walk in, get their hair cut, and have shoes and suits custom made by Vietnamese shoemakers and tailors, all while meeting a

Little Saigon, California

Figure 4. "Asian-style" architecture imbues the landmark front entrance of Frank Jao's Asian Garden Mall, more commonly known as "Phuoc, Loc, Tho." From *Paris by Night 77*, "30 Nam Vien Xu."

friend for lunch. On the lower level, the food court offers Vietnamese food of all varieties. From convenient prepackaged rice noodle dishes, sweet candied coconut cakes, sour, pickled, and salty snacks, to croissants and French-Vietnamese cold-cut sandwiches, full-service foods such as *pho* (Vietnamese beef noodle soup), Chinese food, and even French baked goods, these small, usually family-run stalls have everything available. To drink, there is fresh-squeezed sugarcane juice, Vietnamese iced lattes, and all kinds of tropical fruit smoothies. In Little Saigon one can find anything that was available in the original Saigon and more.

On the upper level of Asian Garden lies the core of the mall: the renowned jewelry center famous for its wholesale prices. Former jewelers from Vietnam practice their craft by employing new technology in jewelry making and design in small, individually rented booths, while itinerant jewelry peddlers walk from booth to booth showcasing their goods. Displays of overwhelmingly radiant luxury items make the jewelry center a place of business where goods are sold, bought, and traded, as well as a place where Vietnamese American socialites shop and flaunt their wealth.

As the largest shopping mall in all of Little Saigon, Asian Garden attracts Vietnamese people of varied socioeconomic backgrounds. Visitors from all over stroll around the mall to people watch, eat from Vietnamese food-to-go snack shops, make purchases, receive various services ranging from photography to insurance information, and most of all, sample new music blaring from the record stores lining the entire mall. As many as four small record stores and three mega music centers are located inside the mall. Each store proudly displays large posters of Vietnamese entertainers on the glass windows and walls. In fact, music and media productions are so integral to the commercial vitality of the mall that Little Saigon has become known as the "Vietnamese Nashville" by the dominant media.[36] Stores stock every kind of electronic media production, including bootlegged copies of American music and imported music and videos from Vietnam. Most of the stores' revenues are generated from recordings made by the Vietnamese American music industry located in Orange County. The work of Vietnamese American singers and performers are displayed publicly on large posters, especially in larger stores where big-screen TVs play videos of the latest releases. Tourists come from throughout the diaspora to purchase CDs, videos, tapes, karaoke discs, and DVDs of their favorite Vietnamese American musical performers.[37]

Despite Jao's insistence on the mall's "Asian" designation, persistent signs of Vietnamese culture, particularly cultural consumable goods such as food, music, and video, dominate all his malls. In addition, an overwhelming number of Vietnamese American shop owners rent his retail spaces and mainly Vietnamese shoppers patronize their stores. Overlooking Jao's vision of the pan-Asian enclave, local residents and visitors, intentionally or inadvertently, refuse to refer to his mall as Asian Garden. Rather, everyone calls it *"Phuoc, Loc, Tho"*—a name derived from the three statues of Asian gods representing, "good fortune, happiness, and longevity" standing at the front entrance of the property.

Adventures in Bridge Building

Jao's remarkable entrepreneurial spirit refuses to succumb under pressure from the Vietnamese American community. When an economic downturn appeared imminent in Little Saigon in the mid-1990s and Orange County suffered the biggest municipal bankruptcy in U.S. history, Jao conceived several plans to revitalize the enclave economy. Determined to open Little Saigon to outsiders, Jao once again proposed to expand his malls by welcoming popular corporations such as Barnes and Noble and Starbucks Coffee to attract the younger generation to return and shop in Little Saigon.[38] When these ideas for expansion failed in 1996, he single-handedly sought to give Little Saigon a facelift and a new identity as a tourist destination by proposing to build a 500-foot-long, thirty-foot-wide pedestrian bridge that would connect his two malls, Asian Garden and Asian Village, on the main strip of Little Saigon's commercial district.

Jao believed that his Harmony Bridge would become a new "symbol of Little Saigon" that would "enhance the identity of the district."[39] However, the project met impassioned resistance by members of the Vietnamese American community who thought the architectural design of the bridge was "too Chinese." Asserting that the bridge represented "an insult to Vietnamese culture," community activists Mai Cong and husband Dinh Le formed the Ad Hoc Committee to Safeguard Little Saigon to stop Jao from once again "impos[ing] his vision of diversifying the district at the expense of Little Saigon's identity."[40] Jao responded to these allegations by denying the relevance of an ethnic conflict and insisting that protesters were simply "jealous of his achievements." Jao continued by declaring, "If a person has hatred in the heart of his old country, it should not be brought over to the United States. When we are here, we are Americans, we should not carry on a history of hatred against each other."[41] Using multicultural discourse to quell and divert ethnic tensions, Jao argued and positioned Vietnam as unfree and oppressive. Correspondingly, he implied that Vietnamese immigrants should not replicate the behavior of such a nation and transfer those malicious attitudes to American society. By constructing the United States as a democratic nation thriving on capitalism and free enterprise, Jao effectively erased the appearance of any tension embroiled in ethnic conflicts.

Jao's public gesture toward reconciliation may appear admirable and conciliatory, but he comes from a position of power in the community. Jao is not just a wealthy entrepreneur; he is also an ethnic Chinese refugee from Vietnam who possesses flexible cultural citizenship.[42] Situated in a privileged position in the overlapping diasporas, Jao can claim multiple identities as a Vietnamese refugee, a Chinese American, a diasporic Chinese and/or Vietnamese subject, and as an ethnic American. Anthropologist Aihwa Ong's study of the Chinese diaspora provides insight into how a man like Jao might succeed as a citizen in a Western democracy and as an entrepreneur in the global economy. She writes:

> Overseas Chinese manipulate their image as internal outsiders in the West by producing discourses of themselves as productive and law-abiding minority citizens. They actively deploy images of themselves as skillful handlers of money, trading minorities, and middlemen in global corporate and media discourses, thus intervening in the epistemological field within which they must situate themselves in the West.[43]

Jao employed flexible strategies to further his business goals and moved between global and local discourses as he constructed his identity. For example, though Jao repeatedly insists in interviews that he "doesn't know anything about politics," his identity politics have been notably deliberate and his business decisions have always been politically savvy.[44] With his wealth and power, Jao befriended a number of politicians over the course of his lifetime as a capitalist commercial developer.

On the day I interviewed Mr. Jao, City Councilmen Frank Fry and Tony Lam had appointments with him and were present at his office. Kathy Buchoz, former mayor of Westminster and current vice president of Jao's company, whom I also interviewed, believes that he hired her because she has "a positive relationship with a lot of Vietnamese businesses, and the Vietnamese community itself." Mr. Jao has admitted publicly that he contributes heavily to the "probusiness" Republican Party.[45] In February 2003, President George W. Bush appointed Jao to be a board member of the Vietnam Education Foundation, an organization that spends $5 million on educational exchanges between the United States and Vietnam.[46]

Although Jao projects himself as an apolitical businessman, his most criticized political act involved a decision over turning the spelling of his surname from the Vietnamized version *Trieu* to *Jao*, the Mandarin Chinese version.[47] Jao defended his name change by referring to the history of forced assimilation Vietnamese rulers imposed upon the ethnic Chinese whereby sinicized names were given Vietnamese spellings. Jao asserts that his name change was not an abandonment of Vietnamese ethnicity; rather, it was merely a reverting back to his "true" Chinese name.[48] Suspicious of Jao's intentions, however, the Vietnamese American community interpreted Jao's name change as a rejection of his Vietnamese past. Nonetheless, Jao's new name opened opportunities and allowed him to position himself as a Chinese American, a strategic move that facilitated his business ventures abroad as well as dealings with other Chinese immigrants from Taiwan and Hong Kong. Many ethnic Chinese immigrants from Vietnam believed that affiliating with the Chinese diaspora opened economic doors to the East and the Pacific Rim. Jao's new identity allowed him to pass as an overseas Chinese. In the context of the early 1990s and the rise of the economic "tigers" in Southeast Asia, Jao's flexible identification granted him access and the ability to float between different worlds and succeed financially in all of them. Among Jao's business circle is longtime business partner

Roger Chen, a Taiwanese American who owns the lucrative 99 Ranch supermarket chain, which is present throughout Southern California. Jao does not deny the importance of his Vietnamese compatriots, but his transnational and global business ties to Asia seem overwhelmingly significant in developing his local stronghold.

Jao credited the basis of his wealth not from actual capital assets but from the belief in the *promise* of financial success his numerous development projects could offer. He explained that obtaining loans from banks posed a tremendous challenge for refugees in the early 1980s. However, the preconceived notion of excessive overseas Chinese wealth investing in his development projects from abroad enabled him to syndicate plans and obtain loans from banks.[49] Trusting that his real-estate developments would reap benefits from such investments abroad, financial institutions lent Jao money to build his real-estate empire. Jao claims that he relied mainly on investors from the refugee community and maintains that a majority of his business partners are Vietnamese Americans. Nevertheless, overseas Chinese from Hong Kong, Singapore, and Taiwan have also had a notable presence in Little Saigon's economy. Jao's financing has been reported to come from Chinese investors living in Indonesia as well as China.[50] Additionally, reporter Christa Piotroski notes, "75% of Little Saigon's total income is deposited into the accounts of Hong Kong Chinese."[51] Jao's transnational Chinese affiliations, imagined or real, have indeed enabled him to become one of the most successful commercial real estate developers in Little Saigon.

As a controversial ethnic Chinese figure in Little Saigon, Jao has often faced opposition from the community. Acrimonious protests from Vietnamese American community leaders forced Jao to abandon the Harmony Bridge project that he and his partners financed. But Jao continued to pursue other projects that proudly displayed his Chinese heritage. Expanding his Asian Village Mall, Jao added a courtyard equipped with kiosks to rent out to small businesses, extending to the New Saigon Mall, another indoor mall that sold cultural items, including Vietnamese artwork. Along the parking lot, Jao also installed an impressively long mural that narrates the history of Vietnamese civilization and an allotment of statues imported from China representing Vietnamese and Chinese historical and mythic figures. Here, Jao also paid tribute to Confucius, the Chinese philosopher who many believe to be the most influential figure in Vietnamese history. This public homage to Chinese and Vietnamese art and history, however, failed to produce profits. With no revenue, Jao converted the space of the New Saigon Mall into a housing project for senior citizens, another astute business decision to meet the needs of the community.

Jao's projects, including the elaborate display of statues of Confucius and his disciples (a symbolic gesture of China's most influential tenets imposed on Vietnam) may be interpreted as a form of silent protest against his Vietnamese critics.[52] At the same time, however, Jao's plans for Little Saigon have always been impassioned, desiring the enclave to reach the level of recognition as Chinatown or Little Tokyo. His attempts to make Little Saigon a pan-Asian cultural and commercial district can also be read as a gesture to appease both his Chinese investors and his Vietnamese customers as well as draw in more American tourists. The embittered rhetoric over the bridge controversy reveals Little Saigon's position as a site of postcolonial ethnic conflict and a point in the overlapping diasporas where cultural nationalism, ethnicity, and class differences converge.

Little Saigon symbolically represents the reconstituted nation, yet resurrecting the lost capital city in the United States demands the reconciliation of a number of vestiges from the past. First, the presence of ethnic Chinese and their economic power consistently posed obstacles to assertions of Vietnamese cultural nationalism. With business acumen, Chinese Vietnamese Americans not only managed to retain the economic prowess they once held in old Saigon, but also possessed the flexibility to identify with other diasporic and overseas Chinese and/or Vietnamese as well as the more established Chinese American community. Past experiences with migration and mobility have allowed the Chinese to cope with transience while imagining themselves as part of a larger overlapping diaspora. As a scholar of Vietnamese immigration, Chuong Hoang Chung calls the ethnic Chinese "twice minorities," meaning that the multiple minority status that the ethnic Chinese experience in different locales helps them become more adept at surviving migration processes.[53] Moreover, the Chinese occupation and colonization of Vietnam left an indelible legacy of Chinese influence on the Vietnamese population. The entangled past of these two ethnic groups has fostered an interdependency whereby the economic sharpness of the Chinese instilled a stronger and more persistent cultural identity for Vietnamese in their insistence on difference.

Despite shared experiences of war, migration, and resettlement, the Vietnamese have vied for a place to call their own since their arrival in 1975. Chinese presence and prominence have plagued Vietnamese cultural purists who have felt a necessity to construct Vietnamese uniqueness amid multicultural Southern California. It is important to point out that they imagined physical, geographical space to build cultural institutions that would enable the production of public images as well as the preservation of historical memories. Little Saigon became the foundation and site where Vietnamese American voices began to emerge.

Blending East/West Architecture

The suburban outgrowth of the Vietnamese community has left the exterior appearance of Little Saigon's malls and businesses resembling a simulated postcolonial Saigon, complete with Asian and French colonial architecture. Oriental accented structures blended with French colonial design mark the overall characteristics of many of the mini-malls erected in the enclave. These buildings are further enhanced by French colonial décor, pagoda-like arches, statues of central figures in East Asian philosophy and religion, and curved rooftops reminiscent of Chinese-style architecture. Little Saigon has become such an integral part of Westminster's landscape that the city places special architectural requirements on the construction of commercial buildings in the area.

Developed in 1993 as a preventative measure in the aftermath of the aforementioned controversial battle between the ethnic Chinese and the ethnic Vietnamese, the *Design Standards Manual of the City of Westminster* offers elaborate explanations on how to construct sites of commerce that will conform to city regulations. It states that any new or existing developments in the community planning area of Little Saigon must adhere to the following requirements: "The design theme shall incorporate architectural elements similar to those found on buildings constructed in Vietnam in the early 1900s in the French Colonial tradition" or "follow a traditional Chinese architectural theme" because "this style of architecture is used on many religious buildings in Vietnam."[54] Disavowing Vietnam's multilayered history of colonialism, the City of Westminster supports an Orientalist style of architecture that adds "multicultural flavor" to suburban sprawl. In theory, the architecture of the standing structures in Little Saigon would ideally be characterized by both "Western" and "Asian" elements replicating that of the original Saigon, but in practice the bricolage of ornate decorations are mere "ethnic" backdrops for neon signs with Vietnamese-, Chinese-, and French-named businesses. These businesses form the market that both produces and consumes the ethnic goods available locally but which can be traced back to Asia. It is through the economic ties to Asia and the Pacific Rim that commerce in Little Saigon has maintained a steady base since the early 1990s.

Owing largely to these transnational flows of goods and services, Little Saigon has grown to become a tourist destination that receives approximately 300,000 visitors annually, far from its original purpose. Little Saigon initially developed to meet the myriad needs of the Vietnamese refugee and immigrant community. The material and emotional desires of those who had abruptly fled their homeland included access to ethnic foods and groceries as well as mutual assistance and social services conducted in Vietnamese. These necessities eventually evolved into a larger project of establishing commercial and communal roots in the United States, made possible by America's flexible capitalist system of accumulation and expansion. From nostalgia and memory, Vietnamese Americans attempted to recover the territorial loss they experienced as refugees by rebuilding their lives in the United States. Born out of an intensified longing for the homeland, Little Saigon gradually became a place for people to reminisce about the old country, a place that reminds them of the original Saigon. In an interview, Le Thi Thach, an elderly woman from San Diego, told a reporter, "I come here to remember Saigon. Everything is Vietnamese here and everyone speaks Vietnamese."[55] The Vietnamese language is spoken throughout the area, the aroma of all types of Vietnamese food lingers, and the sound of Vietnamese music resonates from record shops. Parents bring their children to be immersed in what they believe is Vietnamese culture, groups of elderly men gather to play Chinese chess at tables surrounding the mall, and monks from the local temple seek donations from the entrance. Small-business ownership opportunities have also revitalized traditional trades where former craftspeople could reapply their skills for particular consumers who wish to purchase custom-made suits, traditional costumes, dresses, handmade shoes and other items that mainstream American markets fail to provide Vietnamese consumers. The group of small niche markets and shops in the early 1980s, however, unexpectedly developed into an entire district now known as Little Saigon.

Constructing the Leisure Industry

In only twenty years, Vietnamese immigrants made Orange County into something completely different than it was before their arrival. According to Lisa McGirr, the strict moralism that dominated the population during the first half of the twentieth century prohibited saloons and other drinking establishments as well as any public displays of sexual behavior.[56] Conservative establishments and institutions no longer hold the influence they once did as ethnic businesses began to populate the region.

In its present form, Little Saigon is surrounded by mini-malls and small businesses signifying what Saigon would have been like if the South had won. Walking through the interiors of the shopping malls of Little Saigon, one can feel momentarily transported back to Vietnam—a Vietnam frozen in time by the legacies of war and escapist spaces of entertainment.

Resurrecting the original Saigon involved more than the reconstruction of shops and restaurants; it demanded a full makeover of the cultural landscape in Little Saigon. Formerly dubbed the "Paris of the Orient," French colonial Saigon paralleled the original "city of lights" in form and content. Like Paris, Saigon possessed cultural worldliness as well as a vibrant nightlife that included cafés, bars, dance clubs, and nightclubs with live entertainment. The increased militarization of Vietnamese society during the 1960s and early 1970s as well as the influx of American soldiers who brought with them American popular culture, however, transformed Saigon into an urban entertainment district that depended on prostitution and other exploitative sex industries that were vital to the wartime economy. Although Little Saigon is absent of these types of raucous forms of entertainment, due in large part to its suburban location, Vietnamese entrepreneurs have attempted to revitalize a culture industry resembling that of wartime Saigon.

Accommodating the many Vietnamese Americans who work in the area, Little Saigon has also witnessed a boom in business establishments that fulfilled their desires for entertainment and leisure after the workday, which usually ends around six o'clock at night. With the hegemonic presence of French and American colonialism as well as a wartime past in its recent memory, Little Saigon provides entertainment venues for its residents and its visitors to forget their woes. So, as in wartime Saigon, life in Little Saigon demands escape through nighttime entertainment. The new simulated version of Saigon, however, is much more subdued and exists within the legal bounds of respectability. As Stanley Karnow, a former American journalist who traveled to Vietnam during the war observes, "Unlike old Saigon, a raucous wartime tenderloin of bars and nightclubs, Orange County is quiet—except on Saturday nights, when the action can be found at such discos as the Ritz."[57] Nevertheless, not unlike Saigon, nightclubs and dance studios have surfaced as a favorite pastime for many Vietnamese Americans between the ages of thirty and fifty.[58] While the social activity of ballroom dancing and nostalgic tunes of Vietnamese music gather middle-aged Vietnamese men and women together in dance studios, young people, many of whom have returned to work in the community, are also expressing interest in dance for social reasons.[59] Nighttime entertainment enables Vietnamese people to meet each other and get together, carving out space for their own uses. The wide-ranging cultural and entertainment activities available in Little Saigon require a study of their own, but the mere creation of these forms of nighttime and leisure entertainment reflects Vietnamese American desires for pleasure.[60] For example, cabarets and nightclubs bearing names that recall old Saigon like "The Ritz" and "Majestic" exist as venues where Vietnamese entertainers famed for performing during wartime Saigon attract customers seeking nostalgia and distraction from everyday life.[61] This longing to revive the pastime activities of Saigon—not of the French colonial period prior to the 1950s but of the U.S.-controlled 1970s—indicates that the recent wartime past remains integral to the construction of the community's cultural identity.

The vibrant spectacle of nighttime entertainment has made Orange County, California, the capital of Vietnamese exilic cultural production. An article in the *Los Angeles Times* notes:

> By the 1980s, the Vietnamese who came to Orange County had started to build an impressive infrastructure for arts and entertainment in Little Saigon itself. Now, record shops line the streets, and the vast majority of the product sold there is recorded locally, in one of a dozen or so high-tech studios. The thriving nightclub scene draws young and old, and a music video production business exerts influence in Vietnamese communities around the world.[62]

As the center of entertainment production, Orange County attracts Vietnamese performers from all over the diaspora to come and record and perform in the local nightclubs. This thriving niche industry allows former entertainers to earn a living and rebuild their careers in the United States.

When Vietnamese society was ravaged by war between the 1960s and 1970s, the nation's youth used popular culture and a new form of music called *tan nhac* to maintain a vibrant and lively atmosphere. Created by and for the young generation, *tan nhac* consisted of pop songs that addressed themes such as patriotism, resistance, struggle, and love.[63] Amid wartime Saigon, an energetic youth subculture embraced modernity and progressive elements from Western cultural influences, particularly from the American counterculture movement, and incorporated them in their music. Metropolitan youth carved a colorful nightlife where music entertainment took center stage. Musically, rock music and antiwar songs dominated the scene as prominent songwriters such as Trinh Cong Son wrote for his muse, the renowned Vietnamese female vocalist Khanh Ly, to perform for young urban professionals in Saigon. In 1971, Vietnam even had its first rock festival featuring bands from South Vietnam and other Asian nations to benefit the families of Vietnamese soldiers killed in the war.[64] The presence of American soldiers on Vietnamese soil also created venues of cross-fertilization that enabled Vietnamese youth, particularly musicians, to entertain American soldiers who toured Vietnam.[65] Vietnamese youth preferred to entertain in bars and nightclubs frequented by American military personnel due to fewer restrictions placed on artistic expression at these venues. Vietnamese bands such the CBC and the Uptight showcased their talents to Americans by performing pop music covering performers such as Elvis Presley, Neil Diamond, and Carlos Santana, bellowing rock songs such as "American Pie," "Song Sung Blue," and "Black Magic Woman."[66] The cultural exchanges demonstrated by these performances not only reveal the fluidity of some Vietnamese cultural forms but also set the stage for a hybrid musical culture to flourish throughout the Vietnamese diaspora.

Although music penetrated the wartime economy as a cultural practice, it became particularly essential in the daily lives of Vietnamese refugees after their flight from Vietnam and resettlement elsewhere. Vietnamese musical culture survived the migration process as one of the strongest cultural institutions in the lives of the refugees because it helped them cope with difficult experiences of loss and exile. To pass time in the refugee camps, the detainees entertained one another by organizing music performances with both amateur and professional talents, as many Vietnamese musicians also lived as refugees.[67] When the refugees began to carve a space for music production after resettling in the United States, the process not only gave meaning to the Vietnamese Americans, but also endowed them with ownership of the pleasure they seek to be distinctively theirs alone. As in Vietnam, music provided a similar function for the immigrants and refugees to carve identity by fusing politics with culture and functioning as a tool to further political goals and social agendas for its community members.

Infusing the Cultural and the Political

The Vietnamese community quickly recognized that securing its economic and cultural institutions required active participation in the democratic process. The battles waged to protect and preserve Vietnamese ethnic identity amid multicultural Orange County not only consolidated the community but also staged a rehearsal for its political claims on

Southern California's future. In 1992, Tony Lam became the first Vietnamese American to hold elected public office, serving as councilman for the City of Westminster. Lam's presence as a city council member paved the way for others who would later become significant figures in local politics. By the year 2000, three Vietnamese American men secured their places in local politics: Andy Quach, planning commissioner of the City of Westminster; Lan Quoc Nguyen, member of the Garden Grove Unified School District Board of Trustees; and most notably, Van Thai Tran, who first served as mayor *pro tempore* for the City of Garden Grove and later became the first Vietnamese American to serve as a representative in the California State Assembly. It may appear that the ascension of Vietnamese American politicians occurred quickly, but the community and individual Vietnamese American politicians have collaborated with Orange County's local and state representatives for decades. It is undeniable that Van Tran's past experiences as intern and aide to a number of Republican politicians, including U.S. Congressman Bob Dornan and State Senator Ed Royce, bolstered his political success.

Despite these grassroots efforts, the event that would propel the Vietnamese American community into the public eye was an incident of community surveillance and diasporic politics. According to political scientist Christian Collet, "a 1999 protest outside a Little Saigon video store became a turning point in the community's politics."[68] The first mass public demonstration of Vietnamese Americans in Little Saigon occurred not against dominant structures of American society, but against a compatriot who imprudently displayed a poster of the communist leader Ho Chi Minh and the communist Vietnamese flag at his place of business. The perpetrator claimed he only intended to start a dialogue with his community, but thousands of Vietnamese Americans protested for weeks outside the store because they believed its owner was a communist sympathizer. While this event garnered mainstream media attention, it also thrust the Vietnamese community into the limelight as the quintessential crusaders against communism. Moreover, it launched a group of young community activists into the spotlight, including Van Tran and a number of other would-be local politicians.[69]

Riding on the coattails of their visibility, young Vietnamese American community leaders began organizing at the grassroots level to educate their compatriots and the American public about the ills of the Vietnamese communist regime. These efforts not only served to explain and rationalize the impassioned protests against communism during the rallies, but also ensured a bright political future for the young leaders. Consequently, one organized response that emerged from the protests was the free "Rock-N-Vote" concert that promoted voter registration.[70] Modeled after MTV's "Rock the Vote" campaign, a group of Vietnamese American activists recruited hundreds of top Vietnamese entertainers for a live performance, while local and state political representatives from both political parties made appearances at the event. The free concert, aimed at garnering the youth vote, attempted to raise awareness of the critical mass of Vietnamese Americans in affecting mainstream politics. The carefully planned concert took place at the campus of the University of California at Irvine's Bren Events Center, where organizers distributed thousands of voter registration packets and successfully registered over 5,000 Vietnamese Americans for the 2000 elections.[71] Linking music and politics proved not only a powerful strategy for naturalized and American-born Vietnamese citizens to participate in the political arena, but it also consolidated their power as a voting bloc in Orange County. Vietnam's musical past has always been intricately tied to its political and social history. However, because music is often associated with entertainment and pleasure, it has not been critically studied and linked to politics. From the Rock-N-Vote event, I learned that music and musical performance functioned as cultural forms that distinctly shaped the construction of Vietnamese identity in the United States. Moreover, cultural workers such as performers and entertainers consciously or unconsciously served as ambassadors to the political process.

The success of Rock-N-Vote undoubtedly garnered political support for Vietnamese American candidates. In election year 2006, an unprecedented number of eighteen Vietnamese American contenders sought public office. While this occasion marked the coming-of-age of Vietnamese political participation in formal U.S. politics, it also witnessed a disappointing setback—only three candidates won—the incumbents mentioned above.[72] This disappointing outcome serves as a telling reminder that Vietnamese Americans live in a multicultural milieu historically dominated by whites and populated by Latinos. A significant number of Latino immigrants live and work in Orange County, and many of them work for Vietnamese-owned businesses. According to the 2003 Community Indicator Report of Orange County, non-Hispanic whites comprise over 50 percent of the population, whereas nearly 32 percent are Hispanic and approximately 12 percent are Asian/Pacific American.[73] Along with the changing demographics, the area's quarter-century-long stronghold on conservative politics came to a surprising halt when Loretta Sanchez defeated six-term Republican incumbent Bob Dornan in a controversial election for California's Forty-Seventh District in the late 1990s. Stunned by his loss, Dornan alleged that Sanchez's victory was a result of voter fraud and that illegal voters cost his election. However, a congressional investigation found no proof of irregularities and Sanchez has kept her seat representing the significant district in Orange County since 1996.[74]

When Republican candidate Tan Nguyen attempted to unseat Democratic Congresswoman Loretta Sanchez using similarly racist tactics in 2006, he embarrassingly failed, and seemed to have brought other Vietnamese American candidates down with him. Newcomer congressional candidate Tan Nguyen was a political unknown until his office mailed 14,000 flyers to Democratic voters with Spanish surnames warning immigrants that if they voted, they could possibly face imprisonment or deportation. This scandal gave Tan Nguyen unwanted publicity, prompting him to fire the staff member responsible as well as to organize a rally to support his candidacy. The motley crew of followers who came out to support Nguyen included a karaoke performer who sang a remake of Tammy Wynette's "Stand by Your Man," changing the words to "Stand by Our Tan."[75] This familiar marriage of popular culture and political culture harkens back to Hillary Clinton's political gaffe when as First Lady she inadvertently offended the country singer and those on the right by referencing Wynette's song in an interview with *60 Minutes* dismissing allegations of her husband's first public adulterous affair. Nguyen, however, proudly embraced the tune, making it his new campaign song.[76] Political observers claim that Tan Nguyen's dirty politics caused a setback for other Vietnamese American candidates in the 2006 elections because voters confused the common last name *Nguyen* with Tan Nguyen's campaign.[77]

Loretta Sanchez emerged victorious this time because she had learned to work with the Vietnamese American community in Orange County, building coalitions and supporting their issues. She reached out to Vietnamese voters through Vietnamese-language printed ads as well as through her commitment to championing human rights in Vietnam. Sanchez's firm congressional hold in Orange County proves to be an important reminder that local politics is not only about ethnicity but also about balancing issues. Politics in Orange County is more complicated than it appears—alliances and rifts shift as much as the fault lines inherent in the geography. Loretta Sanchez's Democratic stronghold may indicate that voters occasionally lean left, but these numbers belie the fact that the Republican Party has wooed Vietnamese American citizens since the Reagan era. Reagan's legacy as an anticommunist crusader along with his probusiness policies left a lasting imprint associating Republicanism with anticommunism and fiscal conservatism. Reagan's iconography and myth-making led Vietnamese Americans to believe that the Republican Party held a firmer, more powerful stance against communism than the Democratic Party; as such, their support for the Grand Old Party has been overwhelming.[78] More-over, social and fiscal conservatism are values with which many hard-working immigrants identify. As Michelle Park Steel, a first generation Korean American immigrant, a member of the Board of Equalization, and California's highest-ranking Republican woman, observes, Asian Americans are registering vot-ers, raising money for voter education, and more recently, winning elections as Republicans.[79] These gestures toward including Asian Americans and electing Asian American candidates are proven effective strategies that Republicans have been employing to reach out to formerly untapped and seemingly apoliti-cal populations. As staunch anticommunist activists, Vietnamese Americans, like Cuban Americans, have been able to enter mainstream politics, paving a path for multicultural inclusion through conservative channels.

Van Thai Tran's ascendency into formal politics attests to the success of these strategies. In 2010, Assemblyman Van Tran seized the opportunity to unseat Loretta Sanchez, Orange County's only Democratic member of the House. This time, however, it was Sanchez who committed the racial blun-der by saying in a Spanish-language interview that "the Republicans and the Vietnamese" are trying to take control of her seat. Tran accused Sanchez of inciting "racial rampage" and causing irreparable damage with the Vietnam-ese American community. Sanchez faced one of the toughest political battles in her career, but still ended up winning the election by 10 points.[80] Sanchez's victory demonstrates the strength of the issues as well as the unpredictability of voters. Nevertheless, race and ethnicity remain contentious issues shaping local politics in multicultural and mulitiracial districts like California's 47th.

Conclusion

Located in Orange County's city of Westminster, Little Saigon is a modest ethnic enclave whose burgeoning business district has placed Vietnamese immigrants on Southern California's map. Unlike other ethnic and racial-ized communities that thrive in urban centers, the Vietnamese area of commercial development flourishes amid one of America's most politically conservative suburban communities. Although the Orange County of yesteryear would have never approved of the dramatic changes these immi-grants have made to the land, the multicultural Orange County of today has welcomed the productive developments. The area officially known as "Little

Saigon" is a two-mile stretch bordered by Westminster, Bolsa, Magnolia, and Euclid Avenues. The streets are lined with approximately 2,000 small businesses that generate roughly $50 million in sales annually.[81] Along Southern California's complex highway system, large green freeway signs alert and direct motorists to the area.[82] When approaching Little Saigon in local traffic, giant billboard ads greet visitors in Vietnamese language on Bolsa Avenue—the main boulevard in the heart of Little Saigon where Vietnamese strip malls line the commercial district. The unique geo-social space is much more than just a cultural tourist attraction or an "ethnic" commercial district. Sociologists call the commercial belt the "model urban village enclave" that is replacing the community previously provided by ethnic ghettos.[83] The *Los Angeles Times* refers to Little Saigon as "the center of exile politics, home to a flourishing entertainment industry that produces music, videos, and films, and headquarters for 13 Vietnamese-language radio stations, dozens of magazines and several daily newspapers."[84]

The Vietnamese immigrant community has done more than alter the cultural, ethno-social, and finance-scapes of Southern California.[85] Its presence provides a model for understanding diaspora in the age of transnationalism as it is linked to the marketing of nostalgia in the postrefugee period. For many Vietnamese people dispersed all over the world, Little Saigon exists as both a recognizable destination of pilgrimage and a site that markets and sells cultural identity. Perhaps more than fulfilling commercial and consumerist desires, it has become a place that nurtures political, social, cultural, and emotional needs—essentially, a place that replaced the lost nation. With few economic goals toward mainstreaming, the majority of the revenue generated from tourism comes not from non-Vietnamese, but from Vietnamese exiles from all over the globe.[86] As such, Little Saigon serves as a Vietnamese-oriented international tourist district where the culture of the diaspora thrives.

Urban planners and economists have criticized Little Saigon's "inner-focused" way of doing business, attributing its lack of popular crossover appeal to "the lingering attitude towards the Vietnam War and immigrants in general."[87] What these outside observers fail to note are the various ways in which Vietnamese Americans are culturally and politically engaging with American society. In 2008, a *Los Angeles Times* article cites, "one-third of Westminster's 96,000 residents are Vietnamese American. And they make a sizable voting bloc: Nearly 40% of Westminster's registered voters are Vietnamese American, according to a 2006 Asian Pacific American Legal Center study."[88] The Vietnamese American community's resolute determination to hold on to the historical legacies of the war and their collective memory of forced migration stands as a powerful reminder of U.S. involvement and *failure* in Vietnam. Their actions have demonstrated a willingness to reconcile culture and politics in the United States in order to pursue the American Dream. Part of that dream, however, is predicated on bringing freedom and democracy back to Vietnam. Hence, the most remarkable aspect of this community's cultural and political activism over the past thirty years since settling in the United States is its commitment to fighting the communist regime in Vietnam. Enacting citizenship that is compatible with the conservative status quo, the most vocal Vietnamese Americans have actively reenergized and revitalized Cold War politics during a time when the War on Terror threatens to end it.

The arrival of Vietnamese American candidates into mainstream politics is not a local phenomenon. Rather, they have risen to political prominence in a number of urban areas across the nation: Boston, Houston, New Orleans, San Jose, and Seattle, to name a few. Nevertheless, I maintain that Vietnamese Americans have benefited from working through overlapping diasporas and grappling with their place in multicultural America. I have argued in this chapter that the contested relationship between ethnic Vietnamese and ethnic Chinese provided a stage for the Vietnamese to rehearse a politics and forge a cultural identity that is distinctly their own. Little Saigon is now a site where cultural production, manufactured nostalgia, and ethnicity can be consumed by the rest of the Vietnamese diaspora. The proliferation of visible and reproducible cultural forms mediated through technology and facilitated by increased globalization has given the means for the diaspora to enhance their visibility and shape their self-representations. These images project an ideal for the community by metamorphosing representations of them from refugees to nouveaux riche bourgeoisie resembling a new American middle class. Carving a distinctive social identity, cultural production allowed for the formation of Vietnamese American identity and a consolidation of political power.

In the next chapter, I examine the performance of cultural identities by closely analyzing the symbolic meanings of gender in ethnic beauty pageants. Although a few Vietnamese American women such as Madison Nguyen and Janet Nguyen have made progressive gains in the political arena, I contend that young women are generally excluded from formal politics.[89] Instead, they are central to the construction of nostalgia, imagining community, and enacting cultural citizenship in beauty pageants.

Chapter 3 Pageantry and Nostalgia: Beauty
Contests and the Gendered Homelar

BEAUTY CONTESTS may appear frivolous and trivial, but as a cultural practice they stage complex struggles over power and representation. Some feminists have argued that beauty contests are ideological regimes that reinforce dominant constructions of gender and idealized forms of femininity. Yet these organized events are much more complicated than just outright attempts to objectify, control, and commodify women's bodies. Scholars of beauty pageants have begun to bring forth the contradictions inherent in the beauty contest by situating them in multiple systems of culture, struggles for power and control, and discursive fields of practice.[1] While many have located beauty pageants in dominant discourses of nationalism all over the globe, few have addressed the significance of local "ethnic" beauty pageants. What happens when racially and ethnically marginal immigrant communities organize their own beauty pageants to commemorate their version of "the nation"? Which elements are different and which remain the same? How can we make sense of this need for beauty pageants in immigrant communities, and what do the contests come to represent?

Despite the increasing accommodation toward multiculturalism and the crowning of nonwhite contestants in American national and state beauty pageants, racist practices remain prevalent in perceptions of beauty in general and beauty pageants in the United States. As Sarah Banet-Weiser points out in her study of the Miss America pageant, "The presence of non-white contestants obscures and thus works to erase the racist histories and foundations upon which beauty pageants rest."[2] Moreover, because mainstream pageants tend to reaffirm whiteness and dominant understandings of American citizenship, they can sometimes conflict with cultural goals and beliefs of ethnic and immigrant communities. As such, beauty pageants in general serve different purposes for ethnic and racialized communities in the United States. And though some aspects of "ethnic" beauty pageants replicate larger American national and state pageants, they also simultaneously articulate alternative cultural practices that counter the dominant discourse from which they are excluded.[3]

To resolve these exclusionary practices that disqualify Asian women from representing the "nation" by virtue of their race, Vietnamese Americans have organized their own beauty pageants to provide alternative spaces in which "ethnic Vietnamese" women have the opportunity to participate and to reign as beauty queens for their ethnic community.[4] This chapter examines the complex ways in which the Vietnamese diaspora construct cultural identities and imagine their lost nation through pageantry. I argue that young women play an essential role in the imagined community because they simultaneously represent tradition and modernity in beauty pageants. These pageants not only stage gender politics of the community but also dramatize the various ways in which Vietnamese American citizenship is realized through the performances of young female Vietnamese bodies. It is through the bodies of Vietnamese women that nostalgia is symbolically invoked and cultural nationalism forged.

The Pageantry of the *Ao Dai*

Beauty pageants of the Vietnamese diaspora are different from all other beauty pageants because of one significant cultural fashion component: the *ao dai*, or traditional Vietnamese dress.[5] The basic *ao dai* for women is a long, flowing dress worn over long, full palazzo pants. Although it varies in style, the formal dress most often seen on display for competition is a form-fitting tunic that slits into front and back panels from slightly above the natural waistline down to below the knees. The *ao dai* has a long and complex history that mirrors Vietnam's national and colonial history. Developed from Chinese court clothing, it originally was a dress worn by royalty. However, by the early twentieth century it had become a fashionable clothing item for the "modern" Vietnamese woman. Because the garment is difficult to perform work in, middle-class women and adolescent schoolgirls most commonly wore it. Others, including men, only wore *ao dai* on holidays and special occasions.

Although the *ao dai*'s mandarin collar and panel designs reveal remarkable Chinese and French fashion influence, the Vietnamese insist that the garment is uniquely and authentically Vietnamese. Symbolically, the *ao dai* invokes nostalgia and timelessness associated with a gendered image of the homeland for which many Vietnamese people throughout diaspora yearn. Journalist Nam Hoang Nguyen has observed that the emblematic meanings associated with the *ao dai* have been "perpetuated by countless puppy-love, maudlin poems and novels that engraved, for the most part, the traditional Vietnamese concept of female beauty: innocent, frail, chaste, shy, and soft-spoken."[6] The *ao dai* conjures up romantic images of a Vietnamese past that is pure, innocent, and untainted by war.

Vietnamese *ao dai* beauty pageants are one of the most visible examples of Vietnamese immigrants trying to negotiate the process of assimilating into bourgeois American culture while remaining ethnically Vietnamese. These pageants have become permanent fixtures in Vietnamese American festivals and celebrations since the late 1970s. Their cultural origins, however, are not from Vietnam. Rather, they are an invented tradition created by Vietnamese immigrants in the United States.[7] Beauty pageants in Vietnam tend to place emphasis on a woman's physical appearance. *Ao dai* beauty pageants, however, recognize the "overall beauty" of young women. This includes her public speaking skills, her appearance and gait in *ao dai*, and most important, her ability to retain her ethnic and cultural heritage. Unlike the beauty pageants that take place in Vietnam, pageants hosted in the diaspora celebrate Vietnamese cultural *difference* in an effort to preserve "Vietnamese culture and tradition through beauty pageants."[8]

Ao dai beauty pageants are significant not only because they bridge symbols of the past with bodies that represent the future, but also because they work ideologically to evoke an "imagined community" that authenticates the persistence of Vietnamese ethnicity and carves out cultural roles for young Vietnamese women between ages eighteen and twenty-six.[9] *Ao dai* beauty pageants have become ritualized events that dramatize major debates concerning nationalism, ethnicity, gender, sexuality, and other issues Vietnamese Americans and other Vietnamese in the diaspora face. Indeed, they are crucial to the production of new hybridized gender and ethnic identities. In fact, later we will see another kind of hybrid beauty, one that is defined through plastic surgery and other postmodern technologies.

Imagining the Homeland and Enforcing Exile

The creation of Vietnamese beauty pageants outside the Vietnamese nation, along with the nostalgia they invoke, enables the imagining of communities and fosters the growth of nationalism among exiled Vietnamese scattered throughout the diaspora. *Ao dai* beauty pageants are not mere diasporic cultural productions created for the purposes of "cultural preservation." Held in large public auditoriums and civic centers, they also provide a forum for overseas Vietnamese to contest the racial politics of dominant

American beauty pageants and challenge the limitations the communist regime placed on cultural practice in Vietnam. When the Vietnamese refugees fled Vietnam, they never completely severed their ties with the existing nation of Vietnam. With relatives and sentimental memories remaining in Vietnam, the cultural politics between the exile communities are always in dialogue with those of the current nation. Moreover, because these communities are in exile, the imagined nation is both ambiguous and ambivalent in relation to the former nation and the new nation in which they have resettled. Since fleeing Vietnam, overseas Vietnamese have staged countless public protests to criticize what they deem as corrupt and inhumane conduct by the communist government.[10] At the same time, Vietnamese exiles throughout the world have also expressed strong opinions to instruct the governments of their new countries of settlement on how to relate to the Socialist Republic of Vietnam. Formerly barred from and presently reluctant to physically return to the homeland, Vietnamese exiles emotionally and metaphysically reconstruct, through cultural celebration and pageantry, the Vietnam they lost. Holding beauty pageants has become one of the most powerful ways for Vietnamese communities to publicly assert feelings of cultural nationalism as well as anticommunism. Through beauty pageants, the anticommunist political voice of the imagined community in exile is reaffirmed and the existence of communities in the United States and throughout the world is validated.

Organized in both northern and southern California in 1977, the first *ao dai* pageants were immediate cultural inventions. They were as much a response to the new Vietnamese government's imposition of a dress code on the South Vietnamese as they were an effort to preserve and claim the Vietnamese national dress. When the world of the elites and their "bourgeois decadence" collapsed in Vietnam during the mid 1970s and early 1980s, the status-laden *ao dai* also lost its position as the official national dress of the Socialist Republic of Vietnam. On men, the *ao dai* was seen as representing the "old regime."[11] On women, it represented the extravagance and futility associated with capitalist wastefulness. According to fashion freelancer Lan Vu, "the *ao dai* receded into the background, making appearances only at family gatherings and special occasions" after 1975 when "the Communists ordered everyone to wear the basic work outfit of buttoned top and pants."[12] Though the communists in power never made it illegal to wear an *ao dai*, anyone caught wearing the garment risked surveillance that could even lead to home searches. Vietnamese immigrants remember that the strict regime made it very difficult for anybody to don the *ao dai* because it drew so much attention. For these reasons, the *ao dai* became a hidden material object shielded from public display. However, the more the communist government seized the *ao dai*, the more overseas Vietnamese insisted on preserving their national dress along with other items of material culture, such as the striped flag of the former Republic of Vietnam, as national symbols of the defeated nation. As in the period of decolonization when the *ao dai*, according to Van Ngan, became "a symbol of silent opposition to French colonialism," *ao dai* pageants became a symbol of Vietnamese American protest against the communist forces that displaced it.[13]

Selecting the *ao dai* as the national symbol for the "imagined" Vietnam invokes both classed and gendered articulations of nationhood. The *ao dai* was the official wardrobe of Vietnamese elite men and women. The long and fluid dress accompanied by a pair of lengthy flowing pants requires not only superfluous lengths of cloth to produce, but also custom tailoring. As such, the *ao dai* can be an expensive commodity to own. Working-class men and women could only afford to don the *ao dai* for special occasions such as weddings, funerals, and holidays. Because Vietnamese immigrants brought the *ao dai* with them, the garment continues to make appearances at these same occasions throughout the diaspora. However, significantly more women than men wear *ao dai* today. Throughout its history, the *ao dai* for men remained fairly unchanged in style, and as Vietnamese men adopted Western styles of dress the men's *ao dai* almost entirely disappeared. *Ao dai* fashion for women, on the other hand, not only exhibited regional distinctions but also stylistic change over time. In the 1990s, the Vietnamese communities throughout the diaspora witnessed the resurgence of *ao dai* fashion among younger women, partly spurred by the exilic music and entertainment industry. Though this may indicate that young Vietnamese women are rediscovering their roots through the *ao dai*, community beauty pageants may have also contributed to the construction of this classed and gendered expression of ethnic and national identity.[14]

Forming Partnerships through Culture and Capital

Originally conceived in the late 1970s both to preserve Vietnamese culture through amateur performance and to raise funds for refugees and orphans, *ao dai* pageants of the late 1990s have turned into commercial enterprises that rely not only on the sponsorship of professional businesses, but also on professional talent to entertain audiences throughout the pageant. As annually organized gala events that claim to "bridge together the uniqueness of the western culture and the diverse cultural richness of the Vietnamese communities," beauty pageants receive sponsorship from numerous small Vietnamese American businesses and organizations as well as larger American private corporations.[15] The size of the pageants often depends on the amount of support organizers can muster from business and commercial sectors. However, many pageants have grown into commercial industries that link communities and various economies at both the local and global levels. Organizers work with ethnic businesses, promising to "promote partnerships among the Vietnamese community and America's private corporation[s] or foundation[s]."[16] Some pageants offer "benefit packages" that give sponsors "opportunities to break into the multi-*billion* dollar Vietnamese consumer market by direct marketing of products or services at the actual event."[17] In the 1990s, transnational corporations such as AT&T also seized the opportunity to sponsor Vietnamese pageants as a crucial element for winning the business of Vietnamese worldwide.[18] Transnational corporations particularly profit from conditions of exile and diaspora. Telecommunications companies, for example, strive to close the space-time continuum among overseas Vietnamese and their relatives in the homeland by advertising long-distance telephone connections. Although the financial contributions made by transnational corporations remain considerably less than those of ethnic businesses, the investment interests in overseas Vietnamese communities speak to the potential significance they will play in the future of transnational capitalism.

The videotaping and mass marketing of *ao dai* beauty pageants by the Vietnamese American entertainment industry reveal the extent to which technology has transformed preexisting modes of communication in a context of transnationalism and global capitalism.[19] New media and digital technologies have made it possible for all Vietnamese who cannot attend live beauty pageants to enjoy hours of the gala event without having to leave the comfort of their own homes. At a cost of only fifteen to twenty-five dollars, the affordable videos enable working-class Vietnamese who may not be able to afford attendance at a live show to participate in and be a part of the imagined community. The videos not only feature beautiful young Vietnamese women in the pageant but also contain a variety show featuring famous professional Vietnamese singers performing song and dance routines. Packaged in colorful shrink-wrapped boxed sets and decorated with collaged images of contestants and performers, beauty pageant videos are available for sale in most Vietnamese-owned record stores, and in some areas they can also be bought at local Vietnamese businesses such as small markets.[20] Beauty pageant videos are the perfect vehicle for advertising ethnic businesses as well as transnational corporations because they can reach a wide audience. Although it may be difficult to trace the actual distribution of any given pageant video (as piracy is a common practice), it is not impossible to imagine the possibilities of its cultural and political impact, particularly to the Vietnamese in diaspora. Rich in symbolism and imagery, the pageant videos work on multiple levels to stage highly contested meanings of gender, culture, ethnicity, nationalism, and identity among the Vietnamese in exile. In addition, they sell ethnic-specific products and advertise in ways that attract the Vietnamese consumer.

Commemorating Migration through Pageantry

The remainder of this chapter seeks to provide a close reading of a commercially produced video recording of the eighteenth annual *ao dai* pageant held in Long Beach, California, in 1995. Entitled *20 Nam Chiec Ao Dai Vien Su*, or *The Dislocation of the Ao Dai in Faraway Lands*, this pageant commemorated the twentieth anniversary of Vietnamese migration. Organized by college students and alumni of California State University, Long Beach, and sponsored primarily by Vietnamese American business elites of Southern California, this *ao dai* beauty pageant featured a host of prominent Vietnamese American entertainers. The juxtaposition of the variety show and the beauty contest created a highly glamorized spectacle that encouraged community members to attend and contribute funds. What made this pageant unique was the extraordinary use of the *ao dai* to unearth feelings of nostalgia.

The commemorative ceremonies opened with a sensational performance by Thai Thanh, a seasoned female performer who has entertained generations of Vietnamese. Standing on an elevated platform behind the contestants, she sang the classical Vietnamese operatic ballad "Hoi Trung Duong," a song about the three main rivers located in the northern, central, and southern regions that geographically connect the nation of Vietnam. On stage dancing in front of the vocalist were twenty-one young female contestants, wearing three regional styles of dress that symbolically represented the three regions to which the song alludes. Physically, Thai Thanh embodies the maternal past. Revered and respected, she is the allegorical figure who narrates the national history of Vietnam for the future generation of Vietnamese Americans, represented by the contestants as well as younger members of the audience. For the older generation, she tells a familiar tale, conjuring up images of a unified "homeland" and using allegory to induce memory and nostalgia.[21]

In addition to joining three politically and culturally diverse regions into a unified Vietnam, the historical narrative in the song "Hoi Trung Duong" imagines a mythical homeland void of regional, religious, political, ethnic, and linguistic differences. Preferring to recognize the unified historical Vietnam over the partitioned Vietnam of the Geneva Accords in 1954 and the current Socialist Republic of Vietnam, overseas Vietnamese envision and remember a harmonious nation before the war and before their subsequent displacement. Such nostalgic longings and politically salient representations of the Vietnamese past have become essential themes in Vietnamese American celebrations. Without these recurring images of a mythical and unified homeland, Vietnamese communities throughout the diaspora would not coalesce and attend cultural events such as the *ao dai* pageant. The pageants are thus produced for the overseas communities to consume as well as learn about new cultural practices of different local Vietnamese American communities.

The *ao dai* pageants construct a nostalgic nationalism and reaffirm Vietnamese identity. Vietnamese Americans also celebrate regionalism and their ability to accept and embrace historical and regional differences. The pageants work in a way that enables viewers to inhabit multiple subject positions: as members of the imagined nation, as distinct peoples from different regions, and as Vietnamese refugees who left their homeland and resettled elsewhere in the world. In the context of the 1995 Long Beach pageant, this was achieved through the wearing of the *ao dai* by the contestants; as the young beauties danced in the opening act, wearing different regional *ao dai*, they created the illusion that it was possible to map the bodies and the identities of the young women directly onto the various regions of the Vietnamese nation.[22] Through these efforts to create unity and cooperation amid difference, the performance revealed a desire to link diasporic Vietnamese globally. The metaphorical erasure and disavowal of regional and local distinctions, in essence, dramatize the organic wholeness of the "imagined community." Wherever in the world the *ao dai* beauty pageant video may have traveled, it created the space and spectacle for the Vietnamese in the diaspora to imagine themselves as a united whole.

Central to this vision of collectivity was the displaced *ao dai* and the diasporic communities that the *ao dai* symbolized. Rather than focus on the narrative of migration, the beauty pageant charted the historical transformations of the *ao dai* and its resiliency as a sign of cultural persistence among the Vietnamese in exile. Organizers and contestants repeatedly asserted that, in spite of the fashion changes the *ao dai* has endured; its original form remains the same. Likewise, despite the tumultuous history the Vietnamese have undergone, they insisted that their "core cultural values" remain the same. The traditional dress was thus employed as a metaphor to give meaning to the experiences of migration and cultural change among the Vietnamese throughout the diaspora.

The Spectacle of the Nation in the Female Body

Ao dai beauty pageants are public rituals dedicated to venerate the endurance of "Vietnamese culture." As community rituals, they ensure the continuance of gendered Vietnamese cultural practices. Making the female *ao dai* central to the ritualistic imaginings of a nostalgic and unified homeland necessitates a discussion about the discourse over the female body and what it represents.[23] Whereas women are often marginalized in politically significant ceremonies, the body chosen to represent the Vietnamese nation in this civic event is significantly a female one. Though the *ao dai* is the traditional Vietnamese dress for both men and women, Vietnamese American men are not obligated by the community to preserve Vietnamese culture by wearing the *ao dai*. Vietnamese American women, on the other hand, are *expected* to wear this cultural symbol. A woman's refusal to wear the *ao dai* can be interpreted as a lack of effort and allegiance to Vietnamese culture; conversely, her willingness to embrace the *ao dai* becomes a major source of ethnic pride for herself as well as her community at large.

By making the *ao dai* the quintessential symbol of Vietnamese culture and the primary focus of the pageant, the sexist agenda of publicly displaying and judging young women's bodies is disavowed, masked, and legitimated by cultural practice. The *ao dai* is a form-fitting dress, often made with transparent fabrics that require custom tailoring. For a flattering fit, a woman must have a thin, slender, yet curvaceous body. The shape of the female body is accentuated but remains hidden as the dress clings tightly to it. The *ao dai*, in essence, produces a certain type of sexual body. This sexualized image, however, is contained within the bounds of respectability and curbed under the sign of the "cultural." No contestant who flaunts her body would be awarded the crown. Even so, the overt expression of female sexuality surfaced frequently throughout the Long Beach beauty contest. Though most beauty pageants allow contestants to introduce themselves and say their own names, the contestants in the *ao dai* pageant were introduced to the judges and audience in this first round. Dressed in compulsory white or sometimes pastel-colored *ao dai*, young Vietnamese women in the pageant marched out onto the stage, representing the timeless image of adolescent schoolgirls. Whereas the first round presented the women uniformly and homogenously, the second round of the competition featured the contestants in *ao dai* that each had selected to reflect her personal style. In the third round, the women were clothed in Western evening gowns, a segment of the competition that is borrowed from other mainstream pageants and that reveals the Vietnamese aspiration to enter the American bourgeoisie. Evening gowns are accoutrements of elite American women.[24] Requiring Vietnamese American beauty queens to wear them in pageants conveys a desire to become part of the elite class in the United States. Moreover, the Western evening gown is the perfect modern American counterpart to the traditional Vietnamese *ao dai* because both are fashionably middle-class. After modeling in three rounds of competition, three of the twenty-one contestants were selected to the final round, in which the young women were asked to speak for the first time during the pageant to demonstrate their ability to verbalize and perform under pressure. More important, they were also required to answer questions in Vietnamese.

Realizing that they would not be given the opportunity to express themselves through speech unless they made it to the final round of competition, many contestants used their bodies to win the attention of the audience. This was done most blatantly during the Western evening gown competition in which the young women showed off their bodies in sexy, backless, body-flattering, and tight-fitting evening gowns. The contestants with the skimpiest dresses gained loud applause, uproarious cheers, and catcalls from members of the audience. Those displaying hyperfemininity by swaying their hips and gliding across the stage received similar ovations. One contestant even wore a tiara on her head and took off the cape of her flashy metallic gown as if she were a model strutting on the catwalk (see Figure 5). Since they could only represent themselves through their bodies, the contestants in the *ao dai* pageant took their chances and transgressed the boundaries of respectability by asserting themselves despite the consequences. While the audience mainly consisted of family members and young college students who cheered for their friends on stage, the judges tended to be leaders of the community such as lawyers, doctors, businesspeople, and even former beauty queens. Consequently, transgressors were met with audience approval but judge disapproval, and although transgressors were never disqualified from the competition, losing the contest could have been the result of their actions.

Figure 5. The crowd explodes with cheer as contestant Vo Thi Ngoc Loan sashays down the runway in a metallic silver gown and seductively removes the cape that drapes her strapless evening gown while showing off a tiara already fixed on her head. From "20 Nam Chiec Ao Dai Vien Xu" *Hoa Hau Ao Dai Long Beach*, Ky Thu 18, Diem Xua Productions.

Defining Characteristics of the *Ao Dai* Queen

Although the contestants seemed empowered to challenge the bounds of respectability in some aspects of the pageant, the *ao dai* contest could also be interpreted as an attempt to regulate women's sexuality to the extent that it imposed a moral code of sexual conduct on young Vietnamese American women who are considered in danger of becoming "too American." With the influence of mainstream American media and popular culture, the older generation invariably fears the loss of "culture" among the youth. *Ao dai* beauty contests provided a safe venue for young people to learn about and preserve Vietnamese culture while engaging in the Western practice of pageants. The pageants not only provide young people, such as the college students at the California State University, Long Beach, the opportunity to organize for a major "cultural" event; they also designate young Vietnamese American women a cultural role in the Vietnamese immigrant community. Anthropologist Jesse W. Nash observes that, though the community values old men, "the young women represented the links to the future, the hope of [the] community."[25] When asked what the beauty pageant meant to her, one 1996 contestant stated, "This pageant, *Hoa Hau Ao Dai*, is not about one beautiful person wearing *ao dai*, rather it is about the collective group of people coming together to profess their love for the Vietnamese culture and people."[26] Along with this declaration of "love for the Vietnamese culture and people" is an assertion of cultural citizenship. All the contenders for the crown demonstrated civic pride and commitment to social responsibilities by endorsing social platforms that worked to either help Vietnamese refugees or end poverty in Vietnam. Many of the women who participated in the pageant claimed to have done so because they believed it was a good way to raise funds to help Southeast Asian refugees.[27] Taking part in Vietnamese cultural events such as the *ao dai* beauty pageant thus steered young women away from the corrupting forces of American culture and kept them "pure" and "Vietnamese."

As far as social causes go, *ao dai* pageants gave young Vietnamese American women the chance to "give back" to the Vietnamese community or to uplift the nation from years of communist oppression, but the sine qua non of the *ao dai* queen is her feminine beauty. In his study of what he calls "Vietnamese values," Nash also notes that "the loveliest girls in the community participate in the religious ceremonies, the handsomest women are called to positions of authority, and the prettiest girls adorn every procession or parade."[28] Though Nash never clearly defines Vietnamese beauty per se, he further observes that the Vietnamese appreciation for beauty is not purely aesthetic but must be accompanied by "a delicate walk," "a good posture," and "a soft voice."[29] Chi Nguyen, Miss Tet Vietnam of Northern California in 1992, provides an *ao dai* queen's perspective. She explains that "the Vietnamese standard of beauty is based on *cong* (domestic skills), *dung* (physical beauty), *ngon* (speaking skills), and *hanh* (pose and modesty)."[30] Aside from performing these essentialized forms of ethnic femininity, the contestants also need to show grace, elegance, poise, and innocence. The queen is meant to embody idealized forms of femininity as well as project a particular image of beauty—an image with multiple valences that simultaneously evokes nostalgia and the "natural" beauty of the "motherland," as well as a beauty connected to the "modern" that negotiates living in the context of the West. To win, a contestant must delicately balance the values associated with the Vietnamese immigrant community as well as ethics associated with an American upbringing. One Long Beach contestant stated, for instance, that her ambition is simply to "always be happy." This overly "American" aspiration, which idealizes pleasure and self-fulfillment,

Figure 6. A new queen is crowned at the eighteenth annual "Hoa Hau Ao Dai" Long Beach Pageant in 1995. From "20 Nam Chiec Ao Dai Vien Xu," *Hoa Hau Ao Dai Long Beach*, Ky Thu 18, Diem Xua Productions.

does not correspond with the appropriate "Vietnamese" code of femininity, which values devotion to the family over the self. Maturity and intelligence were also valued attributes the judges favored. The final winner was a poised young woman who aspired to become a doctor and practice in the Vietnamese community in Southern California. She not only demonstrated commitment to Vietnamese culture and community, but also possessed the ability to negotiate both Vietnamese and American cultural values by showing gracefulness and professionalism.

Authenticating "Inauthentic" Ethnic Identities

The stated goal of every Vietnamese American beauty contest is to extol the virtues of Vietnamese culture through the *ao dai*. With the absence of both talent and swimsuit competitions, notions of liberal individualism are suppressed and downplayed by pageant organizers. Nonetheless, individual identities and subjectivities of the Long Beach contestants constantly emerged throughout the pageant despite the repeated use of the contestants and their bodies as symbols of Vietnamese regional and national culture. By virtue of her presence in the pageant, each young woman demanded individual consideration in the competition for the crown. Though not permitted to introduce herself, each contestant's name, the city from which she came, and a list of hobbies, goals, and aspirations were announced by the master and mistress of ceremony. Each was allowed to select one *ao dai* and one evening gown of her choice to wear for the pageant.

At the same time, the pageant's location in Southern California and the contestants' upbringing in the United States often interfered with the nationalist and nostalgic myth-making performances. One of these points of "interference" concerns language. Besides highlighting gender and sexuality, the *ao dai* contests encourage young women to articulate an "ethnic" identity through the preservation of Vietnamese "cultural traditions" and the upholding of "Vietnamese values." The search for an "authentic" past is, however, a fruitless one because of Vietnam's complex history of colonialism. What becomes most salient to Vietnamese cultural identity, as defined by the Vietnamese community and its cultural elites, is the ability to retain the "mother tongue." Linguistic knowledge, therefore, is viewed as emblematic of cultural knowledge. One's lack of knowledge of the Vietnamese language can potentially cut one off from the community. Hence, the Long Beach pageant required that the queen be able to speak Vietnamese with fluency so that she would be able to adequately represent her community.

Growing up in the United States, however, has made it increasingly difficult for Vietnamese American youths to retain the Vietnamese language. The demands made by the community and by dominant American culture have compelled many Vietnamese Americans to construct new hyphenated ethnic identities.[31] Participation in the *ao dai* contest permitted young contestants to perform the doubleness of their "ethnic" identity and even subvert notions of cultural authenticity that the community expected each contestant to possess. This subversion was revealed during the most shocking moment in the pageant, when one of the three finalists was interviewed in the final round. When asked a question about Vietnamese American youth, the young woman could not find the words to respond. Betraying what was considered to be authentic, she simply said, "I'm sorry, *em quen* [I forget]." While the contestant's "forgetfulness" may have reflected either her inability to speak Vietnamese or her inability to remember her lines, the young woman had to endure public embarrassment as the audience laughed at her blunder. Nonetheless, the audience could very well be laughing at the judges for selecting the "wrong" contestant to be one of the three finalists because she was able to fool everyone (by appearing Vietnamese without "really being so") almost through the entire competition.

Professional Performers of Cultural Work

Of the various social responsibilities expected of the *ao dai* queen, her most important duty is to safeguard and represent Vietnamese ethnicity in cultural events inside and outside of the community. Unlike contestants in the Miss America pageant, *ao dai* contestants do not have to demonstrate talent beyond performing an idealized femininity. Instead, pageant organizers hire hosts and hostesses as well as a cast of professional performers to do the cultural work of entertaining the audience. The contestants are left to invoke the beauty of the *ao dai* and embody ideal Vietnamese womanhood.

Diasporic Vietnamese media, in the form of variety shows, have grown into huge capital-generating industries worldwide. Produced mainly in the United States, these variety shows consist of musical and dance numbers, comedic and historical skits, and fashion shows exhibiting Vietnamese women dressed in high fashion *ao dai*. I will elaborate on the significance of these shows and chart the development of the variety entertainment industry in the next chapter, but I want to emphasize here that professional entertainers in the beauty pageant perform diasporic identities that both supplement and contradict the goals of the beauty pageants. In this sense, the variety show within the beauty contests can be regarded as a cultural terrain on which men and women, the young and the old, and Vietnam and America struggle for meaning. Entertainers of the older generation express their concerns about the future while they mourn over the lost nation, singing songs about exile and patriotism. The younger generation, on the other hand, typically performs pop songs and remixes of American oldies, rap, and hip-hop. Offering a wide range of musical genres, entertainers aim to satisfy the desires of all audience members.

Just as entertainers were chosen to draw in the audience, the host and hostess for the Long Beach pageant were carefully chosen to be the voice of a least two important groups of the community—older men and young women. In this pageant, two distinguished and familiar members of the community served as the host and hostess. A public personality, Nam Loc is a middle-aged male songwriter who works in refugee resettlement and immigrant assistance for the U.S. Catholic Conference. His counterpart, Thuy Trinh, is a former *ao dai* queen turned television anchor/video jockey who comes into the homes of Southern Californians daily on the Vietnam

Entertainment Program to introduce contemporary and classic Vietnamese music videos on the International channel. With opposing points of view, the host and hostess presented the pageant rules, told jokes, stirred up emotions, invoked memories, exchanged commentary about gender, generation, and society, and introduced both beauty contestants and entertainment stars to the audience. The back and forth banter between the two provide comic relief to the audience. More importantly, Thuy Trinh identified with the women, the contestants, and younger members of the audience while Nam Loc, on the other hand, provided the link to the older generation and the cultural elites running the show. As representatives of two groups differentiated by gender and generation, the host and hostess used their identities as points of departure to debate and highlight tensions within the community without attempting to resolve them.

The "sideshow" both supplemented the pageantry of the *ao dai* contest and made the contradictions surrounding issues of gender and sexuality in the pageant more explicit. As a rule, the Vietnamese American beauty queen cannot be identified with entertainers because young women performers in the variety shows often openly display their sexuality and mimic popular American media stars such as Madonna. The Vietnamese community believed that an *ao dai* queen must not be overly influenced by the American mass media as they can potentially contaminate her "ethnic" self. The queen is expected to exhibit a Western style of beauty but must remain "Vietnamese" enough to represent the traditions of the imagined nation. In contrast, the variety show typically allows professional performers, who are given more flexibility to navigate between cultures, to act out the realities of the young contestants.

Sponsors and the Business of Making *Ao Dai* Beauty Queens

It comes as no surprise that the major sponsors of the beauty pageant were ethnic businesses: food companies, photography studios, and sewing companies, as well as wealthy professional men and women of the community. A Vietnamese *ao dai* tailoring company dressed the contestants and provided them discounts to purchase their own *ao dai*. The hair and makeup was done by Vietnamese-owned L.A. Cosmetics, another big sponsor. The largest contributor, however, was Tham My Vien Bich Ngoc (Bich Ngoc Cosmetic Surgery Center), which donated a total of $10,000 to the *ao dai* pageant, $5,000 of which was awarded to the queen, who unwittingly becomes their spokesperson. In return for their financial support, representatives of companies and businesses are given the privilege of crowning the queens and runners-up. Additionally, they also get a chance to advertise on the final videotaped product.

Though there was never any explicit connection made between cosmetic surgery and the contestants, the Bich Ngoc Cosmetic Surgery Center secured a major advertising spot on the Long Beach pageant video: a five-minute infomercial right at the beginning of the second videotape. The video ad profiled the "before" and "after" plastic surgery experience of an adolescent Vietnamese woman. A close-up image of her "before" face is discriminately scrutinized and criticized by plastic surgeon Dr. Vu Ban, who declares that Asian women are born with imperfect features: an angular face, a flat nose, no folds on the eyelids, an indistinct chin, and acne. The experienced doctor then introduces his affordable method of making a more "natural-looking, beautiful" face that he boasted Asian clientele prefer. The young woman's glowing "after" picture with alterations to the eyes, nose, and chin was shown, and she was interviewed. When asked why she decided to have plastic surgery, she explained that many of her friends had done it and they were pleased with their results. She attested that the doctor's affordable procedure had made her "beautiful," which in turn increased her self-esteem. What can be interpreted from this infomercial is that increased self-esteem and improved psychological well-being can only derive from physical transformation.[32] Moreover, the transformative benefits of cosmetic surgery far outweigh the costs of undergoing an elective medical operation. Choosing cosmetic surgery is thus perceived as a pathway for happiness and belonging.

Indeed, cosmetic surgery has become increasingly acceptable in the Vietnamese American community due to the frequency and ubiquity of these ads. The surgical procedures most often performed include the narrowing of the nostrils and heightening of the nose bridge, creating a fold on the eyelid, and (for women) augmenting the breasts. According to Eugenia Kaw, Asian Americans are more likely than another ethnic group (white or nonwhite) to pursue cosmetic surgery.[33] Participation in the culture of cosmetic surgery can also be interpreted as an entrance to a classed form of assimilation. With the ability to afford plastic surgery, Vietnamese American women can transform their appearance—erasing flaws of perceived imperfection with which they were born.

Whereas definitions of beauty change over time and vary according to context, Western standards of beauty have clearly been imposed upon women of color.[34] The attainment of Western beauty seems to suggest some form of progress to the Vietnamese. In other words, if the goal of

Vietnamese nationalism is to modernize and advance, to perform plastic surgery on the national body can be seen as a means of improvement. In recent years, plastic surgery has literally transformed the faces and identities of many Vietnamese Americans. Nevertheless, as David Palumbo-Liu has observed, the desire to have plastic surgery to alter the Asian body is "not undertaken necessarily to 'be white,' but to partake of whiteness in a selective fashion."[35] This selective participation in whiteness is intimately linked to the narrative of assimilation and the increased commodification of bodies in American popular culture.[36] In the next chapter, I will theorize and interpret the complex meanings of the normalization of plastic surgery as a cultural practice in the Vietnamese community. Nevertheless, it is evident that the partnership forged between the cosmetic surgery industry and the beauty pageant industry indicates that ethnic beauty in the Vietnamese community is becoming more and more hybrid and is realized through science and medical technology. While beauty ideals remain highly contested in the Vietnamese community, most agree that in the pageants a hybrid look is most desirable. This "hybrid look" corresponds to racial, cultural, and class changes in the community. Moreover, possession of Western beauty alone would not suffice for the *ao dai* queen. In order for her to represent the nation and wear the crown, she must *embody* a number of characteristics including civic virtue, intelligence, and a physical beauty that is reminiscent of the "homeland." Her beauty, however, like that of the young woman whose face was completely transformed by plastic surgery, must be a hybrid beauty. It is not necessarily "Western" because it is still "Vietnamese." This hybrid beauty, mapped on to her body, allows her to represent the fusion of the imagined diasporic Vietnamese nation.

Conclusion

Beauty pageants have increasingly become subjects of study in ethnic and minority communities because they stage complex gender struggles over power and representation.[37] The theatrical performances of history, culture, gender, and identity by organizers, contestants, and professional performers in the beauty pageant illustrate the magnitude of the cultural and social work being done in the Vietnamese American community. As a cultural practice, Vietnamese American pageants exhibit tensions between tradition and modernity, grapple to define meanings of sexuality and ethnic femininity, and reveal struggles over the control of the Vietnamese female body. They generate capital and unite different groups of people. However, while *ao dai* pageants have created cultural roles for young women and spaces for them to perform public service, they have also created problems that constrict meanings of Vietnamese womanhood. For example, the notion of a Vietnamese beauty queen imposes certain idealized and unrealistic beauty standards on young Vietnamese American women. As a result, many Vietnamese are turning to cosmetic surgery and relying on it as the acceptable quick-fix solution to obtaining these beauty ideals.[38] And even though pageant organizers disavow the practice of cosmetic surgery, the sponsorship of plastic surgeons reveals that competing notions of beauty exist within the community.

Another example of casting molds for female identity in the community concerns the primary function of *ao dai* pageants. Like other beauty pageants, they involve showcasing young women's bodies on public stages. What is more troubling about this practice is that it is achieved under the guise of cultural preservation and ethnic and national celebration. The glorification of Vietnamese culture naturalizes gender relations as it inscribes young women's bodies, literally and figuratively, to represent male endeavors. This tendency to make women's bodies a spectacle "to be looked at" reinforces male dominance and maintains unequal sex and gender roles for Vietnamese Americans.[39] However, as long as the *ao dai* maintains a central role in signifying the nation, and as long as it depends on a young woman's body to perform it, beauty pageants will play a significant role in determining the rules of gender politics in this cultural nationalist arena.

In the next chapter, I will expand upon my analysis of professional entertainers and explore how the staging of gender, ethnicity, sexuality, and class in a popular musical variety show series impacts the formation of identity for the Vietnamese diaspora. Like *ao dai* beauty pageants, musical variety shows employ nostalgia and desire to construct new, bourgeois diasporic subjectivities for Vietnamese. Considered together, these cultural productions consolidate a diasporic consciousness, one predicated on commodity culture.

Chapter 4 Consuming Transcendent Media: Videos, Variety Shows, and the New Middle Class

THE EYES OF THE SPHINX glimmer in a night filled with shining stars as dancers dressed in "Egyptian" costumes move their hands in a serpentine fashion. A contemporary tune plays against this "ancient" backdrop as Vietnamese American singing sensation Thien Kim enters the scene, reclining on a chaise carried by male servants. Made up to look like an Egyptian princess, Thien Kim is dressed in robes and adorned with gold jewelry. Her performance of a song entitled "*Doi Em Nhu Cat Kho*" ("My Life Is Like Dry Sand") commences as she alights from her chaise and walks across the backs of her slaves to her throne. Three white, male little people appear, playing servants and jesters to the Egyptian princess, who is unsatisfied with the luxuries her life has to offer. As she finishes her song, the camera zooms out to reveal a colossal stage with a large television screen; then it pans across a packed and appreciative audience. The little people then escort the mistress of ceremonies, Nguyen Cao Ky Duyen, to the podium. Her cohost and master of ceremonies, Nguyen Ngoc Ngan (no relation), makes a grand entrance riding a camel onto the stage. The two cohosts joke about Ngan's height, but the scripted dialogue quickly turns to the lyrics of the opening song. The performance allows the MCs to admonish viewers that wealth and material objects do not necessarily bring happiness. Dramatized by the figure of the lonely Egyptian princess, they point out that even her abundant surroundings bring misery. Although the musical show produces image excess—an elaborate set, lavish costumes, and a celestial ensemble of Vietnamese celebrities from all over the diaspora—such cautionary remarks are delivered to convey a simple moral lesson. Typical of the videos produced in the *Paris by Night* series, this opening scene trades in contradiction, exposing the complex and often paradoxical ways in which the Vietnamese experience in diaspora is mediated and showcased.

Paris by Night is a series of commercially produced videotapes of Vietnamese variety show performances consisting of elaborate musical and dance numbers, comedic skits, and fashion shows featuring Vietnamese women in traditional dress.[1] Many Vietnamese, if they do not own the videos themselves, have seen them on television screens at Vietnamese business establishments or heard them referred to in conversation. As postrefugee commodities, these videos are arguably the most popular cultural products circulating throughout the Vietnamese diaspora. They have entertained nearly 2.5 million overseas Vietnamese audience members worldwide and 72 million via a semi-legal "gray market" in Vietnam.[2] Designed to capture a wide niche of the Vietnamese diasporic audience, these colorful spectacles of song and dance offer over two hours worth of amusement for about $25 USD. Nearly 100 video sets in the series have been produced since the early 1980s, and in 2003 the introduction of the DVD format began to phase out VHS videocassettes.[3] The portable forms of entertainment may be purchased in local ethnic Vietnamese-owned businesses throughout the diaspora and on the Internet. A production

Figure 7. The 2010 releases of two competing diasporic Vietnamese music entertainment production companies, Asia and Thuy Nga rival each other but offer much of the same forms of pleasure. Note the prominence of maps and memories in both. *Asia* recalls the "timelessness" of the last fifty-five years of history for its theme while *Paris by Night* emphatically asserts, "I am Vietnamese" in their ninety-ninth show. Author's collection.

unique to the Vietnamese diaspora, these musical variety shows are often staged at theaters and auditoriums located in tourist cities, or other areas where large populations of diasporic Vietnamese reside and are recorded for wider distribution and consumption. The success of the *Paris by Night* series has not only generated a mass audience base for touring Vietnamese concerts but also inspired the creation of several rival production companies and video series such as *Asia* (Asia Entertainment), *Van Son* (Van Son Entertainment), and *Hollywood Night* (May Productions).

This chapter examines the cultural and representational work of niche media and videotexts produced by and for the Vietnamese diaspora. Combining images and sounds, music videos provide refugees and immigrants much more than pleasure and entertainment in a familiar language. These media technologies enable new ways of literally envisioning Vietnamese culture in exile, carving out spaces for the articulation and formation of postrefugee gender, ethnic, and cultural identities. As such, these inexpensive, accessible, and highly mobile technologies have become tools which Vietnamese Americans use to grapple with various issues including gender, sexuality, acculturation, assimilation, and the generation gap. These Vietnamese video and niche media productions employ the variety show form to construct song-and-dance spectacles invoking an idealized, nationalist vision of an exile community advancing under capitalism. I argue that Vietnamese cultural productions privilege a "new" diasporic Vietnamese subjectivity, shedding an "impoverished refugee" image for a new hybrid, bourgeois, ethnic identity.

Music Revival in America

Vietnamese refugees began rebuilding and carving elaborate alternative structures for Vietnamese-language media and entertainment almost immediately after resettling in the United States. The humble beginnings of this niche industry can be located with refugee musicians, who recorded and distributed audiocassettes of music that reflected their exile status. Although these singers and entertainers initially struggled in their professional adjustment to life in the United States, due in part to the lack of venues in which to perform, homemade audiocassette recordings of Vietnamese music allowed them to eventually regain their former audiences. Their music offered both scathing critiques of the communist government and melodies that took listeners back to a time when peace existed in Vietnam. These sorts of productions garnered the most support from the exile community, enabling many former singers to revive and reclaim their celebrity.

Free from the surveillance of the communist regime, artists and musicians also experimented with other forms of music they were exposed to before the fall of Saigon, including Western musical genres such as rock and roll, disco, and Latin rhythms such as cha-cha, tango, and rumba.[4] In addition to incorporating music from previous eras, musicians and performers also fused aspects of American popular culture with their repertoire and made a conscious movement to become part of their newly found homes. Despite their low production values, homemade audiocassette tapes of Vietnamese music offered a medium that enabled fans to voice political critiques against the communist regime, to express their sentiments on exile, and to negotiate their new identities.

Enter the VCR

Whereas music provided solace for the exile community, the audiovisual capabilities of the videocassette recorder (VCR) changed people's relationship to these cultural forms. In 1988, an estimated 65 percent of television households in the United States had VCRs. By 1997, nearly 90 percent of American homes were equipped with VCRs.[5] These machines revolutionized home entertainment, bringing commercial-free films and programs into domestic spaces and giving television viewers control over what they consumed. While most Americans used the VCR to perform two main functions—shifting viewing time and watching prerecorded audiovisual material on videotapes—groups of recent immigrants saw much more potential. For them, the VCR not only provided access to a world of entertainment and leisure in their native language but also functioned as a tool to preserve ethnicity, strengthen nationalism, and forge ties with the home country. As the video scholar Dona Kolar-Panov argues in her study of Croatians in Australia, the VCR "allows for the production and reproduction of nostalgia and provides for the creation of personal [as well as collective] pastiche of images and sounds as no other medium has done before."[6] The VCR brought new meaning to home entertainment in non-English-speaking households while video, as a reproducible technology, became a portable global commodity connecting immigrants to their homelands.

Like other immigrants, Vietnamese exiles were eager to use video technology to document their lives through the practice of exchanging "video letters."[7] But, unlike other immigrants who welcomed the potential for transnational exchanges between the diaspora and the homeland, Vietnamese exiles vehemently rejected cultural productions that originated in the Socialist Republic of Vietnam, believing that the work created there was tainted by communist ideology. With few alternatives outside of mainstream American media and limited English-language comprehension, many Vietnamese newcomers turned toward imported kung fu films and dramatic epic serials from Hong Kong and Taiwan as a main source of entertainment. Chinese films dubbed in Vietnamese enjoyed much popularity among Vietnamese immigrants and refugees, especially romantic soap operas and kung fu dramas set in ancient China. Jesse Nash's study of this phenomenon argues that Vietnamese adoration of dubbed Chinese films stems from their reaffirmation of traditional Confucian values.[8] Unlike most American television shows and movies, which seem to glorify individualism, Nash suggests that Chinese films play an important role in helping parents educate their children by modeling Confucian ideals such as filial piety and family loyalty. Additionally, Stuart Cunningham and Tina Nguyen's research reveals that Vietnamese Australians preferred dubbed films from Hong Kong and Taiwan because they contain material and settings "where Asian faces and values predominate."[9] Although ethnic and cultural differences between the Chinese and Vietnamese are at times contentious, racial identification minimized these differences, allowing many ethnic Vietnamese to enjoy media centered on Chinese subjects.

The success of dubbed dramatic videos from Hong Kong and Taiwan paved a way for Vietnamese exiles to apply video technology to actively construct new cultural forms for their own ethnic group. By the late 1980s, glamorous images of Vietnamese performers in music videos began to replace the politically overt voices of dissent recorded on cassette tapes. This is not to say that politics disappeared from the music industry with the introduction of video, but that glamour and style diluted traditional notions of politics and gave them a different form. Out of residual nationalist sentiments and the desire to carve out a distinct cultural identity apart from not only communist Vietnam but also multiethnic America, there emerged a vibrant Vietnamese music video industry. This niche industry entertained Vietnamese refugees in the aftermath of resettlement and provided a link to others throughout the diaspora. Advances in stereo, audiovisual, and other electronic media technologies also aided in transforming the modest musical forms that the refugees brought with them into a multimillion-dollar entertainment media industry. Produced mainly in Southern California and available in multiple forms of mediated technology, including cassettes, CDs, videos, karaoke laser discs, DVDs, and video CDs, diasporic Vietnamese musical culture can now be found in Vietnamese homes all over the globe.

Gender, Culture, Class, and *Paris by Night*

The successful progenitor of the contemporary Vietnamese music video industry is Thuy Nga, the corporate producers of the overwhelmingly popular *Paris by Night* video series. Inspired by former military USO shows, MTV, and other variety entertainment from Hong Kong as well as American film and television, *Paris by Night* was born from the entrepreneurial and creative drive of To Van Lai, a former music professor from Saigon. To Van Lai owned a music recording company named after his wife, Thuy Nga, in Vietnam.[10] When the couple fled to Paris after the fall of Saigon, they rebuilt their company under the same name.[11] It was not until 1983, with the assistance of the President of Euro Media Productions Jean Pierre Barry, that the first *Paris by Night* variety show and live recording took place in Paris.[12]

Paris by Night shows and videos made their debut in the United States while the Vietnamese American community was undergoing tremendous change. The increased use of multimedia technology, refugees' upward mobility, and the social, cultural, and commercial development of Little Saigon in Orange County, California, contributed to making *Paris by Night* videos a huge success. The creation of Little Saigon as an ethnic

Figure 8. A double advertisement for special tapings of upcoming live shows starring the "Divas" of *Paris by Night* on one side, and spectacularly themed, "*Toi La Nguoi Viet Nam,*" or "I am Vietnamese" on the other. Both events were held at Knott's Berry Farm, Charles M. Schultz Theater in January 2010. Courtesy of Amanda Gray.

enclave not only brought new possibilities for imagining community, but also resurrected the old capital in a new physical space, complete with the cultural institutions to foster this imagined community. As I argued in chapter 2, the Little Saigon enclave enabled Vietnamese Americans to geographically anchor their niche media industry. Emerging from this space as tools for constructing and authenticating Vietnamese cultural and political identity in the diaspora, these videos exist as cultural forms distinguished from those of other immigrants.[13]

For instance, diasporic Vietnamese media offered an alternative to dubbed Hong Kong and Taiwanese films, the preferred media choice of Vietnamese immigrants and refugees at the time. In some ways, media consumption mirrored contests over ethnic and cultural identity. While dubbed Chinese films and serials maintained their presence in the entertainment appetite of Vietnamese immigrants, the increasing popularity of *Paris by Night* videos throughout the late 1980s and early 1990s presented stiff competition for the serial films to which Vietnamese immigrants were reportedly addicted.[14] *Paris by Night* performers strategically paid homage to Chinese serials by performing popular theme songs from the dramas. Additionally, serial video addiction was often a topic of comedy skits or worked into the dialogues between the MCs because it became so common among the community. In the end, *Paris by Night* videos proved to be a productive tool for the Vietnamese diaspora to affirm an ethnic identity. The fan base for these videotaped shows grew by word-of-mouth, unifying Vietnamese audiences worldwide to celebrate ethnic pride and reimagining Vietnamese culture through elaborate variety song-and-dance numbers.

The first releases in the series earned a stable audience through their thematic focus on the exile experience. With titles such as *"Gia Biet Saigon"* ("Farewell Saigon"), *"Giot Nuoc Mat Cho Vietnam"* ("A Teardrop for Vietnam"), *"Nuoc Non Ngan Dam Ra Di"* ("The Homeland We Left Behind"), and *"Mua Xuan Nao Ta Ve?"* ("Which Spring Season Shall I Return?"), *Paris by Night* videos used popular memories of the homeland and anticommunism as guiding principles for attracting potential viewers. With the refugee elites of the "first wave" as the primary target audience, the *Paris by Night* series produced propaganda-laden, glorified images of the former Republic of Vietnam. According to Stuart Cunningham and Tina Nguyen, members of the diasporic elites welcomed such representations because they not only addressed their "depth of loss and longing" but also the "still-strong politics of disavowal of the regime's complicity in its own downfall."[15] In reconstructing Vietnam's history of war and conflict, the leaders

Figure 9. Commemorating thirty years abroad, *Paris by Night 77* devotes a considerable amount to history recalling the plight of refugees with film reels of war and footage of "boat people." Here, Khanh Ly's moving performance comes to a dramatic close as bodies tumble before a looming image of barbed wire.

of the former republic emerged as heroic figures whose downfall could be wholly blamed on America's abandonment.[16] But, while such blame is placed on the United States, Cunningham and Nguyen note that these narratives also depict America as a "great and powerful friend" that saved the Vietnamese people.[17]

The efforts of the first wave elites to adjust to American society were circumscribed by popular images of subsequent waves of "boat people" leaving communist Vietnam. The mainstream media of the mid- to late-1980s depicted the influx of asylum seekers from Southeast Asia as a social problem draining the resources of the United States and characterized these refugees as welfare dependents and gangsters.[18] In countering these images, Vietnamese show producers veiled immigrant anxiety about refugee dependency. What shaped many representations of diasporic Vietnamese videos was not only an urge to cure homesickness but also a longing to become part of the American nation. Introduced to U.S. ideology and consumer capitalism in Vietnam, immigrants and refugees began to associate assimilation with conspicuous consumption. Ronald Reagan's anticommunist and procapitalist politics of the 1980s particularly appealed to the elite refugees of the first wave, and his conservative politics seemed to promise access to the American Dream.[19] This Reagan-era bourgeois indulgence and its celebration of consumer capitalism consequently shaped many of the images of glamour and opulence that *Paris by Night* would later produce and reproduce. In reconstructing Vietnamese cultural elements and selectively poaching from American popular culture, producers and entertainers used this hybrid cultural terrain to create and sustain a fantasy of "Vietnamese America," reinterpreting history and molding new cultural identities through the strategic marketing of desire.

These projections not only altered musical tastes and preferences among Vietnamese immigrants, but the glamorous images also began to replace the overt voices of political dissent. Sold as commodities of cultural preservation as well as leisure and relaxation, these videos granted many Vietnamese people pleasure and forms of escapism, while they also functioned ideologically to promote a successful middle-class assimilated image. As such, Thuy Nga's videos gave Vietnamese viewers variety entertainment updated and translated with the most recent trends in mainstream American culture, film, television, and fashion, all the while assuring viewers that these translations were compatible with "authentic" Vietnamese culture.[20]

By the late 1990s, Thuy Nga Productions had established distribution headquarters in metropolitan cities in France, Australia, and in Little Saigon in the United States. With a focus on the contemporary Vietnamese diasporic experience, *Paris by Night* videos began to shift the themes of their titles away from the political. More frequently, producers began organizing musical arrangements around prosaic themes with titles such as "Tinh Ca" ("Songs of Love"), "Tien" ("Money"), *"Anh Den Mau"* ("Stage Lighting"), "Vao Ha" ("Holiday"), and "Thoi Trang va Am Nhac" ("Fashion and Music"). Additionally, *Paris by Night* began incorporating *ao dai* fashion shows featuring Vietnamese designers into their productions and traveling all over the diaspora to Las Vegas, Houston, Toronto, and the birthplace of the series, Paris, to perform for far-flung Vietnamese audiences.[21] Releasing over four videos and DVDs annually, each of which cost nearly half a million dollars to produce, and selling an estimated thirty thousand copies of each video, Thuy Nga continues to dominate smaller, rival productions in the diasporic entertainment industry.[22]

Although *Paris by Night* videos have been in circulation throughout the Vietnamese diaspora for nearly three decades, few scholars have seriously considered them as subjects worthy of critical analysis. Neglecting cultural formations and transformations, scholars of Vietnamese migration have tended to focus on the psychological aspects of their experiences, paying attention only to cultural displacement and maladjustments. Reflecting these ideas, scholarship on Vietnamese refugees carried titles such as, *Transition to Nowhere, Hearts of Sorrow,* and *Songs of the Free, Songs of the Caged.*[23] The refugees were often treated as victims because they no longer possessed a national territory in which to plant their cultures. As such, refugee studies scholars pathologized their cultural displacement while at the same time ignoring cultural production created in the aftermath of migration.

When it is not represented as pathological, Vietnamese culture is oftentimes characterized as static, resilient, and unaffected, despite its multilayered colonial past. The anthropologist James Rutledge, for example, observed, "when the Vietnamese refugees left Vietnam they left their country of birth but did not abandon their indigenous culture." Explaining the Vietnamese worldview, he writes: "The Vietnamese view themselves historically, and presently, as harmony-oriented. To the maximum degree possible, Vietnamese people desire to bring peace to other people and to respond to them in the way that bring them the most joy."[24] Such orientalist constructions of the Vietnamese people mask the complicated politics of U.S. military intervention. Moreover, this uncritical description of Vietnamese "indigenous culture" unproblematically idealizes the former world of the Vietnamese and overlooks the nation's history of colonial domination and cross-cultural fertilization.

Disrupting these beliefs through the staging of extravagant fantasy, Vietnamese variety shows offer a different glimpse of Vietnamese immigrant life, challenging the notion that the culture is composed of static tenets simply imported from Vietnam and applied in America. Undermining the idea of resiliency in Vietnamese culture, the cultural forms and objects created from afar exhibit an extraordinary process of relentless borrowing and appropriation to meet the perceived needs of the diasporic community. It is precisely because of this mixing and melding that Vietnamese popular cultural productions are often dismissed as trivial and frivolous pleasures made only for enjoyment.[25] Paying attention to undertheorized sites of the "popular" and the "inauthentic," this chapter examines cultural production and diasporic Vietnamese variety entertainment videos as serious subjects of study. Because these sites of the "popular" are repositories for generative forms of prevalent desires and fantasies, they appeal across gender and class lines to a mass Vietnamese diasporic audience.

Cultural insiders enjoyed *Paris by Night* videos for nearly a decade before these cultural forms caught the attention of a larger public with the controversy sparked by Thuy Nga's release of the special *Mother* video. In August 1997, hundreds of Vietnamese Americans in Orange County marched to the local Thuy Nga headquarters to protest the messages they perceived in the production company's latest release. *Mother* was supposed to be the most innovative and artistic *Paris by Night* video produced thus far. Deviating from the usual live variety format, the feature performances in *Mother* were presented with serious artistic intent, filled with images of Vietnam, and filmed in the style of American music videos. Audiences waited with much anticipation for what Thuy Nga Productions promised to be a very special music video dedicated to Vietnamese motherhood. Containing montages of rare scenery from Vietnam, as well as historical footage of war, the video was not only commemorative, but also instructional and spiritual, highlighting filial connections between mothers and children.[26]

However, controversy erupted when viewers saw footage of an American helicopter belonging to the South Vietnamese Army shooting at innocent civilians, interpreting its inclusion as a "procommunist" gesture. When angry fans stormed *Paris by Night* distribution stores to burn the videos, alleging that the images shown in the videos were historical inaccuracies and demanding an apology, the scandal sparked public interest beyond the Vietnamese diasporic community and drew the attention of some mainstream media.[27] *Paris by Night* sales momentarily suffered as fans looked to other production companies for entertainment. However, after Thuy Nga's contracted performers publicly defended the producers for what was explained away as the mistakes of an inexperienced young video editor, the *Paris by Night* series gradually regained its fan base. Nonetheless, the impassioned battle over representation attests to the critical relationship forged between the Vietnamese exile community and these media forms.

In one of the first published studies of diasporic Vietnamese media, the Australian cultural studies scholars Stuart Cunningham and Tina Nguyen provide a helpful analytical framework for interpreting the videos as cultural texts. Cunningham and Nguyen argue that the functions of these video performances can be classified through the categories of heritage maintenance, cultural negotiation, and assertive hybridity.[28] According to them, in assuming a stance against the communist government, these cultural texts maintain a sense of heritage and yet enable processes of cultural negotiation overseas to arbitrate aspects of the colonial past (such as its French and Chinese influences) and the assemblages of Vietnamese cultural and musical forms. At the same time, "assertive hybridity" highlights pastiche in its appropriations of American pop culture.

Performers who represent this "new wave" of assertive hybridity play crucial roles in the formation of a diasporic youth culture, especially in its experiments with gender and sexuality.[29] For the remainder of this chapter, I wish to expand upon Cunningham and Nguyen's observations and pose different possibilities for interpreting the *Paris by Night* video series as they pertain to diasporic identity formation and Vietnamese exilic self-representation.

Vietnamese Exiles as Authentic Vietnamese

The majority of *Paris by Night* fans are between the ages of thirty-five and sixty, but the videos are viewed by people of all ages and are considered "family entertainment." Older audience members who are fluent in Vietnamese tend to be attracted to two types of music depending on taste and preference: traditional Vietnamese folk songs sung in an operatic style called *vong co*, or more modern, Western and European-influenced music with the familiar Latin rhythms of their youth, called *tan nhac*. The elements that draw the younger generation are the dance beats and sounds of familiar American pop songs. As such, *Paris by Night* makes a concerted effort to feature and promote young singers who perform bilingual song and dance numbers "borrowed" from current American pop culture.[30] However, videos seldom showcase works that are "new." Songs are often recycled and sung by multiple artists on different recordings to display the talents of the artists rather than the artistry of the songs themselves. Because copyrights are almost never enforced, these artistic borrowings as well as multiple covers of the same songs are common practice.[31] In his critique of the standardization of Western popular music, Theodor Adorno posits that pseudo-individuation numbs the minds of the masses, who seek leisure to escape from their everyday realities.[32] For Vietnamese exiles, pseudo-individuation is familiar, as Vietnamese tunes provide an escape in nostalgia. Much more than a pastime, nostalgia-laden music requires the standardization of music to locate a sense of familiarity. This allows Vietnamese exiles to commiserate and share in the experience of listening. Although music preference and reception to specific songs are uneven, audiences of Vietnamese diasporic media draw on what is most familiar and enjoy entertainment that transports them to a nostalgic, prior moment untainted by the devastation of war, dislocation, and displacement.

Nonetheless, though much pleasure is derived from these videos, they should not be ignored simply because they afford pleasure. Instead, borrowing a phrase from Dorinne Kondo, Vietnamese variety-show videos should be regarded as "contradictory sites of pleasure and contestation."[33] As I have shown, the videos and their audiences also enforce an ideology of exile. This is most prevalent in the policing of Vietnamese American performers. Honored as celebrities in the diasporic community, entertainers are often invited to fundraisers for charitable causes and even political rallies.[34] But when diasporic entertainers choose to perform in Vietnam, they automatically become outcasts, losing their fan base and popular standing.[35] (Conversely, when singers from Vietnam tour the United States, exiles organize protests and boycotts of their concerts, branding these singers communist spies.)[36] The business of entertainment for Vietnamese Americans is therefore fused with politics, and anticommunist politics dominate every aspect of the industry. While I agree with Cunningham and Nguyen that maintaining an anticommunist stance secures the ideological work of "heritage maintenance," I contend that anticommunist rhetoric also consolidates and strengthens Vietnamese exilic identities, defining for them what is properly "Vietnamese." The idea of return may be possible, but it is not a viable option for the exiles unless the communist government is overthrown. Hence, the struggle to define what is authentically Vietnamese operates through nostalgia. In his study of Iranian nostalgia, Hamid Naficy notes, "for exiles who have emigrated from Third World countries, life in the United States . . . is doubly unreal, and it is because of this double loss—of origin and of reality—that nostalgia becomes a cultural and representational practice among the exiles."[37] A cultural project already thriving on fantasy, the historical past constructed by variety shows is sometimes imagined as untainted by war and devastation. Critical of the existing communist regime, the Vietnamese exiles refuse to look to the homeland nation as a place of "true" culture. For them, authentic Vietnamese culture only existed before the communist takeover in 1975. In *Songs of the Caged, Songs of the Free*, ethnomusicologist Adelaida Reyes argues that Vietnamese exiles hope to preserve "pre-1975 culture" and reinstate it when Vietnam is liberated from communist rule.[38] Operating at the level of the imagination, *Paris by Night* videos satisfy a longing and alleviate an incurable homesickness by employing nostalgia to elude what scholar Ashley Carruthers calls "diasporic anxiety."[39] Similar to the Iranian experience in Hamid Naficy's study, the fetishization of the pre-1975 homeland creates "an electronic *communitas* that bestows a sense of stability and commonality to the exiles" who left Vietnam.[40]

Constructing "High" Culture

While nostalgia for the homeland allows audiences to imagine a national community in exile, *colonial* nostalgia consolidates its class hierarchies. Consider the title of the video series. Paris was the literal birthplace of Thuy Nga's entertainment empire, but the name *Paris by Night* evokes a colonial past, reminiscent of a time when the Vietnamese elite traveled to the metropole to experience the sophisticated glamour of the "city of lights." When referring to the video series, producers and some fans pronounce *Paris* with a French accent, yet *Paris by Night* is not otherwise known as *Paris par Nuit*. This choice of a linguistically hybrid title implicitly invokes the historical relationships between the former Vietnamese regimes with both France and the United States.

Colonial nostalgia is not only a longing Thuy Nga Productions promotes, but also a set of ideological assumptions on which the company thrives. Drawing from Vietnam's colonial past, with its diverse cultural elements, enables producers and entertainers to invent an exilic culture that is disassociated from communist Vietnam. It is important to note that these colonial projects provide cultural forms loaded with signs of class distinction. For instance, almost every video produced after 1990 contains a fashion show modeled by young attractive performers showcasing the talents of young diasporic designers. Literally fashioning a particular bourgeois sensibility enables performers to project an idealized image of Vietnamese identity. Using colonial nostalgia and its images of cosmopolitanism, *Paris by Night* introduces its audiences to a world of fashion, plastic surgery, and commodity fetishism.

Unlike the diasporic music-recording industry of the late 1970s and early 1980s, *Paris by Night* videos grapple with immigrant alienation and displacement in a manner reflecting a newly forged bourgeois identity. In representing the experiences of Vietnamese immigrants in the United States, Thuy Nga producers construct a trajectory of upward mobility. For instance, in a 1995 special edition video commemorating twenty years of migration and exile, the company staged and recorded a montage of documentary-film footage of refugee flight at the famous Shrine Auditorium in Hollywood, former location of the Oscar and Grammy award ceremonies. Serving as a reminder to the live and video audiences of their shared, collective past, images of boat people flashed across a large movie screen, followed by a powerfully sorrowful performance about the exile experience. These stark images were then replaced by narratives of celebration lauding the current success of Vietnamese Americans throughout the rest of the video.

Figure 10. *Paris by Night* 84 "Passport to Music and Fashion" celebrates the successful achievements of Vietnamese American designers, including *Project Runway* winner Chloe Dao, celebrity hair stylist Kim Vo, and famous *ao dai* designer Calvin Hiep. In this singing/ dancing/fashion show performance, female vocalists pose like celebrities while male *Paris by Night* dancers enact the role of paparazzi taking their photos. Directed by Michael Watt (2006).

The Pedagogy of *Paris by Night*

Thuy Nga Productions comes to grips with history and memory particularly through its release of videos that intentionally remind audiences of the past through commemoration. Nevertheless, more contemporary issues of cultural assimilation and acculturation also inform the performances. One reason Vietnamese variety-show videos are immensely popular is because they actively poach American popular culture.[41] Offering their own interpretations and translations, young performers appropriate a wide range of stylistic elements of mainstream music, from contemporary love ballads to rock, hip-hop, and rap. Young Vietnamese American singers often cover the music of pop artists famous in the 1950s and 1960s, such as Elvis Presley and the Beatles, more contemporary divas such as Madonna and Celine Dion, and trendsetters such as Ricky Martin, Britney Spears, and 'N Sync. These performers introduce what they believe exemplifies American culture to Vietnamese audiences. Many bilingual pop songs serve to open parents' eyes to the interests of their Vietnamese American children.[42] By translating what is considered "foreign" culture for parents, *Paris by Night* videos can act as a generational bridge.

Poaching American culture also allows Thuy Nga Productions to familiarize its audiences with middlebrow productions and other minority cultures. In *Paris by Night 46*, Henry Chuc and Dalena perform numbers from Andrew Lloyd Webber's musical *Phantom of the Opera* for Vietnamese audiences, reenacting scenes and translating lyrics from English into Vietnamese. Also known as the artist who brought rap and hip-hop to *Paris by Night* fans, Henry Chuc demonstrated the range of his musical talent by performing the role of the Phantom. Dalena, a blonde, Anglo-American woman whose ability to mimic Vietnamese vocals made her famous in the world of Vietnamese niche entertainment, played Christine, the Phantom's love interest. This ethnic, off-Broadway version of a popular musical provides a glimpse of American culture to which audiences might not otherwise have access.

In a reinterpretation of another famous American musical, *Paris by Night* modified the lyrics to a popular song so that Vietnamese audiences might better relate to its sentiments. Performing scenes from *West Side Story*, Tommy Ngo and Bao Han change a significant line of Stephen Sondheim's lyrics to match the experiences of Vietnamese Americans. In their rendition of "America," *San Juan* is replaced by *Sai Gon*,

I think I'll go back to Sai Gon,
I know a boat you can get on, bye-bye
Everyone there will give big cheer,
Everyone there will have moved here.[43]

Insisting that the refugee/boat people experience is quintessentially part of the American narrative, this performance inserts Vietnam into the American middlebrow imagination for its viewers. Nevertheless, this *Paris by Night* version remains true to the spirit of the original musical recording, complete with social commentary and a scathing critique of American society. Translated through a Vietnamese American lens, this performance of "America" attempted to perform the original choreography while the singers sung with an "immigrant" accent. Dressed in clothing that resembled an amalgam of 1960s-era styles but with Asian accents, Tommy Ngo and his entourage wore kung fu tops with slacks, while Bao Han and her backup performers wore cheongsam blouses with asymmetrical ruffled skirts and high-heeled tap shoes. Their rendition of "America," introduced by the MC as "Life Is Good in America," contains allusions to racial discrimination ("Buying on credit is so nice / One look at you and they charge twice . . . Life can be bright in America / If you're all white in America . . . Lots of doors slamming in our face . . . Better get rid of your accent!"); the housing problems poor immigrants face, ("Twelve in a room in America"); the lack of employment opportunities ("Free to wait tables and shine shoes"); and an overall disillusionment of the unattainable American Dream ("I think I'll go back to Sai Gon / I know a boat you can get on"). And while the male perspective finds fault in American society, the presumably more Americanized women sing the praises of modernity and consumer capitalism ("Skyscrapers bloom in America / Cadillacs zoom in America / Industry boom in America") and other freedoms available here ("Here you are free and you have pride . . . You can have anything you choose").

Film critics and theatre reviewers have noted that the original lyrics of "America" were modified and toned down for the film version of *West Side Story*, so that its critique of American society would not offend mainstream audiences.[44] Staying faithful to the original stage production allows immigrant men to momentarily find fault in American society, only to be countered by young, presumably more assimilated women singing the praises of consumer capitalism and material wealth. As in the original stage production, the immigrant experience is gendered. The critique of American society nonetheless creates ruptures in the normalizing representations of Vietnamese Americans, destabilizing the problematic elitism in many self-representations of Vietnamese Americans. However, certain consumerist desires still define the immigrant experience.

Disruptions in "Vietnamese-ness"

Although a relatively conservative and traditional class of anticommunist elites holds sway over these representations of "Vietnameseness," what it means to be Vietnamese is constantly disrupted in the shows' performances. Musical acts by young artists often destabilize and refashion the categories "Vietnamese" and "Vietnamese American." Cunningham and Nguyen's category of "assertive hybridity" celebrates these liberating aspects of diasporic performances. Encapsulated by the creative work of artists such as Lynda Trang Dai, known as "the Vietnamese Madonna," and others who transcend boundaries of tradition and culture, assertive hybridity enables Vietnamese youth to embrace aspects of Western as well as Vietnamese culture in an unfolding drama of assimilation.

No other feature of the *Paris by Night* series illustrates these ongoing struggles more poignantly than the banter between the master and mistress of ceremonies (see Figure 11). Nearly every *Paris by Night* event is hosted by the prominent poet and political writer Nguyen Ngoc Ngan and his female sidekick Nguyen Cao Ky Duyen, a young lawyer-turned-performer, who is also the daughter of Nguyen Cao Ky, former vice president and air-force commander of South Vietnam. While the duties of the master and mistress of ceremonies generally consist of introducing performers and, when necessary, providing the historical backgrounds for certain types of performances, the MCs also bear the responsibility of setting the overall ambiance, offering moral instruction and comic relief, and staging debates about gender roles. An eminent member of the exilic literati, Nguyen Ngoc Ngan presumes to represent the views of Vietnamese men and the "traditional values" upheld by the elders of the community. Nguyen Cao Ky Duyen, on the other hand, seeks to embody a vibrant youth culture and speak on behalf of Vietnamese women. Sometimes referred to as "the role model for Vietnamese women for the twenty-first century," Ky Duyen is respected by both young and old women alike.[45] At times, the playful dialogue and comedic exchanges between the two resemble the antics of morning-show hosts Regis Philbin and Kelly Ripa. Like the authoritative and cantankerous Regis and the cheerful and jovial Kelly, Ngan and Ky Duyen often contend with issues of power in gender and social relations. They even receive fan mail and requests from the audience to discuss such matters. For instance, in an exchange about the transformation of gender roles in the immigration experience, Ngan brings up the practice of gift giving as an example. Noting that women often complain about men not giving them gifts on holidays such as Valentine's Day and birthdays, Ngan explains that in times of war and economic hardship it was not common practice in Vietnam for husbands to buy gifts for their wives. Ky Duyen responds by asking, "Then according to Vietnamese society in the past, what makes a good husband?" What follows blossoms into a debate about the qualities that define a good Vietnamese man:

NGAN: In the olden days, most men were the heads of their households except for the few men who went astray and became addicted to gambling and alcohol or committed adultery. Thus, men who do not commit these vices are good husbands.

KY DUYEN: You mean men do not have to help with the laundry, wash dishes, or help with the house chores?

NGAN: You are asking for too much. That is, a husband who does not take in a concubine is good enough. If you ask him to do housework and vac-uum, that's too much. We have migrated here and we see that this soci-ety is different. Women here have noticed our American neighbors are so

Figure 11. The Masters of Ceremony Nguyen Ngoc Ngan and Nguyen Cao Ky Duyen take a moment from introducing performers to discuss gendered responses to beauty standards and media images. From *Paris by Night* 71, "20th Anniversary," directed by Kent Weed (2003).

different from our own husbands. For example, if an American man were to see a Vietnamese man driving his wife home from the market and it is raining outside, the Vietnamese man is expected to open the car door for his wife. I don't know about you all, but this is not a practice that Vietnamese men are accustomed to doing . . . . The American man would be surprised to see that the Vietnamese man walked out of the car with umbrella in tote while his wife soaked in the rain.

The audience laughs, and Ngan pleads with the female members of the audience to understand the plight of men:

NGAN: In their transition from Vietnam to America, of course there are certain old habits that are deep-seated. We will change gradually but we can't instantly become gallant like American men because it is not a practice that men of my generation are used to. Perhaps it will be possible for my children's generation to do this.

To which Ky Duyen quickly retorts:

KY DUYEN: This is the first time I have heard it explained to me in this manner. But I have a suggestion to make. We women will consider the situations of our men only when there's a holiday or a special occasion. You need not purchase any gifts for us. We just ask that you give us money so that we can buy gifts for ourselves.[46]

Turning to the audience for assent and applause, Ky Duyen smiles and adds, "This is because whenever men buy things for us, we always have to exchange them, and if they buy diamonds, they're always too small. So if they give us money, it's the only sure thing." Content with her final punch line, Ky Duyen turns a potentially charged discussion that gestures towards feminism into one about female consumption.

After a musical performance by two young singing sisters, Ky Duyen picks up where the conversation ended with a monologue that revisits the discussion on gender roles.

> K Y D U Y E N : The fact is, men do have faults, but the faults are minor. If a man forgets to buy a present for his wife, or isn't gallant or meticulous, that's actually fine. However, I think there are certain things that men should never do. If men ever do these things, we should leave them. First, never hit a woman, and second, do not ever drink excessively. Moderate social drinking is fine but drinking too much is bad, right?

Ngan spontaneously replies, "Yes, I do agree. I dare not do any of those things. I am afraid to hit my wife, and I do not drink alcohol because I get these glances from her." Both the host and hostess put forth a firm stance against domestic violence and alcoholism, but alcohol provides a segue for Ngan to tell a joke about three men at an Alcoholics Anonymous meeting. Unwilling to allow her elder male counterpart make light of the situation, Ky Duyen pushes the conversation back to the changing gender roles of men and women. She prompts, "What do you think is the main difference between Vietnamese husbands and wives now and then in Vietnam?" Ngan confidently explains, "I think the houses in Vietnam were too small. Husbands and wives shared one room with their children." Ngan again proceeds to tell another joke about lovemaking and the lack of privacy parents have when sleeping in crowded quarters and sharing a room with their children.

The typical dialogues between the two MCs often involve issues of migration, the disparities between American and Vietnamese societies, and gender, class, and culture before and after settling in the United States. I quote this dialogue at length to demonstrate that through comedic rupture and recuperation, the master and mistress of ceremonies grapple with issues of gender differences, educating and provoking audience members to discuss on their own the complexities of the immigrant experience. However, the conversations vacillate between seriousness and light-heartedness, often ending in laughter rather than any direct ideological critiques. Rife with humorous exchanges ranging from intelligent to raunchy, the repartee between the MCs entertains as it enables the audience to reflect upon other unresolved differences between Vietnamese American women and men.

The debates about gender roles staged by the MCs reflect a larger concern over meanings of tradition and modernity, often writ large on the female body. The *Paris by Night* stage showcases an incredibly diverse range of Vietnamese femininities, but Nhu Quynh and Lynda Trang Dai exemplify the two extremes. A traditional female vocalist, Nhu Quynh represents an image of the virginal innocence of a young Vietnamese woman (See Figure 12). Lynda Trang Dai, the "Vietnamese Madonna," on the other hand, uses her sexuality (like the original Madonna, the performer) to express her art. Nhu Quynh has been described as "sweet," "pretty," "graceful," and "the girl that every man wants to marry." As the apotheosis of Vietnamese feminine beauty, Nhu Quynh often appears pure and angelic. Her performance of ideal femaleness complements her soothing, melodious voice. Her repertoire mainly consists of folk songs, traditional ballads, and upbeat songs of girlhood innocence. She almost always appears in the traditional *ao dai*, the long,

Figure 12. Nhu Quynh sings and dances with a conical hat representing rural Vietnamese traditions in *Paris by Night* 89 "Korea Live" where the cast performed in front of organized tours of Vietnamese American visitors to Korea. Directed by Seounghyun Oh (2007).

flowing Vietnamese tunic that symbolizes both Vietnamese ethnicity and essentialized, gendered, and classed forms of femininity. In contrast to the female performers who always wear *ao dai* in their acts, Lynda Trang Dai stands out as a symbol of the "Americanized" Vietnamese woman. Notorious for imitating Madonna's song and dance routines, she has been alternately criticized and praised by young and old audiences alike for "lacking originality" and being both "too sexy" and "bold and daring." As a performer who has been able to imitate, amalgamate, and to some extent invent hybridity through cultural mixing, Lynda appears highly original to her fans. In the early 1980s, she became one of the first Vietnamese American female entertainers to shed convention by styling herself as a seductress and "boy toy." Unlike Madonna, who embraces polymorphous perversity, Lynda denies any similarities between her stage persona and her "real life," insisting, "I don't smoke, I don't drink. I'm just your typical Vietnamese girl who wants to look different when she sings."[47] Nonetheless, many viewers refuse to see her sexualized performances as belonging to a "typical Vietnamese girl." Many older Vietnamese people view her as a dangerous influence, yet they tolerate and dismiss her presentations as directed toward the younger crowd. Embodying a youthful style, her acts are believed to inspire young girls to transgress traditional notions of Vietnamese femininity.

Like the original Madonna, Lynda has also transformed herself throughout the years, innovating her performances by incorporating recognizable elements from mainstream popular culture. For example, Lynda has created music by translating an American pop song and hybridizing it with faster, upbeat, danceable rhythms, thereby giving it new meaning. She has experimented with every genre of American music including disco, pop, rock, rap, and hip-hop. For younger people, she is the embodiment of "cool." Throughout her career as a performer for Thuy Nga, Lynda has toned down her sexy image by occasionally dressing herself in the *ao dai*. She married fellow *Paris by Night* performer Tommy Ngo, which in some ways allowed her the artistic permission to display her sexuality more overtly. To the viewing community, flirting with one's husband seems more acceptable even though that means arousing other men. Tommy plays her ideal counterpart onstage and off because of his pretty-boy charm and equally creative devotion to blending Vietnamese music for youth audiences. Tommy and Lynda collaborate on many occasions singing duets and making videos together. Despite these attempts to have a sanitized offstage life, Lynda's image as a sex symbol continues to dominate her reputation (see Figure 13).

Figure 13. Lynda Trang Dai boldly gyrates to the tune of "Fame" on the special twenty-fifth anniversary of *Paris by Night*. The real Lynda (center stage) looks back at herself (here she is wearing her famous "Lynda" jewel encrusted bustier) projected on a larger-than-life screen that reflects and recalls her own famous career. Her performance involved removing layers of clothing while dancing with the most memorable of her past personae, represented by the *Paris by Night* dancers. From *Paris by Night* 71, "20th Anniversary," directed by Kent Weed (2003).

Both Lynda Trang Dai and Nhu Quynh enact diverging qualities of Vietnamese womanhood on stage, but recent events surrounding their maternity have exposed the performative qualities of these musical megastars. Lynda's stage persona as the sexy, flirtatious, femme fatale who often wears outrageously skimpy outfits was tamed when she took a hiatus in 2004 to have her baby. Lynda's decision to have a child was met with approval, but Nhu Quynh's pregnancy stirred controversy because it went against others' expectations. When Nhu Quynh announced her pregnancy in 2007, she did so as an unwed mother-to-be. To make matters worse, she refused to disclose the identity of her child's father, causing an uproar and rapid-fire gossip among many of her loyal fans. Much to the young female vocalist's dismay, the Vietnamese public did not treat her case with open-mindedness and flexibility. Rather, her private decisions became fodder for the rumor mill and stories about her "illegitimate" baby spread all over the

Vietnamese press and the Internet. Nhu Quynh had apparently dated Andy Quach, an aspiring politician in Orange County, but she broke up with him and claimed that her baby's father had the initials "NT."[48] With this tarnished reputation, Nhu Quynh lost her contract with Thuy Nga and was forced to return to Asia Entertainment, a top rival diasporic entertainment company that she had worked for but also sued early in her career. Despite her indiscretions, Nhu Quynh's beguiling charm continues to secure a wide audience. She has since renegotiated and returned to Thuy Nga in time to star in the special "Divas" show (see Figure 8).

The *Paris by Night* stage both guides and regulates dominant gender ideology, especially in light of its purported responsiveness and responsibilities to its fan base. In the above cases, female performers are expected to morally uphold the ideal desires and values of the community. Violating what appears to be the trust audiences have placed on their bodies creates jarring disruptions between performance and reality. While women are expected to stay within the bounds of respectability, men are allowed much

Figure 14. Tommy Ngo and Henry Chuc perform hypermasculinity by paying homage to the action film series *The Matrix* in their dance performance, yet their duet is a song entitled, "Don't Forsake My Heart." From *Paris by Night* 71, "20th Anniversary," directed by Kent Weed (2003).

Figure 15. Ho Le Thu and Nguyen Hung visually illustrate gender relations in this sexually suggestive dance. From *Paris by Night* 84 "Passport to Music and Fashion," directed by Michael Watt (2006).

more flexibility and freedom in their expressions of ideas, politics, and even (hetero)sexuality. The older they are, the more authority they hold over women and the younger generation. Despite the public criticism that the celebrities of the Vietnamese diaspora must endure, in the end, these setbacks do little damage to the entertainers' careers. Transgressions in the name of artistic freedom are still achieved through the sexualized display of female bodies. In the contemporary postrefugee moment of globalized electronic media, the position of these entertainers has in fact been elevated to the point where they are celebrated and admired by the Vietnamese diaspora worldwide. Male and female performers alike are revered for their gift to entertain as well as their abilities to negotiate the contradictions of the modern exilic Vietnamese condition.

Carving Out Spaces for Creative Bodies

The alternative cultural public of the diasporic entertainment industry not only allows exiles to represent themselves, but also provides the only theater for most professional performers of Vietnamese descent to showcase their artistic and musical talents. Boasting quality production values as the most prestigious venue in the industry, the *Paris by Night* stage gives diasporic Vietnamese performers a chance to attain fame and celebrity. In this setting,

Vietnamese bodies are at the center while non-Vietnamese are on the periphery. The privileging of Vietnamese bodies in Vietnamese music video productions is, however, occasionally offset by non-Vietnamese performers who take on "yellowface."[49] One of the most beloved non-Vietnamese performers to ever join the diasporic music industry is Dalena, a blonde, blue-eyed, Anglo-American woman who sings in accent-free Vietnamese. Dalena was discovered by an Asian restaurateur, who gave her a cassette tape of Vietnamese music after learning that she loved to sing in multiple languages.[50] Her ability to mimic and perform Vietnamese vocals catapulted her to the top of the industry, allowing her to play a pivotal role in popularizing Vietnamese diasporic music in the early 1990s. Dalena does not understand the Vietnamese language, but her fascination with and willingness to embrace Vietnamese culture—donning the traditional *ao dai* and singing in a range of Vietnamese genres, including traditional Vietnamese opera—has made her a huge star.

Filmmaker Nguyen Tan Hoang has even made a documentary about Dalena's unconventional stardom as a Vietnamese pop star. In his short film, *Cover Girl: A Gift from God* (2000), Nguyen compiles an impressive montage of Dalena's performances, marveling at her ability to master

Figure 16. Dalena successfully crosses over to become one of the few non-Vietnamese performers who sing in Vietnamese. Not only has she perfected the tones in the language but she has also mastered the gracefulness of the movements. Dalena left Thuy Nga to sing for Asia Entertainment, its biggest rival music production company. From "Huyen Thoai Le Minh Bang" *Asia* DVD 52, Asia Entertainment, directed by Ryan Polito (2006). Courtesy of Son Lieu.

Vietnamese music.[51] Dalena's presence in the Vietnamese entertainment circuit serves a number of functions. She often appears as an ethereal, blonde, feminine figure that is conservatively dressed in Vietnamese traditional clothing. As an Anglo-American woman who embraces Vietnamese culture through the music she sings, she is welcomed into the community. In fact, her perceived love of Vietnamese culture is often used by Vietnamese elders as a way to inspire Vietnamese American youth to retain their culture.

Dalena's success has not been matched by other non-Vietnamese performers, but her "crossover" appeal to Vietnamese diasporic audiences reveals their fascination for "exotic" non-Vietnamese others. Rick Murphy, an Irish American who sings Vietnamese opera; Frank Olivier, a French singer and songwriter; and Lynn, the blonde Anglo-Australian wife of famed performer Cong Thanh, have all made appearances on *Paris by Night* videos. Biracial performers such as Thanh Ha and Phi Nhung have also gained entry into the world of diasporic entertainment for their striking appearances. Although the *Paris by Night* dancers do not occupy center stage, they have played a significant role in bolstering fan loyalty. With their expressive and graceful collective talents, this elite group of dancers assembled by the producers of *Paris by Night* is mainly Asian American of Korean, Filipino, Thai, Chinese, and Japanese descent. Their talents transcend Thuy Nga Productions as they have been on tour with a variety of acts such as Celine Dion, the Spice Girls, and Cirque du Soleil.

While a host of exotic non-Vietnamese others are given the opportunity to work alongside these Vietnamese mega pop stars, one notable "behind-the-scenes" contributor is Shanda Sawyer, a famed choreographer who began working with Thuy Nga in 1995. Under Sawyer's direction, the appearance of *Paris by Night* videos underwent a dramatic transformation, giving it a modern—even postmodern—aesthetic. According to her website, Sawyer's credentials include working for Ringling Brothers and Barnum and Bailey Circus, *Dancing with the Stars* Live Tour, television drama episodes of CBS's *Ghost Whisperer* and NBC's *Las Vegas*, Siegfried and Roy shows, and a number of celebrity holiday specials.[52] Sawyer's influence on the *Paris by Night* stage is remarkable in that she gave it flair, grandeur, and hyperexoticism.

Consistent with its goals to thrill audiences with acts that are out of the ordinary, Thuy Nga Productions, under the direction of Shanda Sawyer, have used little people as well as exotic animals as stage props in the variety shows. Employing strategies of performance as those in nineteenth-century

Figure 17. Boasting high production values, every *Paris by Night* show begins with a spectacular opening act filled with grandeur, various exotic props, and numerous supporting dancers. Here, singer Thuy Tien wears Chinese robes but is surrounded by "Thai" motifs complete with open flames and dancers carrying pythons around their necks. Her performance is immediately followed by fiery magic tricks performed by guest illusionist Franz Harary. From *Paris by Night* 71, "20th Anniversary," directed by Kent Weed (2003).

American circus acts, producers of Vietnamese diasporic videos have not only exploited ideas of exoticism and difference in terms of ethnicity and race, they have also pushed to explore notions of female sexuality as it is linked to the Vietnamese body.[53] I draw these parallels here between the entertainers in Thuy Nga Productions and those of the circus because of the significance of the cultural and ideological labor they perform. I maintain that the *Paris by Night* stage both reinforces and tests the boundaries around notions of ethnicity, gender, sexuality, and identity for the Vietnamese diaspora. As examined earlier, gender struggles are frequently rendered in explicit discussions and debates on stage through musical and comedic performances as well as in the banter between the MCs. Nevertheless, the materiality of the Vietnamese female body is highlighted even more visually in other aspects of the cultural production, including the advertisements.

The various body-conscious commercials and infomercials advertised in the videos reveal that the producers of *Paris by Night* have tapped into the Vietnamese psyche that has learned to become aware of social anxieties. Numerous ads placed in Thuy Nga Productions claim to solve bodily dysfunctions and enhance lifestyle—surgical procedures that cure sweaty palms, exercise devices that slim and trim, lotions and potions designed for and catered to Asian clientele, and exotic products such as royal jelly that promise to bring health and beauty.[54] In fact, the mistress of ceremonies, Nguyen Cao Ky Duyen, has an entire website devoted to marketing these body-enhancing products for hair, skin, face, and overall health. Committed to beauty, wellness, nutrition, and fashion, the online "Ky Duyen House" sells items including handbags, clothing, and accessories as well as designer *ao dai* for the modern but culturally aware Vietnamese bride.[55] One may even purchase books, audio CDs, DVDs, and calendars of pretty girls in *ao dai* or bikinis from this online marketplace.[56] This is developed in line with Thuy Nga's merchandising of *Paris by Night*–related items, including karaoke DVDs, books on tape, and the glossy monthly entertainment magazine *Van Nghe*, which provides updates and behind-the-scenes stories, news, and interviews with the *Paris by Night* performers. As entrepreneurs, Ky Duyen and Thuy Nga Productions are not only commodifying cultural products, they are also selling a lifestyle associated with the celebrity culture of the Vietnamese diaspora. It is important to highlight that this stylish cult of celebrity promoted by Ky Duyen and others has gone online, traversing the diaspora. Constrained by a lack of opportunity to participate in the dominant American market, Vietnamese American entertainers are limited to attaining fame and popularity only within their own ethnic group. Nevertheless, this relatively small group is both global in reach and has an emerging consumer base willing to spend their hard-earned money on lifestyle–enhancing products.

Diasporic Vietnamese recording artists, entertainers, and performers who have achieved star status with their adoring fans in real life have become subjects of virtual admiration for fans. Like Hollywood celebrities, Vietnamese entertainers are generally looked upon by the exile community as icons of success and beauty worthy of imitation. Their bodies are not only made for consumption, they also provide a model of materiality for ordinary Vietnamese. Theorizing celebrity and identity formation, media scholar Neal Gabler suggests that the pervasiveness of entertainment penetrates our desires to the extent that ordinary life becomes a movie and common

Figure 18. A cosmetic surgery ad featuring the services of a "surgeon to the stars" of Hollywood. According to the ad, Vietnamese clients may receive a discounted price of $2,995 for a breast augmentation procedure. These infomercials and others like them appear in almost every *Paris by Night* video placed between Disc 1 and Disc 2 (usually at the beginning of Disc 2). From *Paris by Night* 67 in San Jose, directed by Kent Weed (2002).

people are the stars in them. Gabler explains that ordinary subjects who live life as a movie require the accoutrements of a movie star.[57] To what extent do consumers of Vietnamese popular media live their lives as movies?

To obtain as wide a range of responses as possible, I solicited various online Vietnamese American groups, giving survey participants the option to complete the entire survey in one sitting or in three different parts. The Web survey enabled me to unveil different spheres of discourse that occur in cyberspace and to gauge the role technology played in the formation of exilic Vietnamese identities. Participants in my Web survey revealed that fans of Vietnamese diasporic media are responding to the cult of celebrity and marketing of desire in various ways. Some aggressively identify with the performers and want to be entertainers themselves.[58] Others support the glamorized images of Vietnamese culture, confessing that they "like to look at how people dress" and "copy the good things."[59] Many who responded to my survey were, however, keenly aware that "entertainers are asked to portray an unrealistic lifestyle [that is] often misleading to viewers."[60] A real estate developer from San Jose, California reasons, "I seldom discuss the merit of the videos. I either like it or turn it off or walk away."[61] Another office worker from British Columbia, Canada writes, "I can fast forward the part I don't like."[62]

While media viewers do have a choice, they still must negotiate the representations they confront as consumers of popular culture.

For example, viewers of variety-show videos are frequently bombarded with ads promoting plastic surgery. Rivaling the aesthetic-surgery company discussed in chapter 3, the Hanh Phuoc Victoria Cosmetic Surgery Center supports and sponsors the *Paris by Night* series by advertising in their videos. As an advertiser and longtime sponsor of the video series, Ms. Hanh Phuoc has made numerous public appearances on the shows. She is often shown sitting in the front row as an audience member. In one of the videos, Marie To, daughter of To Van Lai and Thuy Nga and executive producer of the *Paris by Night* series, honors her on stage with an award recognizing her loyalty and support for the production company.[63] It is no coincidence that Hanh Phuoc is also a beauty queen who proudly displays her credentials as such. In 1995, she won the crown for a local (Houston, Texas) beauty pageant for married and mature women, called Mrs. All-Nations Universal and has since used her title to sell plastic surgery.[64] Hanh Phuoc is also the spokesmodel for her business. She often appears provocatively posed in publicity photos showcasing her post-op face and body as if they were products consumers can purchase. These images of her perpetually youthful, smooth, and refined body clearly convey that the Vietnamese body—and, more important, the female body—is directly linked to an investment in general consumer practices and plastic surgery in particular. To maintain this type of lifestyle requires both the embrace of exclusive products and a concomitant willingness to accept technology as a path to transformation.

Despite having the option to fast-forward ads, viewers often take notice. Lan, a working mom and fan of *Paris by Night* videos, observed that the ads are a "waste of her time" but she "can see how [they] can be effective in reaching all the Viet[namese] population."[65] Thuan, a male respondent to the Web survey wrote: "I think it is overwhelmingly clear that Vietnamese people are really into this and that is strange." When asked, "Would you consider having plastic surgery to enhance your looks?" he answered, "yes."[66] Tricia, a college student, asserts, "It's amazing what technology can do for a person. I think that what they said about the surgeries can happen without a shadow of a doubt."[67] And like the vast majority of respondents who expressed their opinions in my survey, *Paris by Night* fans believe Vietnamese people, especially the performers who are under constant public scrutiny, should have aesthetic surgery so that they can have "more confidence" on stage. Those who objected to plastic surgery cited only health and safety reasons for not going under the knife.

The Reformed Refugee Vietnamese Body

Vietnamese immigrants are astoundingly familiar with Hollywood and the practices of American celebrities, particularly since Little Saigon is in such close proximity to the culture of the film industry. Moreover, the gossip stories of American celebrities are often translated in ethnic media, giving Vietnamese readers access to the latest celebrity news, including the stories of body modification in Hollywood. While the performances of diasporic Vietnamese entertainers serve a different purpose for the exile community, their bodies serve as conduits through which the Vietnamese Americans imagine their engagements with questions of cultural assimilation. Within the various spheres of the Vietnamese immigrant community, desires to create an ethnic "American" identity are therefore reflected in public figures featured in popular culture. Like celebrities in Hollywood, Vietnamese diasporic entertainers are looked upon as paragons of immigrant success and models of ethnic beauty. With the power of the entertainment industry behind them, these performers set a different standard for how Vietnamese Americans might construct their own identities. Yet numerous performers, particularly female entertainers, have physically altered their faces (especially eyes and noses) and bodies to achieve their desired success. As proponents of plastic surgery and the cosmetics industry, performers project an idealized image of beauty that seems to inspire other Vietnamese to transform their bodies to attain success. It is no coincidence that Vietnamese cosmetic surgeons often advertise their businesses in ethnic media. The normalization of plastic surgery in the Vietnamese immigrant community, however, goes beyond simple mimicry of the behaviors of Hollywood celebrities and Vietnamese diasporic performers. This practice to forge new identities through surgical procedures is endorsed and embedded in the cultural productions themselves.

To understand these trends, I suggest that the strategies used to transform the Vietnamese body are intricately linked to the process of recovering from a war-torn past and becoming middle-class ethnic Americans in the United States. Vietnamese identities are embodied in ways that are complicated by cultural processes and rooted in a history of terror that begs for the reformation of the body. The history of plastic surgery provides a compelling link and antecedent to this phenomenon. As a new medical technology formed from circumstances of war, plastic surgery was applied to soldiers who were wounded on the battlefield.[68] Plastic surgery reduced the scars of war and rehabilitated those who were physically injured, allowing them to be reintegrated and re-assimilated into society. In his analysis of the practice of plastic surgery in East Asia, David Palumbo-Liu calls attention to the fact that "the high point of surgery began as a public relations program of the United States occupational forces in Korea." Palumbo-Liu examines an essay by army surgeon D. R. Millard, who was sent to Korea to "help reconstruct war-damaged bodies," believing that the "rehabilitat[ion]" of the bodies would rehabilitate the state.[69] Like the "war-damaged bodies" from the Korean War, the war-scarred bodies of Vietnamese Americans are being rehabilitated through science. Medical professionals who perform plastic and cosmetic surgery are clear in distinguishing cosmetic procedures that are done for cosmetic purposes from plastic surgery that is done for rehabilitation. It is much more difficult to determine the motivations behind the increased normalization of plastic surgery among Vietnamese immigrants. Nevertheless, plastic surgery appears to hold the promise of inclusion by rendering the scars of past, be they metaphorical or real, less visible.

The process of becoming more "American" or "Western" is being mediated and increasingly realized through technology, and more specifically, surgical techniques in aesthetic surgery. Documenting the cultural history of aesthetic surgery, Sander Gilman explains in his book *Making the Body Beautiful* that in the late nineteenth century, aesthetic surgeons began altering the body to make it appear more "healthy" and therefore, citing Michel Foucault, more "racially acceptable" according to dominant racial ideologies at the time. Gilman further argues that the trope of "passing," alongside the historical construction of race, not gender, is the most useful model for understanding historical and contemporary meanings of aesthetic surgery.[70] Gilman's research provides an insightful framework that can be applied to the rising practice and acceptance of cosmetic surgery among Vietnamese Americans. Employing science and medical technology, Vietnamese self-reformation through aesthetic surgery allows former refugees to remake their bodies and to racially reinvent and reconstruct identities that transcend from the haunting images of the past. As a modern technology that has transformative capabilities, plastic surgery both literally and figuratively fulfills the desires for assimilation through the face and body.

Plasticity and Commodity Culture

One way to interpret the normalization of cosmetic surgery in the Vietnamese immigrant community is to consider the practice as a form of class inclusion and assimilation into American society. Cosmetic surgery has become a common operation among those who can afford it.

Though men are only gradually adopting these practices, many upwardly mobile women have undergone major cosmetic surgery to shed their Vietnameseness in exchange for a new, hybrid identity constructed through both Vietnamese and mainstream American cultures. In "Notes on Deconstructing the Popular," Stuart Hall highlights the contradictions between capital and culture, emphasizing the stakes capital has in changing identities while simultaneously creating and marketing new ones.[71] Hall's astute observations can be applied to the flexible accumulation of capital among Vietnamese immigrants and the new plasticity of Vietnamese identity in commodity culture. As new subjects embodied in cosmetic surgery, Vietnamese diasporic identities become flexible and malleable. While the processes of constructing, adapting and adopting new identities are inevitable, this form of violence done to the body has become an alarming trend in Vietnamese communities worldwide. Popular cultural forms of the Vietnamese diaspora have not only legitimated the social practice of plastic surgery but have also encouraged it.

Conclusion

It is important to keep in mind that while *Paris by Night* videos present Vietnamese Americans as having transcended their refugee origins, they do not abandon or disavow this history. But the image of the Vietnamese as frail, powerless "boat people" is found only as historical footage. According to these videotexts, these suffering bodies have been transformed into healthy ones, displaying not only middle-class respectability but also material excess. Playing with these ideas about poverty and progress, *Paris by Night* 57, a show entitled "Thoi Trang va Am Nhac" ("Fashion and Music"), features another debate between Ky Duyen and Ngan about fashion, socioeconomic status, and the value people place on appearances.

KY DUYEN: My dress is designed by Calvin Hiep [a Vietnamese American fashion designer who designed many of the costumes worn by the *Paris by Night* cast]; Ngan's tuxedo was purchased from the swap meet.

NGAN: You are mistaken. I rented it.

KY DUYEN: Then we better not get it dirty.

NGAN: In Vietnam, we learned that we simply "eat to satisfy hunger, wear clothes to keep us warm," so that you do not die from hunger or freeze to death in the cold. But as we have progressed, the words have changed to "eat for gratification, dress to look good," now that we have all that life has to offer. But before, when we were poor, we adhered to the proverbs, fables, and folktales we learned about in grade school. We used to be humble about the food we eat, grateful for every grain of salt. But now when we are asked to go out for a meal, we ask what kind of food are we eating. Is it lobster or steamed fish? When others give us gifts, such as a tie or a suit, we now ask, what label or which designer made the clothes? Is it Calvin Klein or Donna Karan? We have now progressed to a higher level, so we no longer have to "eat to satisfy hunger and wear clothes to keep us warm." We now eat well, and dress for appearances. We are now at a point were we can be fashion conscious.

KY DUYEN: Are you saying that you have to be wealthy in order to have fashion? Then countries that are poor do not have any sense of fashion?

NGAN: Yes, that's generally true. If you went to a poor country and gave its people a choice between diamonds and salt, they would take the salt instead of the diamonds.

KY DUYEN: Not me, I would want the diamonds. It doesn't matter how poor I am, I would still take the diamonds. *[Chuckles]* But you are correct. Society in general does value outward appearances more. But for the Vietnamese people, perhaps the West may have influenced us; therefore, we think that appearances are very important. But as you claim that we suffer in our wealth, I think that we have suffered through our poverty as well. What's worse is we suffer from the fear of others knowing that we are poor. And we may be poor, but when we are in public, we have to dress nice and try to drive an expensive car, right?

NGAN: Yes, that is one of the problems Vietnamese culture suffers from.[72]

Both Ky Duyen and Ngan agree that members of the Vietnamese diaspora have "progressed" to the point where relevant concerns are reduced to conspicuous consumption and possession of material objects. Ky Duyen attributes these anxieties not only to the immigrant experience, but also to Western influence. It is the fear of the judgment of others from within and without the community that drives Vietnamese immigrants toward excess and materialism. As a popular cultural production, *Paris by Night* videos dramatize these urges and desires, presenting Vietnamese Americans as a successful immigrant group, replacing the image of the poor refugee with that of the new "model minority." And through a cautious acceptance of the model-minority label, Vietnamese Americans insert themselves into a mainstream discourse on race in popular culture.

Popular media of the Vietnamese diaspora have played a critical role in transforming Vietnamese culture in diaspora, producing both liberating and repressive possibilities. As a venue for the creative talents of people in the

Figure 19. A newcomer to the *Paris by Night* stage prepares to sing a before a packed live audience. Phuong Thu from *Paris by Night* 77 "30 Nam Vien Xu," directed by Michael Watt (2005).

diasporic community, the variety show as a cultural form has contributed to the construction of an alternative public sphere that promotes a sense of ethnic pride. At the same time, however, exilic media culture has also packaged representations that not only have problematic gender and class implications, but also present an illusion of access. The Vietnamese entertainment industry has objectified women's bodies, glamorized high fashion, and supported plastic surgery through massive and repetitive advertising. Aspiring to reproduce bourgeois tastes, these shows also project unattainable visions of assimilation for those immigrants and refugees who lack access to social, cultural, and economic capital. In their capacity as a popular cultural apparatus for linking diasporic Vietnamese, the *Paris by Night* videotexts have established hegemony over other forms and practices articulated by Vietnamese subjects who view themselves as peripheral to this particular vision. Their dominance in the diaspora continues to submerge other forms of independent art and culture expressing Vietnamese American experiences.[73]

Conclusion   Transnational Flows Between the Diaspora and the Homeland

WHEN THE UNITED STATES lifted economic sanctions against Vietnam in the mid-1990s, it was inevitable that cultural products from the communist nation would enter American soil. Popular culture, particularly music and audiovisual media, filtering in from an invigorated Vietnam caused a rift between two generations of Vietnamese Americans. The *Los Angeles Times* described it accordingly:

> To young Vietnamese Americans, it's the hottest music around. To older generations, it's nothing more than Communist propaganda. And to a Little Saigon music industry once hailed as 'the Vietnamese Nashville,' it could spell doom . . . The shift in taste is emerging as a hot political issue. Local radio stations don't play the music, even though it sells out in stores. At demonstrations, protesters stomp on the Vietnamese products. And many residents simply clasp their hands over their ears when the music from Vietnam plays.[1]

Although these transformations have been taking place for nearly a decade, the older generation still fears that cultural production from the former homeland threatens to corrupt the consciousness and aesthetic taste of American-born, American-raised Vietnamese youth, while the younger generation views the material as novel and culturally authentic. Arguing that Vietnam remains a steadfastly communist nation with a corrupt government that abuses its populace, members of the older generation disparage what they believe to be a unidirectional flow of cultural production and question why materials entering the communist nation are so heavily regulated by the repressive regime. They protest not only the political but also economic implications of young Vietnamese Americans flocking to buy cheap music and other cultural products imported from communist Vietnam. While these trends mark a turning point in transnational cultural flows, they also signal a gradual decline of the Vietnamese diasporic culture industry. The staying power of the entertainment media empire built by the diaspora is being challenged by cultural production from the homeland as record sales and audiences begin to wane after enduring nearly three decades of undeniable success. Considering these new developments, how can we think about migration and the movement of bodies in relation to the flow of cultural products? How are diasporic communities responding to the people and culture of Vietnam as they re-enter the world stage both as cultural and economic forces? How can we think about exile as geo-political boundaries begin to blur? Is reconciliation impending between the homeland nation and the diaspora? Are these signs marking the end to an era of diasporic triumph, or has competition reached new levels in the global capitalist arena? What are the full implications of these trends that mark the return of the homeland nation-state as it confronts the people of the Vietnamese diaspora? These and a host of other questions have begun to surface as I conclude this study.

The forces of globalization have undoubtedly created new tensions between the diaspora and the homeland nation. Diasporic publics formed through popular entertainment and niche media industries reveal the ambiguous nature of these tensions. This ambiguity is further muddled by new advancements in technology such as the Internet and forces of global capital flowing beyond national boundaries. While changes are occurring on both sides, I locate the expressions of diasporic anxieties in the practices of media consumption and resistance, especially as they are played out in public discourse. Throughout this book, I have unlocked key issues involved in the complex processes of identity formation by examining various sites of culture and media circuits. I have found that much of the discomfort and ambivalence about diasporic community has been articulated in terms of gender and sexuality. As cultural forms, bodies, and ideas circulate more freely in the age of transnational and global capital, the diaspora's authenticity, as well as its claim to Vietnamese-ness, is being challenged by the homeland nation. In this concluding chapter, I examine the interactions between the local and the global as they negotiate the future of the Vietnamese people in both the homeland and the diaspora.[2] Based on my observations of live traveling concert performances and data analysis collected from responses to an online survey, I suggest that the moral imperative to be productive citizens in the Vietnamese diaspora, coupled with the desire to be victors against the communist regime, fosters an environment of surveillance that keeps the community in check. Community policing, therefore, emerges from the need to morally regulate and control

Vietnamese bodies as they respond to new forms of consumption, commodification, modernization, and, most important, globalization.

I wish to return to the images I introduced to my readers in the beginning of this book where I discuss the diametrically opposed representations of the Vietnamese refugee as the destitute immigrant and the modern diasporic subject. At some level, Vietnamese realities exist at both ends and in between this spectrum. My research as a participant-observer unveils these aspects of community formation. In the following, I document the experience of a Vietnamese concert in Chicago, a large American city located in the Midwest, as a counterpoint to my analysis of Vietnamese in California. Unlike the population in Orange County, California, Vietnamese audiences in Chicago seek pleasure amid a mosaic environment where Vietnamese culture exists on the margins. In a metropolitan setting with a relatively small diasporic population, organized music variety shows provide an outlet for Vietnamese immigrants and refugees to gather socially and connect with one another through leisure. Data gathered through participant-observation and informal interviews I conducted while attending four live Vietnamese concerts in the course of two years reveal that these performances provide not only pleasure, but also an opportunity for members of the community to connect and collectively affirm their cultural identity.[3] The dynamic interactions between performers and audiences, however, reveals the contradictory ways in which culture is defined and perceived in the diaspora. The live setting prompts an awkward acceptance of performers testing boundaries, while the Internet allows for contestations and open challenges.

Nostalgia and Innovation: Inside the Traveling Performances of the Vietnamese Diaspora

The Vietnamese community in Chicago gathers socially for a night filled with song, dance, and live entertainment at the "Gala Show" twice a year, Memorial Day weekend in May, and Labor Day weekend in September. Organized and sponsored by a coordinator with connections to Southern California "industry performers" and local ethnic Vietnamese merchants, Chicago's Gala Shows feature a lineup of popular touring Vietnamese entertainers made famous by *Paris by Night, Asia, Van Son, Hollywood Night* and other copycat music performance series. Though not as elaborate and spectacular as the multi-million dollar productions recorded for video or DVD consumption, the Gala Shows promote touring Vietnamese singers and give them an opportunity to earn additional income and promote their latest work.[4] For Vietnamese audiences and adoring fans, the

Figure 20. A widely circulated poster advertising the Gala Show in Chicago held on Memorial Day weekend, Sunday, May 26, 2002. These posters plaster the ethnic businesses frequented by the local Vietnamese community. Author's collection.

shows provide a chance to be close to celebrities and idols of the diaspora and watch them perform live. In the course of my research, I attended four live concerts, three of which were held at the famed Aragon Ballroom, a renowned venue in Chicago's Uptown neighborhood often used by mainstream American music acts. When the Vietnamese community is unable to reserve the Aragon, the concerts are staged at the Chicago Amory Park, an indoor facility resembling a large gymnasium that hosts other community events such as the annual Tet Festival.

The Vietnamese immigrant community in Chicago has created a vibrant ethnic enclave in the city's northwest side with social networks and cultural institutions. With a population of approximately 15,000 and substantially fewer venues for cultural events and Vietnamese-language media outlets, Chicago's Vietnamese immigrant population embraces cultural forms produced from the Vietnamese American "center" on the West Coast with much zeal. Unlike Vietnamese Americans in California who have direct access to a culture industry—complete with nightclubs and live entertainment—the Vietnamese community in Chicago rarely has the opportunity to enjoy the pleasures of exilic cultural productions on a daily basis. The Gala Shows provide one of only a few opportunities for Vietnamese Americans in the Midwest to be part of the larger audience of diasporic Vietnamese cultural production.

Though Chicago lacks the rich and dense cultural characteristics of other regions where Vietnamese people have resettled, popular culture of the Vietnamese diaspora occupies many public spaces in the enclave economy. The Gala Shows affect local Vietnamese business establishments in various ways. Restaurants frequently play music and variety shows on big-screen television sets and display advertisements featuring images of Vietnamese American celebrities on storefront windows. These "celebrities" from California are so effective in attracting large crowds that they are invited to perform at special benefit concerts for every organization from the Vietnamese Catholic Church to community-based social service organizations such as the Vietnamese Association of Illinois.

Of all community-organized events in Chicago, the Gala Shows are the best-attended social gatherings, drawing thousands of Vietnamese Americans from all over the Midwest. Offering a night filled with entertainment that the Vietnamese community can claim as their very own, the Gala Shows bring together people of all ages, from small children as young as five to elderly adults in their seventies. Couples, groups of young boys and girls, and friends alike look forward with great anticipation to seeing their favorite diasporic Vietnamese pop stars. Dressed in a medley of styles ranging from casual to flashy, sexy, gaudy, and outrageous, attendees come to see and be seen. Because fans are often permitted to approach the stage to hand the performers flowers or various gifts ranging from cold drinks to teddy bears, it becomes imperative for attendees to be dressed in their very best.

The Aragon Ballroom exudes formality and boasts Romanesque architecture, but the Vietnamese cultural event creates an ambiance of a busy marketplace where petty economic opportunities abound inside the grand ballroom. Vietnamese food such as spring rolls and sweet snacks and beverages from soybean milk to beer are sold at every event. A picture booth, set up by a professional studio photographer, captures the special occasion on camera, while a flower vendor sells single-stemmed red roses to fans who present them to their favorite performers on stage. Even the entertainers themselves have vending areas to sell compact discs that they personally autograph during intermission.

As the show commences, popular Vietnamese American entertainers sing, dance, and perform songs appealing to audiences at the request of the fans. Attendees could be exposed to almost every musical genre from traditional Vietnamese music called *vong co*, a musical style equivalent to African American blues, which sings of pain and suffering, to 1970s disco and contemporary soft rock and rap. Vietnamese American performers sing ballads about love and war that bring tears to the eyes of elders. They also perform bilingual covers of American popular songs from mainstream artists such as Celine Dion and Enrique Iglesias. At a concert I attended in May 2001, a fashion show modeled by young Vietnamese American women exhibited the latest collection from a Vietnamese American designer.

In another show, the entertainers performed a comedic sketch that portrayed conflicts and misunderstandings illustrative of the generation gap. The motley cast of performers at these live concerts and variety shows enables the boldest public displays of Vietnamese American identity. Simultaneously, they bring the latest trends in mainstream American culture into the community and translate them for newer immigrants and elders.

The Gala Shows serve various entertainment functions for Vietnamese audiences in Chicago. Eagerly awaiting the night's entertainment, a young man who attended one such event with his girlfriend and a group of friends from church told me he had come because he wanted to "dance and listen to music."[5] Treating the venue as if it were a nightclub or a social gathering for the Vietnamese community, this concertgoer seized his last chance to enjoy the summer in Chicago before he went back to school in Indiana, where Vietnamese music is less accessible. Others regard the Gala Shows as a rare opportunity to meet their favorite Vietnamese American celebrities in person. Teenage girls swoon over their favorite singing idols, and young men fantasize about the female singers performing on stage. On one occasion, a young woman in her twenties drove all the way from Kentucky with her mother and cousin so they could see the Vietnamese American singers "in person." Ecstatic to have the chance to take a photograph with her favorite songstress, the woman raved all night about how beautiful the singer was. She also commented that she had only watched the Vietnamese pop stars on video and listened to their CDs, and that it was "worth it to drive that many hours to see how they 'really' performed."[6]

Unlike the starstruck youth who excitedly cheer on celebrities of the diasporic Vietnamese performing circuit, people of the older generation go to the concerts to remember. Listening to songs transports many people back to a different place in time. Older members of the audience at one concert told me that they often participated in this type of leisure activity when they were young. One man recalled that Saigon provided a number of venues where live bands performed to allow people to forget the woes that the war in Vietnam had brought.[7] Hearing traditional songs also brought tears to people's eyes as they missed their homeland and those whom they had left behind.

Not all performances, however, conjure feelings of nostalgia; some can be deemed inappropriate for the entire family. The variety format seemingly caters to everyone in the audience, juxtaposing "cultural" performances with "trendy," more mainstream, "Westernized" song and dance numbers. Yet adult themes predominate throughout the show. Young female performers often dress provocatively and entice their male fans with racy dance moves. Imitating the dance styles of such American performers as Madonna and Britney Spears, younger female Vietnamese American singers express explicit sexuality on stage. Their sexually suggestive movements to contemporary dance music oftentimes disrupt the act of remembering. Likewise, the comedy skits containing sexual innuendo filled with raunchy adult humor spin the show in directions that do not necessarily move toward cultural preservation.

At one concert, the audience responded to the performances unevenly, sometimes disavowing inappropriateness but praising creativity. In the dark, some mothers covered their children's eyes when the provocatively dressed performers bopped on stage. Young men, however, gawked at them and tried to see beyond the low-cut, cleavage-baring tops. Older members of the audience shook their heads in disapproval, but tolerated these

"Americanized" performances because they also came to see songstresses like Nhu Quynh and Phi Nhung, both of whom dressed in *ao dai* and sang traditional Vietnamese music. Patricia, a young teenager, told me that she respected the performers who used "their talents" like her favorite singer and fashion designer, Bao Han, more than she respected those who used "their bodies."[8] Nevertheless, the very artist that Patricia claims uses her talents also performs in her own scantily clad designs. Sexualized female bodies in variety show performances are therefore, sanctioned by the community under the veil of culture and in the name of leisure. As in the *ao dai* pageants and variety show videos, in live concert performances, the female body is a site for public consumption as well as moral contestation. And in the age of digital technology, these fears and anxieties about Vietnamese celebrity bodies are launched into cyberspace.

Cyber Vietnamese-ness

The Internet has become so integral to the lives of citizens of the United States and throughout various parts of the world that it is difficult to ignore its impact on migrant populations. The recent explosion in studies of new media, especially the effects of cyber-culture on race and cultural identity have only begun to address how people of color are using the Internet.[9] In her recent book, *Digitizing Race*, Lisa Nakamura writes, "Performing close readings of digital visual images on the Internet and their relation to identity, itself now an effect as well as a cause of digitality, produces a kind of critique that takes account of a visual practice that is quickly displacing television as a media-based activity in the United States."[10] For populations that have always been peripheral to television culture, the Internet holds more promise for the articulation of identity. In fact, cyberspace is enabling the Vietnamese diaspora to engage in a number of online activities, including transmitting bilingual news, engaging in political activism, archiving the Vietnamese diasporic experience, learning culture and history, reaffirming cultural and ethnic identities, and voting and polling public opinion. The boundless, deterritorialized space on the World Wide Web is rapidly becoming a virtual social realm for inventing, contesting, and reinventing diasporic Vietnamese cultural identity.

For these reasons, I chose the Internet as a primary mode to survey the fans and audiences of diasporic Vietnamese entertainment media. Not only limited to techno-savvy youth, an increasing number of people have access to this technology, this new borderless terrain where people log in to culture and cultural production and participate in defining what it means to be Vietnamese in the diaspora. The unique space of the Internet casts a wide global demographic net and allows fans to convene at one site. Within this digital realm, posting, chatting, and other modes of communication exist to enable dialogue between strangers who have never or may never meet. Those who willingly enter these sites identify themselves as fans of Vietnamese cultural production.

Transforming the ways in which culture and leisure are experienced, the Internet has contributed to the vast popularization of Vietnamese cultural productions. Internet discussion groups and Web realms have formed over a variety of issues with regard to diasporic Vietnamese popular culture. The Internet has also allowed people from all over the world, including non-Vietnamese, to sample music, view pictures, watch video segments, buy videos, CDs, karaoke laser discs, and experience a wide range of cultural production created by the Vietnamese diaspora. Thus, "Vietnamese culture" can be tapped into and experienced virtually online with the stroke of fingers. In the virtual sphere, followers of diasporic Vietnamese popular culture convene on the Web and form communities based on common interests. Specifically, these Internet domains allow fans from all over the world to exchange information and participate in discussions about culture, music, and identity. Similar to the other spaces of media reception, cyberspace reaffirms community and shapes Vietnamese identity in the diaspora. However, because a certain degree of anonymity exists in this realm, spaces for unrestrained discursive critique have also emerged. Nevertheless, I will demonstrate that despite the possibilities for critique and contestation, the virtual sphere remains a space where identities are regulated and monitored. As with the other spaces of diasporic community, cyberspace protects the tradition of surveillance especially over the increasingly slippery meanings of "Vietnamese-ness" in the wake of participation of those from the homeland country.

Narratives Online

In the three years of posting my Web survey online, I received forty-three completed surveys and eighty-three partial surveys. While most respondents were students or professionals with access to the Internet and the ability to read English, they came from all over the United States and from around the world. From the United States, I received responses from people living in California, Pennsylvania, Texas, New York, Illinois, Florida, Virginia, Kansas, Michigan, Washington, and Arizona. Outside the United States, I received responses from people living in Australia, Canada, Austria, and Germany. One non-Vietnamese respondent who identified herself as Mexican American also filled out my survey.[11] Introduced to diasporic Vietnamese media by her Vietnamese American neighbors, this fan enjoys variety show videos and karaoke DVDs. Her knowledge of the Vietnamese entertainment industry proved to be extensive.

The ages of the survey respondents ranged from eighteen to fifty. Because the electronic survey required English reading comprehension as well as access to and familiarity with the Internet, a majority of those who completed the survey tended to be educated individuals between eighteen and thirty-five years old. Overall, an overwhelming number of the respondents indicated that they were male, and a significant proportion worked in jobs that regularly used computers with Internet access. Participants in the study provided a range of responses and a wealth of information. Some gave terse, cursory answers while others volunteered very thoughtful explications filled with introspective critiques. Prompted by my questions, their narratives reveal personal responses to media reception. More important, their reflections indicate that the Internet is fast becoming a site where the younger generation is resisting dominant media images produced by the Vietnamese diaspora. Expressing deep ambivalence about assimilation, gender ideology, class, and consumer culture, young people are using cyberspace to voice their critiques.

Forging Anonymous Cyber-critiques

Current research on media and digital technology has shown Internet use to be both beneficial and detrimental to public involvement. As a tool for connecting with others, the Internet has the ability to provide information, promote civic engagement, and enable the formation of "virtual communities." Simultaneously, however, the Internet also has the potential to undermine traditional human relationships due to the lack of face-to-face communication. A recent study by communication scholar Dhavan Shah and others concluded that while recreational uses of the Internet foster a sense of social interaction, they "may erode the individual-level production of social capital because these activities are generally asocial or anonymous."[12] But for most diasporic Vietnamese, it is precisely this anonymity—obtained only through the medium of the Internet—that allows them the agency to foster social interaction without consequence. As a site for information as well as leisure and consumption, cyberspace, along with people's recreational use of the Internet, contributes to the social formation of exilic Vietnamese identities by opening virtual spaces of social critique.

Unlike the multi-generational sites I have previously discussed, cyberspace allows for individualized responses that are protected by anonymity. The emergence of online discussion groups and fan communities have literally and virtually forged the space for public debates about self-representation. The results of my Web survey and my study of online participants and fan communities of Vietnamese niche media reveal that the second generation is using cyberspace as an outlet to challenge hegemonic representations. Viewing themselves as peripheral and resistant to the cultural nationalist project of Vietnamese diasporic popular media, many young people have carved alternative virtual spaces of social critique. Commenting on the spectacle of entertainment and the promotion of glamour in diasporic media representations, a graduate student from New York University disparages, "the illusion of a middle-class lifestyle is a disgrace."[13] Another respondent disapproved of the media forms for being "too commercial."[14] When asked about her first impression of Vietnamese exile media, a woman from Australia responded, "I didn't like the image they presented, and I didn't like their interpretation of Vietnamese [culture]. I didn't like the commercialisation, westernisation, overt sexualisation, and somewhat rhetoric banter" [sic].[15] Expressing his overall dissatisfaction, an activist from San Francisco asserted, "Vietnamese-language media, especially entertainment, are so low in quality, very kitschy, moronic at times, overly melodramatic."[16] Likewise, a Canadian engineer jeered at the homogenizing effects of video culture, claiming "it is a good communication tool . . . good at making people think alike."[17]

The critiques of Vietnamese popular media are not limited to cultural representation; in fact, the most intense debates involve race, gender, and sexuality. One respondent observed, "Vietnamese ideas of sexuality come off as very whitewashed. Men are tall and suave, with appearance of wavy hair (what a sham). Women's beauty is too white-inflected."[18] He then cites an example of an Amerasian singer whose talents, he believes, derive from her "high and pointy nose, deep set brown eyes, and pale skin." Feminist critiques have also surfaced challenging the hypersexualized images projected by female performers. One young woman commented, "the women are always in caked-on make-up, shining jewelry, and designer fashion. They also appear demure, soft and sweet. Others who are wild are on the other extreme as rebels against the norm, often looking cheap and fake."[19]

Another man disapprovingly rants, "seeing women dressed scandalously is not how I would like Vietnamese women to be portrayed."[20]

Others are concerned with the potentially immoral and overtly sexual connotations portrayed by younger and more provocative women performers. In response to an anonymous posting by a fan of Lynda Trang Dai, the "Vietnamese Madonna," one former fan writes:

> Lynda is all right. I used to be a big, I mean big fan of hers, but I dunno I dun't think so anymoe, cuz her songs are getting worser, no offense or anything and she fixes her noses soo much that its getting ruined. But I think Lynda should put a little bit more clothing on. Cuz I dunno ma cuzin really likes her, and she's starting to dress like Lynda . . . and she's only 10!! And she wants to grow up and be just like Lynda.

As this fan cautions, entertainers also serve as "role models" for young people. Performers should keep in mind that fans often watch the videos because they "love to see how people dress."[21] Diasporic entertainers, however, rarely abide by the rules of the community. Rather, they follow the guidelines set by Hollywood and respond to a public that demands nothing less. As such, they set a standard based on mainstream celebrity culture for how Vietnamese Americans construct their identities.

Perhaps this disturbing trend is a cause for concern. Young people have begun to question the image production and the commercialization of Vietnamese diasporic culture, particularly with regard to the normalizing practice of plastic surgery among the performers. As one woman apprehensively observes:

> The entertainment industry thrives on selling images so it makes sense that so many people will have plastic surgery. People can do whatever they want, but I think it's a shame that these people who claim to be promoting Vietnamese culture and are so proud of it completely destroy their natural Vietnamese features for something fake and seemingly Western.[22]

Exposing the hypocrisy of the entertainment industry, this commentator is not only cognizant of the hegemony of the culture industry, but is also aware of the problems embedded in the racial politics of cultural representation, particularly in constructing diasporic notions of celebrity. These celebrities may be considered paragons of success and beauty for some segments of the diaspora, but a new generation of Internet users is questioning the top-down images they project as the prevailing dominant visual representations.

It is no wonder they are turning to music produced in the homeland as the voice of authenticity. I return to the questions I posed at the beginning of this chapter to inquire about the need to examine the contemporary flows of people, capital, culture, and ideology.[23] I draw attention to the new tensions that exist between the diaspora and the homeland nation because they have social, cultural, and political implications for transforming ideas, policies, and economies. It is important to note that despite having lived over thirty years away from the homeland, the refugees who left still emphatically reject communism and insist upon an ideological separation between themselves and their former nation. In reality, however, it has been impossible to enforce this type of distance. Cultural productions created by the Vietnamese diaspora have also made their way back to the homeland despite the restrictions and regulations imposed by communist leaders. In fact, diasporic Vietnamese music and other audiovisual productions have proliferated all over Vietnam for the past two decades, even though they are legally barred from entering the country. It was common practice for visitors, convinced that Vietnam's residents were deprived of untainted artistic cultural expression, to smuggle items into the communist nation. Popular music, often in the form of cassette tapes and later CDs, was hidden in suitcases and remittance packages and surreptitiously enjoyed by those who remained in the homeland.

Consuming popular culture from the overseas community became customary even though it carried tremendous risk, especially during the period after annexation between the late 1970s to the late 1980s, when the Socialist Republic of Vietnam exhibited years of introspection, isolation, and stagnation. The fledgling Southeast Asian nation retreated from global view after the communists ousted the Americans and took over the South. Having endured an intensely drawn-out civil war, a significant dispersal of its own population, and a repressive regime that only sang praises to Ho Chi Minh, Vietnam struggled in seclusion with only the assistance of its comrade nations, China and the Soviet Union, for nearly two decades.

Between the late 1980s and early 1990s, however, Vietnam began to witness a revival, a *perestroika* similar to that of its ally and tutor called *doi moi*, or "new world." This social and economic revival plan spearheaded a renaissance in cultural production. The renovation project under *doi moi* not only implemented changes from within Vietnam, but the small communist nation also began opening up to foreign elements and cultural forms once thought to impede or, worse, contaminate its own national development. In particular, Vietnam looked to neighboring modernizing Asian nations such as Korea and Taiwan as well as its former enemy, the United States, for cultural adoption and imitation.[24] At first glance, Vietnam's changing attitude and new cultural policy can be understood as a positive shift toward modernization and progress. Another interpretation of these changes, however, might suggest accommodation or concession to the social, cultural, and economic frenzy resulting from transformations of the *doi moi* era as it ushered in global capitalism.

Indeed the revitalization of the arts in Vietnam can largely be attributed to new flexible state ideology set forth by *doi moi*. Attuned to outside influences, artistic and cultural productions created in Vietnam began making their way outside the nation and into the global market. Art and music produced after *doi moi* appeared to have advanced not only technologically but also aesthetically. A new generation of vocally trained singers began recording music in Vietnam. To the ears of young Vietnamese Americans, music from Vietnam sounds novel and innovative. Its origination from the homeland gives it an aura of authenticity. Listening to the new sounds from the homeland provides Vietnamese American youth with a fresh alternative or perhaps a site of resistance to the music of their parents as well as dominant U.S. popular culture. Most important, because it is so inexpensive, it is even more accessible than music produced by U.S.-based Vietnamese recording artists. Imported CDs cost as little as $2 each, whereas those recorded and produced in the United States cost between $6 and $12.[25]

Meanwhile, the cultural and artistic productions made by the diaspora have also gained tremendous popularity in Vietnam. Popular music, full of yearning, appeals to the masses in Vietnam. According to Philip Taylor, the same music created from the "refugees' nostalgia for the past" that had been triggered from the sense of rupture following the communist takeover was in high demand during the 1990s.[26] This demand for nostalgia became so popular that those in Vietnam sometimes had access to pirated new releases *before* Vietnamese Americans ever heard them. It became unfeasible for the communist government to regulate this form of popular cultural consumption, particularly in the southern regions of Vietnam where ties to the diaspora tended to be stronger.

Philip Taylor's work suggests a number of notable changes in culture and cultural transmission between the "home country" and the diaspora. Taylor's ethnographic search for modernity in Vietnam points to the complex ways in which the people of South Vietnam negotiated the government's policies through the contested terrain of popular music.

Taylor notes that in the 1990s, "one could hear Western hits of months old vintage translated into Vietnamese, rearranged, performed and produced in California, and exported for the rapidly expanding home-country market."[27] While Taylor's study implies that music producers of the diaspora are benefiting from the widening market as Vietnamese popular music from overseas penetrates into Vietnam, I remain skeptical about the ease of these transnational flows.[28]

It is undeniable that cultural forms created both in Vietnam and in the diaspora have come to bear a remarkable likeness. In various venues and formats from music videos, karaoke discs, comedy skits, and even *ao dai* beauty pageants, Vietnamese cultural productions appear similar. Sometimes the only major difference between the products from Vietnam and the products made in the United States are the performers. Other slight but notable distinctions are in brand recognition and price points. With an edge on access to new technology, entertainment companies established in the diaspora such as Thuy Nga, Asia, and Van Son have higher production quality and have become household names, whereas Vietnamese productions often lack any branding and tend to be very inexpensive. Despite these distinctions, sellers of Vietnamese popular media have started to group cultural materials by genre and not by where the products are made. This blurring of categories, particularly on Internet websites, has created anxieties, especially among those in the diaspora who insist that they own the authentic voice of the Vietnamese.

Vietnamese producers and entertainers throughout the diaspora are fighting a losing battle to protect their work from relentless copyright infringements. This loss can be measured not only in monetary value but also in the potential to reach the markets in Vietnam. The obstinacy of the diasporic community to restrict the entertainers from performing in the communist nation has had a real impact on the diaspora's culture industry. Enforcing an imposed position of exile, the Vietnamese community in the United States has explicitly restricted entertainers from publicly performing in the homeland. The community policing is so strict that those who have performed in Vietnam have been equally rebuked and even accused of betraying democratic causes and colluding with the communist government. This inflexible posture exhibited by the Vietnamese American community's unwillingness to move forward despite the homeland nation's evolving cultural milieu parallels what Sunaina Maira calls immigrant "cultural fossilization."[29] What is distinct about the Vietnamese case, however, is that the ideological debate is articulated in *private* and *public* terms.

This private/public split is undergirded and made more complex by anticommunism, commodity circulation, and consumption, all of which remain ripe for further investigation. Nevertheless, my research suggests that key differences in exile and diaspora are operationalized situationally through public and private discourse. For example, despite the *public* politics of staunch anticommunism that enables Vietnamese Americans to self-impose an existence of exile, they still *privately* travel to Vietnam and have the freedom to do so. While some may view this decision to travel back to Vietnam as a compromise (as traveling back to the "homeland" connotes an implied willingness to participate in the socialist political economy), the community regards this as permissible when it is done for "personal" reasons. The corollary to this also applies to Vietnamese citizens and diplomats who visit the United States. When they travel as private tourists to areas such as the Little Saigon district in California, the Vietnamese American community deems this socially and politically acceptable. However, if U.S. officials recognize diplomats from Vietnam as state representatives, the Vietnamese American community will undoubtedly organize protests against these *public* performances of political reconciliation, as they did against George W. Bush's welcoming of Prime Minister Phan Van Khai in June 2005. Although the Bush White House defended its position to host the senior Vietnamese official in order to mark the tenth anniversary of the normalization of diplomatic ties between the United States and Vietnam, the Vietnamese American community criticized the Bush Administration for allowing a Vietnamese government official onto U.S. soil.[30]

Anticommunist politics have functioned as a distinct marker of cultural identity for the Vietnamese diaspora. The public and often most vocal desire to steadfastly embrace anticommunist sentiments has heightened, especially during a time when commodities, people, and cultural forms cross borders and defy territorialization. Some Vietnamese Americans have chosen to enforce a compulsory identity that associates the community with that ideology. The anxiety generated by Vietnamese cultural production flooding the shores of America presents a threat to the strength of the Vietnamese diaspora in the age of transnationalism and the exceptional neoliberal policies of the Vietnamese nation-state. In particular, the cultural policies conceived after *doi moi* garnered exceptional responses in Vietnam that quickly reverberated throughout the rest of the diaspora.

Aihwa Ong has suggested that the spirit of neoliberalism has enabled communist regimes to compete with and participate in global capitalism.[31] These exceptions have not only allowed Vietnam to emerge as an economic and labor force for the twenty-first century, they are also blurring the lines between the diaspora and the homeland in a powerful way.

Neoliberal discourse is creating the illusion that Vietnam is moving toward a more capitalist economy. As such the diaspora is responding more flexibly, forging new transnational strands and connections. Under advanced capitalism, digital technology, and transnational commerce, diasporic cultural productions have inspired and influenced the culture of the homeland in surprising ways. I alluded above to Vietnamese American youth buying CDs, videos, and films from Vietnam. However, an unexpected trend has also emerged among older generation Vietnamese immigrants who are now approaching middle age. They too are grudgingly and gradually accepting cultural production from the homeland in the privacy of their own homes. In a number of interviews I conducted for my research, people privately confessed that they enjoyed music and films produced in Vietnam.[32] They reason that communist propaganda no longer infuses the arts produced in the former home country and that the new generation of performers, raised in the aftermath of war and during *doi moi*, are classically trained in music and vocals. In comparison, the new singers featured in the diasporic industry have only risen to fame that comes from having practiced on karaoke machines. Disparaging this model of American success where people are "discovered" rather than "trained," some members of the Vietnamese community are beginning to accept music and finding pleasure in cultural imports from their former native country. Yet this new preference is embraced with much caution, as a majority still frowns upon the communist regime and the human rights violations of its government.

Ideology and Desire

This book has illuminated the various ways in which popular culture and niche media created by and for the Vietnamese diaspora have contributed to the construction of racialized, gendered, and classed identities for this minority group. Part of the need to construct identity through media channels and cultural forms stems from a response against dominant discourses that portray the Vietnamese as refugees requiring sympathy and assistance. Countering these notions of dependency, self-representations produced by Vietnamese Americans insisted upon promoting an assimilationist image of success attained through consumption and material excess. The refugees from Vietnam believed that their escape from communism granted them not only a second chance at freedom, but also the limitless opportunities to participate in a free-market capitalist society.

As the cultures of the diaspora and the homeland become less distinguishable in the global economy, why does anticommunism have the same salience in the public discourse of the diaspora? I argue that anticommunist discourse is rooted in a very distinct history tied to consumer culture, particularly in the second half of the twentieth century. Since the beginning of the Cold War, specifically the moment of Nixon's "kitchen debate" with Nikita Khrushchev, where the U.S. president established that the essence of American freedom laid in consumer goods, American freedom has been associated with consumerism.[33] When U.S. goods were introduced to the Vietnamese people during the period of American military intervention, first-world luxury became synonymous with capitalist freedom.[34] Consequently, Vietnamese refugees and immigrants quickly learned, even before they migrated, that the vision of a successful and secure life included the accumulation of wealth and material goods. Once they arrived in the United States, they strove to participate in consumer culture with the hopes that this would lead them to wealth, independence, individuality, and upward mobility. Like other immigrants before them, Vietnamese refugees and immigrants sought to become Americans through various forms of consumption.[35]

The American Dream for Vietnamese refugees and immigrants was generated and powered by nostalgia and a stake in both the sameness and the repetition of nostalgic experiences as well as the novelty of a cultural identity invested in consumption and commodity capitalism. In seeking to fulfill the American Dream and become modern American subjects, Vietnamese immigrants thrived on nostalgia and wanderlust, but desired to secure a middle-class identity. Nostalgia's role in cultural retention and maintenance has sustained an entertainment industry that supports an ideological stance against communism. While communism may be a source of conflict among the Vietnamese, I have demonstrated throughout this book that the quest to participate in and preserve a culture of capitalism has brought about new challenges in the Vietnamese diaspora.

One particular dimension of these challenges involves the negotiation of desire. Desires resonate in many of the media forms produced in the diaspora. Like the cultural products themselves, people's desires for nostalgia, consumption, and belonging circulate throughout the diaspora. Imagined and constructed through these complex experiences, Vietnamese cultural identity is therefore formed out of a set of strategic and problematic relationships. In the preceding chapters, I argued that creative popular expressions and performances function in various ways—as cinematic historical archives documenting the transformation of Vietnamese migrant culture, as entertainment and leisure, as representations of transcendence that resist dominant images of a refugee past, as media that facilitate assimilation, and as tools for expressing modern diasporic Vietnamese subjectivity. The Vietnamese diaspora is responding to these new formations by regulating itself as part of the process. Advances in technology coupled with flows of global capital have created a paradox of sorts. The Internet, for example, has forged spaces for resistance against the now hegemonic cultural forms of the Vietnamese diaspora, yet responses by the diaspora to police these spaces of resistance demonstrate the diasporic community's anxieties about the increasingly blurring lines between itself and the homeland state. It is not surprising that these responses coincide with the opening of the homeland nation and resulting porous borders ushered in by globalization. The movement and migration of things, people, capital, and ideology back and forth compels the diaspora to further enforce the tradition of surveillance upon its members. This is not to say that community policing has been entirely successful; rather, it functions as a characteristic of the future of Vietnamese diaspora—one that is beginning to heal from the rupture of the trauma that caused the dispersal of its people in the first place.

By examining these various sites of culture, popular niche media, and lived experience, my study has investigated the historical trajectory of a displaced population and demonstrated how new subjectivities are formed in maintaining the work of capitalist development and cultural citizenship in the Vietnamese diaspora. While representations offered by the Vietnamese culture industry of the diaspora at times reinforce dominant gender and class ideologies, the contradictory messages embedded in these same representations have also opened up a terrain for new discourses in the formation of identities. Aided by video, digital, and other advanced technologies such as the Internet, a new mode of social critique has also begun to emerge. Perhaps these critiques may lead to a political break from the past, but it certainly is reanimating tensions felt on both sides. While the future remains to be seen, the migratory path of Vietnamese diasporic cultural production, mirroring the people, attests to the fluidity of Vietnamese culture itself. Neither static nor pure, Vietnamese culture has always been in flux—an unstable process that is always in motion. The cultural productions created by the Vietnamese in diaspora emerged from their conditions as subjects of U.S. imperialism, as refugees, as migrants, as exiles, as Vietnamese Americans, and as global subjects.

Acknowledgments

THIS BOOK began as a personal journey to critically understand the transforming world around me, but it quickly evolved into an intellectual pursuit that forced me to engage, interrogate, and theorize the entangled histories of Vietnam and the United States as well as the lived experiences of survivors of an unpopular war. The narratives collected in these pages provide powerful examples of a community in transition. I am grateful to have met so many people along the way who were willing to share their perspectives and stories. I did my best to render their accounts accurately and respectfully.

At the University of Michigan, where this project began, I had the fortunate opportunity to work with a handful of brilliant scholars who eventually became my trusted mentors. Susan J. Douglas, George J. Sánchez, Catherine Benamou, David Scobey, and Roger Rouse provided guidance and intellectual support. Susan Douglas, in particular, encouraged me to be bold and to think creatively. She continues to give me invaluable advice regarding career and family. I hope one day I can follow in her footsteps by successfully balancing a lucrative career with a happy and fulfilling family life. George Sánchez taught me to trust my instincts and urged me to think broadly without compromising individual voices. I credit him for energizing me every time we met and I thank him for his astute advice and wise strategies. I am grateful to Jack Tchen for his support and willingness to serve on my dissertation committee despite the distance between us. Both he and Catherine Benamou offered insightful comments on my dissertation, which eventually became this book.

I would not have imagined pursuing a career in academia had it not been for the inspiration of my undergraduate professors. At the University of California, San Diego, Stephanie McCurry, Dorothy Ko, Lisa Lowe, Rachel Klein, Vicente Rafael, Yen Le Espiritu, and Lisa Yoneyama introduced me to the world of knowledge-seeking in ways I never knew existed. I owe them for introducing me to academia and continuing to support me to get to where I am today. I did not get the chance to work with George Lipsitz while we were both at UCSD, but he is an incredible scholar as well as one of the most gracious and generous human beings I have ever met. George took time to read earlier versions of my manuscript, provided thoughtful and detailed comments, and injected a sense of gravity to this project.

The emotional and intellectual support of my friends has sustained me throughout the years. Grace Wang has been like a sister to me. She was there to help me through rough patches and celebrate minor victories. It is comforting to know that I could always count on her to lift my spirits during my moments of insecurity and self-doubt. Her great sense of humor brings laughter and her feedback is always reassuring. Helen Jun also made me smile and taught me to not take myself too seriously. I will always be indebted to Helen for her timely assistance in getting me back on the academic track. My constant and enduring friendships with Anna Pegler-Gordon, Daryl Maeda, John McKiernan-Gonzales, Nicole Stanton, Larry Hashima, Sonya Smith, Paul Ching, and Jennifer Beckham helped me through graduate school and beyond. Were it not for academic conferences, I would not be able to share and test out my ideas with friends and colleagues. The Michigan connection runs wide and deep. I always find pleasure catching up with Kate Masur, Ines Casillas, Pablo Ramirez, Alex Textor, Carla McKenzie, Colin Johnson, Cynthia Wu, Richard Kim, Barbara Kim, Robin Li, Natalia Molina, Tom Guglielmo, Maria-Teresa Macedo, Adrian Burgos, Barbara Berglund, Tom Romero, and Nick Syrett. I appreciate the friendships I have found in colleagues I have met over the years. I thank Adria Imada, Glen Mimura, Julie Sze, Emily Ignacio, Ana Aparicio, Hung Thai, David Hernandez, Mimi Thi Nguyen, Thuy Linh Tu, Jim Lee, Mariam B. Lam, Thuy Vo Dang, Viet Nguyen, Lan Duong, Linda Trinh Võ, Nina Ha, and K. Scott Wong for providing me intellectual rigor and camaraderie.

Anne Frank is now enjoying her retirement, but her work at the Southeast Asian Archive at the University of California, Irvine, was remarkable. She went above and beyond to get me the materials I needed when I conducted long-distance research. She took me seriously when others did not. Active and committed to her work, Anne pointed me to valuable sources that I used, which enabled me to build my own archive of materials.

Working at the University of Texas at Austin challenges me to be a better researcher, writer, and teacher. I am lucky to be in the company of committed and prolific scholars such as Janet Davis, Elizabeth Engelhardt,

Shirley Thompson, Steve Hoelscher, Julia Mickenberg, Bob Abzug, Jeff Miekle, Mark C. Smith, Stephen Marshall, Neil Foley, Randy Lewis, Cary Cordova, Naomi Paik, Madeline Hsu, Lok Siu, Julia Lee, Sharmila Rudrappa, Kimberly Alidio, Kt Shorb, Madhavi Mallapragada, and Shanti Kumar. The amazingly dedicated staff in my home department of American Studies and the Center for Asian American Studies makes the campus a pleasant place to be. I give special thanks to Cynthia Frese, Kenyatta Dawson, Barbara Jann, Valeri Nichols-Keller, Ella Schwartz, and Stephanie Kaufman for their daily hard work.

Colleagues I met around campus challenged me to think about interdisciplinarity and helped me figure out ways to better articulate the arguments in this project. I have enjoyed illuminating conversations with Jemima Pierre, Erika Bsumek, Carolyn Eastman, Jennifer Fuller, Karl H. Miller, Polly Strong, Gretchen Ritter, Deborah Paredez, Frank Guridy, Laurie Green, Tiffany Gill, Mia Carter, Lisa Moore, Brian Bremen, John Gonzalez, Jennifer Wilks, and Ellen Cunningham-Kruppa.

Janet M. Davis provided great encouragement and comments on earlier drafts of this book. Her work on the circus was not only influential but also very helpful for me in thinking through gender, sexuality, and performance. I value her mentorship and guidance and have benefited from her generosity and good spirit. I am also grateful to Shirley Thompson, Julia Mickenberg, Madeline Hsu, and Elizabeth Engelhardt for taking time to read and comment on various chapters of this book. I especially thank Lok Siu for our budding friendship and her insightful interpretation of my work. Her arrival to UT has been wonderful. She kindly read chapters of this manuscript and offered extremely helpful suggestions and thoughtful feedback.

Students are a joy to work with as they keep my mind fresh and preserve my enthusiasm for a life of learning. I thank Christina Garcia, Jacqueline Smith, Rebecca D'Orsogna, Irene Garza, Eric Covey, Katie Feo Kelly, John Cline, Audrey Russek, Andi Gustavson, Josh Holland, John Gronbeck-Tedesco, Greg Carter, Kelly Chu, Linda Ho Peché, Lily Laux, Amanda Gray, Allison Wright, Kassie Clark, and Jake Maguire for keeping me focused and engaged with critical ideas. I learned a lot from my former undergraduate students, particularly from the handful who made up the Asian American studies posse. Carole Sun, Courtney Banayad, Kathy Phan, and Anh Pham continue to remind me of the importance of teaching. They all are now successful in their chosen paths but I am glad to inform them that this book is finally complete. I am most thankful for the meticulous editorial work of Amy Ware, whose fine editing skills polished off this manuscript. Amy worked tirelessly to bring clarity and logic to some of my otherwise vague and dense writing. Finally, I owe gratitude to David A. Martinez for his quick, yet careful compilation of the index and his critical eye at crunch time.

Friendships I have formed outside of academia have helped me hone my writing skills for a more general audience. I want to send special thanks to Sue Park, Moses Lee, Gwen Hamilton, and Ed and Marsha Aguirre, who will be proud to hold this book in their hands. Michael Bostrom read drafts of this book in its formative stages. Davis Truong, Daniel Truong, and Jennifer Ngo generously shared their collection of videos and DVDs with me. Tam Van Nguyen and Patricia Nguyen gave me insights on the Vietnamese community in Chicago. Rob Duncan and I worked at the Vietnamese Association of Illinois together while I conducted research for parts of this book.

I also thank the handful of people who kept me healthy and centered. Kewal Hausmann is the best yoga teacher on the planet. Geri Jones heals me whenever my body tenses up and goes out of whack, which is quite often. My doctors Nancy Binford and Robyn McCarty took care of me through my pregnancies and beyond.

After the birth of my first child, I met a group of mommies who became an unbelievable source of support and inspiration. Molly Leder Hepkin, Jonelle Seitz, Sara Evans, along with Lauren Honza guided me through the challenging maze of parenting when I became overwhelmed with work and family. They are wonderful mothers to their awesome children. I also thank my childcare providers—Angeline Stidham, Stephany Urrea-Visbal, Korina Loera, and Wendy Worden—who took great care of Sophie while I wrote the bulk of this book.

I met the great William Germano who dispensed sharp criticism and sound advice on publishing during a workshop provided by the University of Texas. It was he who gave me the great title for my project.

I wish to thank Ann Phong, whose gorgeous art graces the cover of this book. I am eternally grateful for the generosity of this artist who willingly collaborated on this project without one bit of hesitation. I am hopeful that her talent will be recognized widely and her message taken seriously.

I reserve a million thanks to Adam Brunner for being an extraordinary editorial assistant. He was always responsive, patient, encouraging, and supportive. His constant professionalism remains unmatched. He truly believed in this project from its very beginning, and I am grateful to had the opportunity to work with him during his tenure at the University of Minnesota Press. Kristian Tvedten provided invaluable assistance and wonderful momentum to help push me through the final stages of this project. I am thankful for his discerning eye and useful feedback. Richard Morrison oversaw the entire project with great care and reassured me of the importance of this work. I very much appreciate his support and encouragement.

This book benefited tremendously from the comments and suggestions of anonymous reviewers and readers. I thank them for the close attention they gave to my manuscript. Their suggestions were insightful, engaging, and constructive. In the end, their feedback guided me through the revision process and helped me write a better book.

In this field, one of the most important things a research scholar can never have enough of is time. Miraculously, I was able find focus to write while on maternity leave. I was fortunate to have this writing time extended with a Dean's Fellowship and a Summer Research Assignment. The College of Liberal Arts also granted me a generous Subvention Grant to help underwrite the production costs of this book. I am grateful to have this institutional support from the University of Texas, Austin.

I would not have been able to write this book without the love and support of my family. I am grateful to my parents, Nhung Truong and Mo Lieu, for all they have done for me and for our family. They made the ultimate sacrifice when they chose early retirement to come live with me and my husband to raise their grandchildren. They relocated from the familiar surroundings of Southern California to come to Austin, Texas. I can never repay them for the help they have given me. My mom made healthy and delicious meals to nurture us. My dad helped out by taking my daughter to school, doing household chores, and running endless errands. They both have shown nothing but love and adoration for their grandchildren.

My parents introduced me to Vietnamese cultural productions when I was a teenager, and we continue to talk about "Vietnamese culture," but I am a bit more cautious and a lot more critical of popular culture than they ever were. My mom was not only a guiding force but she also often served as an informant whose knowledge base was impressive and extremely useful. I hope one day she and my dad will attempt to read this book so they understand my perspective and why I am weary about teaching my children these mediated versions of "Vietnamese culture."

My blissfully wakeful children Sophie and Ethan have brought pleasure and new challenges in my role as a parent. They taught me how to set my priorities, manage my time, and find inner peace and patience. I learned to set aside work to play with them. They are beginning to play with each other now and it is most gratifying to watch them adore and love each other as they interact and grow up together. I hope their closeness will resemble the relationship I have with my brother, Son Lieu, who I thank for adding laughter and levity to my life by making fun of the things I do. He is the best uncle my kids could have, and he continues to provide a good ear and a shoulder to cry on whenever things got difficult for me. Surprisingly, among his many talents Son is also a tech geek who helped me learn to do visual "screen grabs" to accompany the text of this book.

I owe my deepest love and gratitude to my soul mate Toan Leung, who has been there for me every step of the way. Toan made sure I got rest and optimal writing time, especially in the last stages of this project. His patience, honesty, and kindness always brought calm to our otherwise hectic lives. He was right when he said it takes a lifetime to love someone. I am fortunate to have found that someone in him. I am glad we grew up together and have been there for each other for more than half our lives. I can't believe we are all grown up now, building our family together. He is an amazing father to our children and a caring provider for our family. I count my blessings every day that I get to spend with him, which is rare considering how much he works.

Lastly, LuLu and Sun Tzu slipped down the totem pole after Sophie and Ethan arrived but they continue to bring sweet happiness and a bit of ruckus to our growing family.

All mistakes made in this book are mine and most of them are likely from the fact that I have been deprived of a full night's sleep for the past four years.

Notes

Introduction

1. Edward Said, *Orientalism* (New York: Vintage Books, 1978).

2. I will use the terms *Vietnamese exile performers, exilic performers, diasporic performers,* and *Vietnamese American performers* interchangeably throughout my work. Vietnamese exilic performers, unlike the Vietnamese nationals with whom they disidentify, come from all over the world as refugees who escaped Vietnam in and after 1975. A majority of them have since immigrated to the United States and resettled in Southern California's Little Saigon, the entertainment capital of the Vietnamese diaspora. Exile performers tour the globe entertaining fans dispersed all over the world, but they are not allowed to return to Vietnam. If they decide to return and perform for Vietnamese audiences in Vietnam, they will not only have placed their careers in jeopardy but also have risked the chance of being branded as "communist sympathizers" by the exile community.

3. Nancy Fraser, "Rethinking the Public Sphere," in *Habermas and the Public Sphere*, ed. Craig Calhoun (Boston: MIT Press, 1992), 142.

4. Hamid Naficy, *The Making of Exile Cultures: Iranian Television in Los Angeles* (Minneapolis: University of Minnesota Press, 1992).

5. Monique T. D. Truong, "The Emergence of Voices: Vietnamese American Literature 1975–1990," *Amerasia Journal* 19, no. 3 (1993): 27–50.

6. The 1990s signified a new transition in Vietnamese society in which the government adopted *doi moi* or "new society," a *perestroika* for Vietnam whereby a different attitude opened up the nation to cultural and social influences from abroad.

7. Scholars and authors who meditate on "transnational" Vietnamese relations have pointed to the liberal potential of these flexible flows, but some also warn of the potential dangers of the discrepant disparities between those who live in Vietnam and those who have left. See Caroline Kieu Linh Valverde, "Making Transnational Viet Nam: Vietnamese American Community Linkages though Money, Music and Modems" (PhD diss., University of California, Berkeley, 2002); Hung Cam Thai, *For Better or For Worse: Vietnamese International Marriages in the New Global Economy* (New Brunswick, N.J.: Rutgers University Press, 2008); Andrew Lam, *Perfume*

Dreams: Reflections on the Vietnamese Diaspora (San Francisco: Heyday Books, 2005); and Andrew Pham, *Catfish and Mandala: A Two-Wheeled Voyage across the Landscape and Memory of Vietnam* (New York: Picador USA, 2000).

8. Stuart Hall, "Notes on Deconstructing the 'Popular,'" in *People's History and Socialist Theory*, ed. Raphael Samuel (London: Taylor & Francis, 1981), 227–41. In his chapter entitled "The Sweet Buy and Buy," George Lipsitz stresses the fact that the greatest profits no longer come from marketing the same item to more and more consumers, but rather from the creation of specialty markets that derive their profitability from differentiation. George Lipsitz, *American Studies in a Moment of Danger* (Minneapolis: University of Minnesota Press, 2001), 261.

9. Fredric Jameson, "Reification and Utopia in Mass Culture," in *The Jameson Reader*, ed. Michael Hardt and Kathi Weeks (1979; repr., New York: Wiley-Blackwell Publishing, 2000), 123–48.

10. Adelaida Reyes, *Songs of the Caged, Songs of the Free: Music and the Vietnamese Refugee Experience* (Philadelphia: Temple University Press, 1999), 143.

11. Ibid., 35.

12. Raymond Williams, *Marxism and Literature* (New York: Oxford University Press, 1978).

13. At the start of this project, videocassette was the preferred form of media for this community. As videocassette technology becomes increasingly outdated, it is replaced by DVDs and video CDs (VCDs).

14. Robert Scholes, "Power and Pleasure in Video Texts," in *Videos, Icons, and Values*, ed. Alan M. Olson, Christopher Parr, and Debra Parr (New York: SUNY Press, 1991), 85.

15. Benedict Anderson, *Imagined Communities: Reflections on the Origin and Spread of Nationalism* (London: Verso, 1993).

16. Lisa Lowe, *Immigrant Acts: On Asian American Cultural Politics* (Durham, N.C.: Duke University Press, 1996), 22.

17. Arjun Appadurai, *Modernity at Large: Cultural Dimensions of Globalization* (Minneapolis: University of Minnesota Press, 1996).

18. I see my work to be in conversation with texts that have been published in the last decade that do address these intersections. These include: Sunaina Maira, *Desis in the House: Indian American Youth Culture in New York City* (Philadelphia: Temple University Press, 2002); Rick Bonus, *Locating Filipino Americans: Ethnicity and the Politics of Space* (Philadelphia: Temple University Press, 2000); Arlene Dávila, *Latinos, Inc.: The Marketing and Making of a People* (Berkeley: University of California Press, 2001); Lisa Nakamura, *Digitizing Race: Visual Cultures of the Internet* (Minneapolis: University of Minnesota Press, 2007); Sandya Shukla, *India Abroad: Diasporic Cultures of Postwar America and England* (Princeton, N.J.: Princeton University Press, 2003); Robert G. Lee, *Orientals: Asian Americans in Popular Culture* (Philadelphia: Temple University Press, 1999); Mimi Thi Nguyen and Thuy Linh Nguyen Tu, eds., *Alien Encounters: Popular Culture in Asian America* (Durham, N.C.: Duke University

Press, 2007); Shilpa Davé, LeiLani Nishime, and Tasha G. Oren, eds., *East Main Street: Asian American Popular Culture* (New York City: NYU Press, 2005); and Rachel Rubin and Jeffrey Melnick, *Immigration and American Popular Culture: An Introduction* (New York City: NYU Press, 2006).

19. William Liu, Mary Ann Lamanna, and Alice K. Murata, *Transition to Nowhere: Vietnamese Refugees in America* (Nashville, Tenn.: Charter House, 1979); Darrel Montero, *Vietnamese Americans: Patterns of Resettlement and Socioeconomic Adaptation in the United States* (Boulder, Colo.: Westview Press, 1979); and Paul Rutledge, *The Vietnamese Experience in America* (Bloomington: Indiana University Press, 1992).

20. Liu, *Transition to Nowhere* and Montero, *Vietnamese Americans*.

21. Most notable are the writings of Yen Lê Espiritu, Linda Trinh Võ, Viet Nguyen, Lan Duong, Mimi Thi Nguyen, and Thuy Vo Dang. Two important anthologies have been published documenting these transitions in the field: Yen Lê Espirtu and Nguyên-Vo Thu-Huong, eds., "30 Years AfterWARd: Vietnamese Americans and U.S. Empire," special issue, *Amerasia Journal* 31, no. 2 (2005) and Linda Trinh Võ, ed., "Vietnamese American Trajectories: Dimensions of Diaspora," *Amerasia Journal* 29, no. 1 (2003), ix–xviii.

22. Roy Rosensweig, *Eight Hours for What We Will: Workers and Leisure in an Industrial City, 1870–1920* (New York: Cambridge University Press, 1983); Kathy Peiss, *Cheap Amusements: Working Women and Leisure in New York City, 1880 to 1920* (Philadelphia: Temple University Press, 1986); and John Kasson, *Amusing the Million* (New York: Hill and Wang, 1978). All these works illustrate the need to study leisure in working class and immigrant cultures. Works in immigration history and the formation of ethnic identity that examine leisure and cultural transformation have been critical to shaping my thinking on the Vietnamese American experience. These texts include: George J. Sánchez, *Becoming Mexican American: Ethnicity, Culture, and Identity in Chicano Los Angeles, 1900–1945* (New York: Oxford University Press, 1993); Elizabeth Ewen, *Immigrant Women in the Land of Dollars: Life and Culture on the Lower East Side, 1890–1925* (New York: Monthly Review Press, 1985); Andrew Heinze, *Adapting to Abundance: Jewish Immigrants, Mass Consumption and the Search for American Identity* (New York: Columbia University Press, 1990); and Lon Kurashige, *Japanese American Celebration and Conflict: A History of Ethnic Identity and Festival in Los Angeles, 1934–1990* (Berkeley: University of California Press, 2002).

23. Naficy, *The Making of Exile Cultures*.

24. Rutledge, *The Vietnamese Experience in America*.

25. Eric Hobsbawm and Terrance Ranger, eds., *The Invention of Tradition* (Cambridge, U.K.: Cambridge University Press, 1992).

26. Here I build upon Amy Kaplan and Donald Pease's call to critically think about the history of U.S. imperialism and more recent works that closely examine U.S. imperialist expansion through cultural production. See Melani McAlister's illuminating book, *Epic Encounters: Culture, Media, and U.S. Interests in the Middle East, 1945–2000* (Berkeley: University of California Press, 2001), for an in-depth

discussion of the reasons why the United States has been involved in the Middle East since 1945. See also Christina Klein's *Cold War Orientalism: Asia in the Middlebrow Imagination, 1945–1961* (Berkeley: University of California Press, 2003).

27. I borrow the term *suburban warriors* from Lisa McGirr's study to illustrate the continuity of the fight against communism that Vietnamese refugees took on after their arrival in Orange County: McGirr, *Suburban Warriors: The Origins of the New American Right* (Princeton, N.J.: Princeton University Press, 2001).

28. Ella Shohat, "By the Bitstream of Babylon: Cyberfrontiers and Diasporic Vistas," in *Home, Exile, Homeland: Film, Media, and the Politics of Place*, ed. Hamid Naficy (New York: Routledge, 1999).

29. Jürgen Habermas, *The Structural Formation of the Public Sphere: An Inquiry into a Category of Bourgeois Society* (Cambridge, Mass.: MIT Press, 1991); and Calhoun, ed., *Habermas and the Public Sphere*.

1. Assimilation and Ambivalence

1. Suzanne Oboler's work on labeling Latinos informs my thinking about this term: *Ethnic Labels, Latino Lives: The Politics of (Re)Presentation in the United States* (Minneapolis: University of Minnesota, 1994).

2. Nina Glick-Schiller, "U.S. Immigrants and the Global Narrative," *American Anthropologist*, New Series, 99, no. 2 (June 1997): 404–8.

3. Paul Rutledge, *The Vietnamese American Experience* (Bloomington: University of Indiana Press, 1992), 5.

4. Yen Le Espiritu, "Toward a Critical Refugee Study: The Vietnamese Refugee Subject in U.S. Scholarship," *Journal of Vietnamese Studies* 1, no. 1–2 (February/August 2006): 410–33. Espiritu makes important suggestions as to how to approach these subjects and points to an emerging body of scholarship that is transforming the field.

5. Ronald Takaki, *Strangers from a Different Shore: A History of Asian Americans* (Boston: Little, Brown, and Company, 1989), 448. In his book, Asian American historian Ronald Takaki reported that only 603 Vietnamese people were living in the United States in 1964. In 1974, when the population multiplied to 15,000 due to increasing numbers of scholars and wives of American servicemen immigrating to the United States, still no one paid much attention to them. The existing pre-1975 group of Vietnamese Americans received such little attention that it was almost invisible even after their compatriots arrived in 1975. Significantly, the historiography on Vietnamese settlement in the United States overlooks this population as well. However, new historical research is unearthing their ambivalent yet significant position in U.S. and Vietnamese American history. See Vu Hong Pham, "Beyond and Before the Boat People: Vietnamese American History before 1975" (PhD diss., Cornell University, 2002).

6. Renny Christopher, *The Viet Nam War/The American War: Images and Representations in Euro-American and Vietnamese Exile Narratives* (Amherst: University of Massachusetts Press, 1995), x.

7. William J. Duiker, *Vietnam: Nation in Revolution* (Boulder, Colo.: Westview Press, 1983), 101. The critically acclaimed American documentary *Hearts and Minds* (1974), directed by Peter Davis, also featured scenes where the Vietnamese bourgeoisie profited from wartime industries.

8. Duiker, *Vietnam*, 101.

9. Ibid., 131.

10. Duong Van Mai Elliott, *The Sacred Willow: Four Generations in the Life of a Vietnamese Family* (New York: Oxford University Press, 1999), 260.

11. Duiker, *Vietnam*, 127.

12. Gail P. Kelly, *From Vietnam to America: A Chronicle of the Vietnamese Immigration to the United States* (Boulder, Colo.: Westview Press, 1977), 52–53.

13. I choose to focus on these early studies that focus on refugee trauma and victimization because they framed the historiography and became dominant narratives of Vietnamese immigration. These studies include: Barry Stein, "Occupational Adjustment of Refugees: The Vietnamese in the United States," *International Migration Review* 13:1 (1979), 25–45; Darrell Montero, *Vietnamese Americans: Patterns of Resettlement and Socioeconomic Adaptation in the United States* (Boulder, Colo.: Westview Press, 1979); and William Liu, Mary Ann Lamanna, and Alice K. Murata, *Transition to Nowhere: Vietnamese Refugees in America* (Nashville, Tenn.: Charter House, 1979).

14. Stein, "Occupational Adjustment of Refugees," 37.

15. These ideas about the unassimilability of Asians became part of the discourse on race into which scholars began to slot Vietnamese immigrants.

16. Stein, "Occupational Adjustment of Refugees," 37.

17. David Palumbo-Liu, *Asian/American: Historical Crossings of a Racial Frontier* (Stanford, Calif.: Stanford University Press, 1999), astutely points out that managing "the 'flood' of refugees from Southeast Asia required a convergence and correlation of the narrative of the model minority (which would assure America that this new population would follow along the path of previous Asian groups) and the narrative of reconciliation and forgetting (or a particular remembering, let us say) of the war in Vietnam, which would assure it the material histories that had delivered the refugees to America's shores would not complicate their subjectification in any significant manner" (234).

18. Kelly, *From Vietnam to America*.

19. See Kelly, *From Vietnam to America*, 36.

20. Ibid., 1–2, 35–36; and "Refugees: Situations Wanted," *Newsweek*, May 19, 1975, 75.

21. Rutledge, *The Vietnamese Experience in America*, 5.

22. Liisa Malkki, "National Geographic: The Rooting of Peoples and the Territorialization of National Identity among Scholars and Refugees," in *Becoming*

National: A Reader, ed. Geoff Eley and Ronald Grigot Suny (New York: Oxford University Press, 1996), 443.

23. John Chr. Knudsen, "When Trust Is on Trial: Negotiating Refugee Narratives," in *Mistrusting Refugees*, ed. E. Valentine Daniel and John Chr. Knudsen (Berkeley: University of California Press, 1996), 13–35.

24. Malkki, "National Geographic," 443.

25. David Haines's analyses of the historiography suggest that disciplinary boundaries and limited federal funding constrained the breadth of early scholarship on refugees: Haines, *Refugees as Immigrants: Cambodians, Laotians, and Vietnamese in America* (Totowa, N.J.: Rowman and Littlefield, 1989), 16–17.

26. Liu, Lamanna, and Murata, *Transition to Nowhere*, 1.

27. I am referring to Liu, Lamanna, and Murata, *Transition to Nowhere*.

28. E. Valentine Daniel and John Chr. Knudsen, ed., *Mistrusting Refugees* (Berkeley: University of California Press, 1996).

29. See Yen Le Espiritu, "Toward a Critical Refugee Study"; Russell C. Leong and Brandy Lien Worrall-Yu, ed., "30 Years AfterWARd: Vietnamese Americans and U.S. Empire," special issue, *Amerasia Journal* 31, no. 2 (2005); Linda Trinh Võ, ed., "Vietnamese American Trajectories: Dimensions of Diaspora," special issue, *Amerasia Journal* 29, no. 1 (2003); and Mimi Thi Nguyen, "Representing Refugees: Gender, Nation, and Diaspora in 'Vietnamese America'" (PhD diss., University of California, Berkeley, 2004).

30. Gail P. Kelly, "Coping with America: Refugees from Vietnam, Cambodia, and Laos in the 1970s and 1980s," *Annals of the American Academy of Political and Social Science* 487, no. 1 (1986): 138–49.

31. "The New Americans," *Newsweek*, May 12, 1975.

32. "Refugees: A Warmer Welcome for the Homeless," *Time*, May 19, 1975, 9.

33. Ibid.

34. Liu, Lamanna, and Murata, *Transition to Nowhere*, 63.

35. The Chinese Exclusion Act of 1882 was the first anti-immigration legislation that barred a group of immigrants from entering the United States based on their race. This act set the precedent for other legislation, including the Gentlemen's Agreement of 1907, which stopped issuing passports to laborers of Japanese descent; the Tydings-McDuffie Act of 1934, which reclassified Filipinos making them non-U.S. nationals; and the National Origins Act of 1924, which ultimately closed the door to "unwanted" immigrants. These harsh laws provided the framework for immigration legislation in the 1960s, which failed to account for many of the categories that would inevitably allow Asian immigrants to enter. See Sucheng Chan, *Entry Denied: Exclusion and the Chinese Community in America, 1882–1943* (Philadelphia: Temple University Press, 1991); Lucy Salyer, *Laws as Harsh as Tigers: Chinese Immigrants and the Shaping of Modern Immigration Law* (Chapel Hill: University of North Carolina Press, 1995); and Erika Lee, *At America's Gates: Chinese Immigration During the Exclusion Era* (Chapel Hill: University of North Carolina Press, 2003).

36. "Refugees" *Time*, 9. Ford draws upon a tradition that has allowed more than two million refugees to be admitted from communist countries. More than half a million came from Central and Eastern Europe while three-quarters of a million each came from Cuba and Southeast Asia. See Aihwa Ong, *Buddha Is Hiding: Refugees, Citizenship, the New America* (Berkeley: University of California Press, 2003), 81.

37. *Time*, "Refugees," 9. Ong, *Buddha Is Hiding*, points out that John F. Kennedy's book, *A Nation of Immigrants* (New York: Anti-Defamation League of B'nai B'rith, 1958), makes a similar argument for welcoming potential newcomers. In the book, JFK notes that the United States should open its doors to the huddled masses, particularly from communist countries, because it can receive the high-skilled immigrants such as scientists, artists, and inventors who can contribute productively to the nation. Ong, *Buddha Is Hiding*, 80.

38. "Hail from the Chief," *Newsweek*, May 19, 1995, 16.

39. Christian Appy, *Working-Class War: American Combat Soldiers and Vietnam* (Durham: University of North Carolina Press, 1993); and George Mariscal, ed., *Aztlán and Viet Nam: Chicano and Chicana Experiences of the War* (Berkeley: University of California Press, 1999).

40. David Desser, "Charlie Don't Surf: Race and Culture in Vietnam War Films," in *Inventing Vietnam*, ed. Michael Anderegg (Philadelphia: Temple University, 1991), 94.

41. Michael Hunt, *Ideology and U.S. Foreign Policy* (New Haven: Yale University Press, 1987), 176–77.

42. Antiwar protesters of color often recognized this aspect of the war, particularly Asian American protesters whose leftist politics would later reveal a lack of full understanding of Vietnamese American anticommunist politics. See, for example, Daryl J. Maeda, "Black Panthers, Red Guards, and Chinamen: Constructing Asian American Identity through Performing Blackness, 1969–1972,"*American Quarterly* 57, no. 4 (December 2005): 1079–103.

43. William Wei, *The Asian American Movement* (Philadelphia: Temple University Press, 1993).

44. Hunt, *Ideology and U.S. Foreign Policy*, 169. Also see *Hearts and Minds* (1974) directed by Peter Davis.

45. Liisa Malkki, "Refugees and Exile: From Refugee Studies to the National Order of Things," *Annual Review of Anthropology* 24 (1994): 500.

46. According the Immigration Act of 1965, refugees who had professional skills, such as doctors, were granted immigrant status and became legal residents. Nonprofessionals and others would be eligible for "legal immigrant status" if they could prove that they were self-sufficient. In financial terms of assets, this meant that they would have to be able to support themselves on $4,000 per family member.

47. Kelly, "Coping with America."

48. Ibid., 140.

49. Malkki, "Refugees and Exile," 504; and Loescher and Loescher, *Global Refugee Crisis*, 4–5.

50. Liu, Lamanna, and Murata, *Transition to Nowhere*; James Freeman, *Hearts of Sorrow: Vietnamese American Lives* (Stanford, Calif.: Stanford University Press, 1989); and Nazli Kibria, *Family Tightrope: The Changing Lives of Vietnamese Americans* (Princeton, N.J.: Princeton University Press, 1993). A notably exceptional study that closely examines how race, class, and refugee management affected the lives of Southeast Asian refugees is Ong, *Buddha Is Hiding*. Ong's scholarship raises critical questions about the field of Asian American studies and the representational politics of Southeast Asian refugees in the historiography.

51. "Obligations to Vietnam's Refugees," the *Washington Post*, May 20, 1979; T. Nguyen, "Voices: Perspectives on the Southeast Asians in the United States," *AsianWeek*, June 17, 1998; and Lowell Weiss, "Timing Is Everything," *The Atlantic*, January 1994.

52. Ong, *Buddha Is Hiding*, 85.

53. Ong makes a compelling argument that Cambodian refugees were trained in refugee camps to replace the cheap labor force in America's postindustrial economy. Ong, *Buddha Is Hiding*, 84.

54. Terry Rambo, "Refugee Camp in Philippines: 'Best and Worst' of Vietnam," *Washington Post*, April 26, 1975.

55. This is also reflected in popular narratives reconstructed by refugees and former refugees. The cinematic version is rendered in *Green Dragon*, DVD, directed by Timothy Linh Bui (2001; Culver City, Calif.: Sony Pictures, 2002).

56. Rambo, "Refugee Camp in Philippines," 35.

57. Ibid.

58. The refugee experience is by no means comparable to that the experience of slavery. However, Saidiya V. Hartman's theorization of post-emancipatory master-slave relations is tremendously helpful in thinking about concepts of self-discipline, conscience, and obligation as they relate to notions of "freedom." Like former enslaved peoples, war refugees from Southeast Asia had to prove to the American public they deserve the "freedom" the countries of asylum granted them: Saidiya V. Hartman, *Scenes of Subjection: Terror, Slavery, and Self-Making in Nineteenth Century America* (New York: Oxford University Press, 1997). I thank Shirley Thompson for suggesting this very helpful text which informed my theorizing of the refugee experience.

59. Historically speaking, the term *economic refugee* could not even be applied to this group of Vietnamese immigrants as it did not come into frequent use until the late 1980s when it appeared that too many "boat people" from various parts of the world were seen as flooding American shores only to escape bad economic situations in underdeveloped nations.

60. Kelly, *From Vietnam to America*, 154.

61. George J. Sánchez along with a number of scholars such as Amy Kaplan, Donald Pease, and Lisa Lowe have examined the history of U.S. imperialism and called for the reexamination of America's imperialist past by questioning the construction of the United States as a "nation of immigrants." See George J. Sánchez, "Face the Nation: Race,

Immigration, and the Rise of Nativism in Late Twentieth Century America," *International Immigration Review* 31, no. 4 (1997): 1009–30; and Amy Kaplan and Donald E. Pease, eds., *Cultures of U.S. Imperialism* (Durham, N.C.: Duke University Press, 1993).

62. This is reminiscent of colonial enterprises where the colonial power leaves and takes with them their servants as a reminder of the colonial relationship.

63. "Refugees: Situations Wanted," *Newsweek*.

64. Ibid.

65. Steven J. Gold, *Refugee Communities: A Comparative Field Study* (Thousand Oaks, Calif.: Sage Publications, 1992).

66. Nathan Caplan, Marcella Choy, and John K. Whitmore, "Indochinese Refugee Families and Academic Achievement," *Scientific American* (1992), 36–42.

67. Linda Trinh Võ, "The Vietnamese American Experience: From Dispersion to the Development of Postrefugee Communities," in *Asian American Studies: A Reader*, edited by Jean Wu and Min Song (New Brunswick, N.J.: Rutgers University Press, 2000); and David Whitman, "Trouble for America's 'Model Minority,'" *U.S. News and World Report*, February 23, 1987.

68. Whitman, "Trouble"; and David Whitman, "Refugees: A Dose of Bootstrap," *The Economist*, April 10, 1982.

69. Ong, *Buddha Is Hiding*, 82.

70. Darrell Montero compares Vietnamese ethnic enclave formation and assimilation with other Asian immigrant groups: Montero, *Vietnamese Americans*, 61–62. Also see Liu, Lamanna, and Murata, *Transition to Nowhere*.

71. William Petersen, "Success Story: Japanese American Style," *New York Times Magazine*, January 9, 1966; and "Success Story of One Minority Group," *U.S. News and World Report*, December 26, 1966. Reprinted in *Asian American Studies Reader*, ed. Jean Yu-wen Wu and Min Song (New Brunswick, N.J.: Rutgers University Press, 2000), 158–63.

72. For a more comprehensive look at how the "model minority" has been deployed, particularly in the field of education, see Rosalind S. Chou & Joe R. Feagin, *The Myth of the Model Minority: Asian Americans Facing Racism* (Boulder, CO: Paradigm Publishers, 2008. Also, Stacy J. Lee, *Unraveling the "Model Minority" Stereotype: Listening to Asian American Youth.* (New York, NY, Teachers College Press, 1996).

73. Sylvia Yanagisako, "Transforming Orientalism: Gender, Nationality, and Class in Asian American Studies," in *Naturalizing Power: Essays in Feminist Cultural Analysis*, eds. Sylvia Yanagisako and Carol Delany (New York: Routledge, 1995), 275–98. Yanagisako was one of the first scholars to critique this practice. Positioned outside of Asian American studies, Yanagisako's insight has been supported by others, such Aihwa Ong. Asian American studies scholars also have begun to challenge this paradigm in which the race shapes the study of the Asian American experience. Scholars such as Kandice Chuh push for a "subjectless" discourse in the discipline: Kandice Chuh, *Imagine Otherwise: On Asian Americanist Critique* (Durham, N.C.: Duke University Press, 2003).

74. Evelyn Hu-DeHart, "Asian American Formations in the Age of Globalization," introduction to *Across the Pacific: Asian Americans and Globalization*, ed., Evelyn Hu-DeHart (Philadelphia: Temple University Press, 1999), 17.

75. Ong, *Buddha Is Hiding*, 86.

76. Ibid.

77. Mimi Thi Nguyen's work addresses how Vietnamese refugees commemorate and negotiate their gratefulness to the United States. See "Representing Refugees."

78. Jade Ngoc Huynh, *South Wind Changing* (Minneapolis: Graywolf Press, 1994); Le Ly Hayslip, *When Heaven and Earth Changed Places: A Vietnamese Woman's Journey from War* (New York: Plume Publishers, 1990); Andrew Pham, *Catfish and Mandala: A Two-Wheeled Voyage through the Landscape and Memory of Vietnam* (New York: Farrar, Straus, and Giroux, 1999); and Kien Nguyen, *The Unwanted: A Memoir* (New York: Pan Macmillan, 2001). For a closer examination of the literature produced at this time period, see Monique T. D. Truong, "The Emergence of Voices: Vietnamese American Literature 1975–1990," *Amerasia Journal* 19, no. 3 (1993): 27–50; and Renny Christopher, *The Viet Nam War/The American War: Images and Representations in Euro-American and Vietnamese Exile Narratives* (Amherst: University of Massachusetts, 1995).

79. Thomas A. DuBois, "Constructions Construed: The Representation of Southeast Asian Refugees in Academic, Popular, and Adolescent Discourse," *Amerasia Journal* 19, no. 3: 1–25.

80. Truong, "The Emergence of Voices." Truong's critique of literary and discursive representations of Vietnamese refugees has been an invaluable article that has inspired later scholarship.

81. Viet Thanh Nguyen, *Race and Resistance: Literature and Politics in Asian America* (New York: Oxford University Press, 2002).

82. Yen Le Espiritu "The 'We-Win-Even-When-We-Lose' Syndrome: U.S. Press Coverage of the Twenty-Fifth Anniversary of the 'Fall of Saigon,'" *American Quarterly* 58, no. 2 (June 2006): 344.

83. Ibid., 345.

84. Ong, *Buddha Is Hiding*, 256.

85. Ibid.

86. Aihwa Ong, *Neoliberalism as Exception: Mutations in Citizenship and Sovereignty* (Durham, N.C.: Duke University Press, 2006), 14. See also Jodi Melamed, "The Spirit of Neoliberalism: From Racial Liberalism to Neoliberal Multiculturalism," *Social Text* 89, vol. 24, no. 4 (2006): 1–24; Helen Heran Jun, "Reading Neoliberalism and Asian American Racialization in *a.k.a Don Bonus* (1995) and *Better Luck Tomorrow* (2002)," Center for Asian American Studies Speaker Series, University of Texas, Austin, March 6, 2009.

87. Christian Collet, "The Determinants of Vietnamese American Political Participation: Findings from the January 2000 *Orange County Register* Poll," 2000

Annual Meeting of the Association of Asian American Studies, Scottsdale, Arizona, May 26, 2000.

2. Vietnamese by Other Means

1. For an in-depth comparative sociological study of Little Saigons in the United States, see Karin Aguilar-San Juan, *Little Saigons: Staying Vietnamese in America* (Minneapolis: University of Minnesota Press, 2009).

2. Lisa McGirr, *Suburban Warriors: The Origins of the New American Right* (Princeton, N.J.: Princeton University Press, 2001), 260.

3. Thuy Vo Dang's work on anticommunism has been helpful for me in thinking about this local crusade against the former regime. See Dang, "The Cultural Work of Anticommunism in the San Diego Vietnamese American Community," *Amerasia Journal* 31, no. 2 (2005): 65–85. Dang's research productively positions Vietnamese Americans in dialogue with Cuban Americans. See, in particular, Guillermo J. Grenier and Lisandro Perez, *The Legacy of Exile: Cubans in the United States* (Boston: Allyn and Bacon, 2003).

4. In a series of conversations on November 11 and November 18, 2001, George J. Sánchez and I developed the idea of "overlapping diasporas." Sánchez's insight on migration and identity formation led me to formulate and conceptualize Vietnamese and ethnic Chinese relations through this framework. Though slightly different in usage, my notion of overlapping diasporas is also borrowed from Earl Lewis, "To Turn as on a Pivot: Writing African Americans into a History of Overlapping Diasporas," in *Crossing Boundaries: Comparative History of Black People in Diaspora*, ed. Darlene Clark Hine and Jacqueline McLeod (Bloomington: Indiana University Press, 1999), 3–32.

5. Stuart Hall, "Cultural Identity and Diaspora" in the *Theorizing Diaspora: A Reader*, ed. Jana Evans Braziel and Anita Mannur (Hoboken, N.J.: Wiley-Blackwell, 2003), 233–46.

6. *Green Dragon*, DVD, directed by Timothy Linh Bui (2001; Culver City, Calif.: Sony Pictures, 2002).

7. Vietnamese Americans fought arduously to fly the South Vietnamese flag and to encourage the American public to refuse acknowledgement of the communist Vietnamese flag. The South Vietnamese flag, or the Vietnamese Freedom and Heritage flag, was officially recognized by the State of California under the governorship of Arnold Schwarzenegger on August 5, 2006. Vietnamese Americans had lobbied the governor of the State of California to formally recognize the Vietnamese Freedom and Heritage flag as the official symbol of the California Vietnamese-American community and to support the efforts of California's Vietnamese-American community to promote freedom and democracy. The Vietnamese Freedom and Heritage flag may be displayed on the premises of state buildings in connection with state-sponsored Vietnamese-American ceremonial events, consistent with rules and protocol regarding the proper display of the United States and the State of California flags, including the provisions of U.S. Code, chapter 1, title 4.

8. Mike Nally, "The Miracle of Little Saigon: Early Beginning," *Business Digest/ Vietnamese Chamber of Commerce in Orange County* (September–October 1984), 20–21.

9. Linda Trinh Võ, "The Vietnamese American Experience: From Dispersion to the Development of Postrefugee Communities," in *Asian American Studies: A Reader*, ed. Jean Wu and Min Song (New Brunswick, N.J.: Rutgers University Press, 2000), 290–305.

10. Chor-Swang Ngin, "The Acculturation Pattern of Orange County's Southeast Asian Refugees," *Journal of Orange County Studies* 3/4 (Fall 1989/Spring 1990): 46–53; McGirr, *Suburban Warriors*.

11. Christa Piotrowski, "The American Dream for Vietnamese?" *Swiss Review of World Affairs*, June 1, 1994.

12. McGirr, *Suburban Warriors*, 269. McGirr notes that much of the county's dynamic growth came from the diversifying economy. In this case, Orange County transformed from an agricultural to industrial economy, allowing gains to be matched by other sectors such as finance, real estate, trade, and services.

13. Yen Le Espiritu, *Asian American Women and Men: Labor, Laws, and Love* (Thousand Oaks, CA: Sage Publications, 1995).

14. Stanley Karnow, "In Orange County's Little Saigon, Vietnamese Try to Bridge Two Worlds," *Smithsonian* 23, no. 5 (August 1992), 34.

15. Orange County's minority population doubled to more than 20 percent between the 1970s and 1980. This also coincided with the rapid growth of the Latino population (McGirr, *Suburban Warriors*, 270).

16. According to McGirr's *Suburban Warriors*, Orange County became the bastion of right wing Republicanism and conservatism with the election of Ronald Reagan to the presidency. Though it may appear that Southeast Asians escaping communism would find a hospitable environment in which to settle in Orange County, the refugees encountered both antagonism and support.

17. Scott Gold and Mai Tran, "Vietnam Refugees Finally Find Home," *Los Angeles Times*, April 24, 2000, A1; and Valerie Alvord, "Refugee Success Breeds Pressure, Discrimination," *USA Today*, May 1, 2000.

18. Sam Lasoff, "Mr. Little Saigon" *Transpacific* 7, no. 3 (July/August 1992): 100.

19. Kathy Buchoz, interview with the author, September 29, 2000, Westminster, Calif.

20. Patrick Andersen, "Orange County: U.S. 'Vietnamese Capital,'" *AsianWeek* 4, no. 19 (January 6, 1983); and Lionel DeLeon, "Education Can Curb Hate," *Los Angeles Times*, September 26, 1999, Orange County edition.

21. Sheila Grissett-Welsh, "Vietnam: The Legacy: Westminster's Little Saigon," *BC Cycle*, April 14, 1985.

22. Michael Peter Smith and Bernadette Tarallo, "Who Are the 'Good Guys'? The Social Construction of the Vietnamese 'Other,'" in *The Bubbling Cauldron: Race, Ethnicity, and the Urban Crisis*, ed. Michael Peter Smith and Joe R. Feagin (Minneapolis: University of Minnesota Press, 1995), 64. Gang wars were also a topic

of intrigue to outsiders and a subject of exploration in fiction. See T. Jefferson Parker, *Little Saigon* (New York: St. Martin's Paperbacks, 2004).

23. See, in particular, Aihwa Ong, *Buddha is Hiding: Refugees, Citizenship, the New America* (Berkeley: University of California Press, 2003). In addition, see Liisa Malkki, "National Geographic: The Rooting of Peoples and the Territorialization of National Identity among Scholars and Refugees," in *Becoming National: A Reader*, ed. Geoff Eley and Ronald Grigot Suny (New York: Oxford University Press, 1996), 434–55; and Malkki, "Refugees and Exile: From Refugee Studies to the National Order of Things," *Annual Review of Anthropology* 24 (1995): 495–523.

24. Jao is most notably present in journalistic narratives of Little Saigon. Although a number of immigrants from Vietnam (including Jao) wanted to develop the land in Westminster, Jao edged above them with his sharp business sense.

25. Lasoff, "Mr. Little Saigon," 41.

26. Frank Jao, interview with the author, September 29, 2000. According to the city of Westminster, the Redevelopment Agency, first formed in 1982 and amended in 1986, 1987, 1989, and 2000, allotted a total of 2,076 acres for redevelopment. The city areas responded to the changes in development made by the Vietnamese American community, and particularly Jao's plans (*Los Angeles Times* Westminster City Council website, http://www.latimes.com/communities/govt/councwmn.htm [accessed November 16, 1999]).

27. Timothy Fong, *The First Suburban Chinatown: The Remaking of Monterey Park, California* (Philadelphia: Temple University Press, 1994), 168.

28. Ramses Amer, *The Ethnic Chinese in Vietnam and Sino-Vietnamese Relations* (Kuala Lumpur: Forum Press, 1991), 11.

29. Ibid., 23.

30. Sucheng Chan, *Asian Americans: An Interpretive History* (Boston: Twayne Publishers, 1991), 157.

31. Ken McLaughlin, "Torn Between Worlds: Chinese-Vietnamese-Americans Confuse Census Takers and Their Santa Clara County Neighbors," *San Jose Mercury News*, April 14, 1996.

32. Lily Dizon, "Acrimony over Project Called 'Harmony,'" *Los Angeles Times*, June 25, 1996, A1.

33. Merrill Balassone, "The Heart of Little Saigon Beats Strong," *Los Angeles Times*, October 23, 2005, K3.

34. David Reyes, "Asiantown: Commercial-Cultural Complex Expected to Anchor Southland's Next Chinatown," *Los Angeles Times*, March 16, 1987.

35. Van Thai Tran, interview with the author, September 29, 2000.

36. Trini Tran, "A Time for Big Decisions in Little Saigon," *Los Angeles Times*, August 23, 1998, Orange County edition.

37. Jonathan Minh Tuan, interview with author, August 2, 2000. I spent several days at Tao Dan, a mega-music center, with its owner and distributor, Jonathan Minh Tuan, who enlightened me on various aspects of the Vietnamese American music business, July–August 2000. During this time, I engaged customers who

came from far-flung places and wanted to bring music and videos back from their travels.

38. Don Lee, "One Man's Vision for Little Saigon," *Los Angeles Times*, August 5, 1997.

39. Enrique Lavin, "Pedestrian Bridge Will Reflect Style of Little Saigon," *Los Angeles Times*, March 30, 1996.

40. Dizon, "Acrimony over Project Called 'Harmony.'"

41. John Nguyen, Kim Khanh Nguyen, Phuong Nguyen, and Son Vu, "The Harmony Bridge" (unpublished term paper, University of California, Irvine, November 26, 1996).

42. Ong, *Flexible Citizenship: The Cultural Logics of Transnationality* (Durham, N.C.: Duke University Press, 1998); and Ong, "On the Edge of Empires: Flexible Citizenship among Chinese in Diaspora," *Positions* 1, no. 3 (1993): 745–78.

43. Ong, "On the Edge of Empires," 769–70.

44. Karnow, "In Orange County's Little Saigon, Vietnamese Try to Bridge Two Worlds," 34.

45. Frank Jao, interview with the author, September 29, 2000.

46. Sam Black, "Little Saigon Investor Investing in St. Paul, Minn." *Los Angeles Times*, June 9, 2003.

47. Bert Eljera, "Big Plans for Little Saigon," *Asianweek*, May 17–23, 1996.

48. Jao, interview with the author, September 29, 2000.

49. Jao, interview with the author, September 29, 2000.

50. Lee, "One Man's Vision for Little Saigon"; and "Jao: The Developer Credited with Master-Planning Little Saigon Looks for Deals in Asia," *Orange County Register*, December 26, 1996.

51. Christa Piotrowski, "The American Dream for Vietnamese?"

52. Eljera, "Big Plans for Little Saigon."

53. Chuong Hoang Chung, discussion with the author, Vietnam Studies Conference: "Moving beyond the War: New Directions in the Study of Vietnam," Philadelphia, April 2000.

54. *The Design Standards Manual of the City of Westminster*, 53–67, devotes an entire section, 17.67.090, to architecture and landscaping requirements for all building or development activities. Prepared by Urban Design Studio, 2000.

55. Seth Mydans, "Vietnam, the Way It Might Have Been," *New York Times*, August 22, 1991, A20.

56. McGirr, *Suburban Warriors*, 31.

57. Karnow, "In Orange County's Little Saigon, Vietnamese Try to Bridge Two Worlds," 28–39.

58. Ibid.

59. Zan Dubin, "Ballrooms Stay in Step with 'National Hobby,'" *Los Angeles Times*, March 14, 1995.

60. A few notable studies of the Vietnamese search for entertainment include: Deborah Wong, *Speak It Louder: Asian Americans Making Music* (New York: Routledge,

2004); and Lan Duong, "Desire and Design: Technological Display in the Vietnamese American Café and Karaoke Bar" in "Vietnamese American Trajectories: Dimensions of Diaspora," ed. Linda Trinh Võ, special issue, *Amerasia Journal* 29, no. 1: 97–115.

61. Tran Quang Hai, "Vietnam: Situation of Exile Music since 1975 and Musical Life in Vietnam since Perestroika," Tran Quang Hai and Bach Yen Researches Website. http://tranquanghai.phapviet.com/english/vnexile.htm/(accessed February 13, 2004.)

62. Zan Dubin and Rick Vanderknyff, "From Isolation to Mainstream: After and Embryonic 20 Years, the Influence of Vietnamese Artists, Musicians, and Writers in Orange County Is Exploding," *Los Angeles Times*, March 12, 1995, A1.

63. Tran, "Vietnam." See also Adelaida Reyes, *Songs of the Caged, Songs of the Free: Music and the Vietnamese Refugee Experience* (Philadelphia: Temple University Press, 1999).

64. "The Saigon Rock Festival Rolls," *Rolling Stone*, July 8, 1971.

65. Tom Marlow, "Yea, We're the CBC Band and We'd Like to Turn You On. We Got a Got a Little Peace Message, Like, Straight from Saigon. Waaaaaaaa Yeaaa!" *Rolling Stone*, November 26, 1970, 28.

66. Ibid.

67. Reyes, *Songs of the Caged, Songs of the Free*.

68. Laura Mecoy, "Vietnamese American Is a Political Pace-Setter," *Sacramento Bee*, March 15, 2004. This controversy and the battles it generated within the community over symbols of communism were discussed and highlighted in a documentary by Lindsay Jang and Robert Winn. *Little Saigon, USA*. NAATA, 2003.

69. These activists include Van Tran, Lan Quoc Nguyen, Trung Nguyen, and Janet Nguyen.

70. I attended several planning meetings for the "Rock-N-Vote" concert in the summer of 1999. All the aforementioned political activists were present at the meetings. Those who spearheaded this event included famed musicians and songwriters who worked with refugee resettlement organizations such as Nam Loc Nguyen and Viet Dzung, along with local professionals who worked in Little Saigon.

71. The event was held on October 17, 1999. In July 2002, Tully Fairgrounds in Northern California hosted a similar event organized by yet another future Vietnamese American political figure, Madison Nguyen. The campaign and concert launched Nguyen's political career by registering 5,000 voters in San Jose, where 10 percent of the population is Vietnamese American (see Erin Sherber, "Madison's Last Stand: Inside the Councilmember's Recall Fight," *Metroactive*, December 3, 2008, http://www.metroactive.com/metro/12.03.08/news-0849.html [accessed April 19, 2009]). Madison Nguyen's rise to political prominence owes a great deal to her active response to a call by the San Jose community to have a stronger political voice. Her fall from politics came when she refused to support naming the Vietnamese retail district in San Jose "Little Saigon." This decision was interpreted by the Vietnamese community to be an expression of sympathy toward the communist regime.

72. Andrew Lam, "Little Saigon Mulls Poor Showing by Vietnamese-American Candidates," *New American Media*, November 9, 2006, http://news.newamericamedia.

org/news/view_article.html?article_id=9a6dd242b80fc882ad0f73caa1447 b3b (accessed December 17, 2010).

73. *2003 Orange County Community Indicators*, 4. A pdf of this study is available at http://www.occhildrenandfamilies.org/CommunityIndicators. aspx (accessed December 17, 2010).

74. Jackie Koszczuk, "Proof of Illegal Voters Falls Short, Keeping Sanchez in House," http://CNN.com, February 7, 1998.

75. Gustavo Arellano, "Their Man Tan: Nguyen Addresses His True Believers," *OC Weekly*, http://www.ocweekly.com/news/fine-print/their-man-tan/26122/(accessed June 19, 2007).

76. In 1992, during a *60 Minutes* interview, Hillary Clinton said she "wasn't some little woman 'standing by my man' like Tammy Wynette." This reference to the famous song involved Hillary Clinton's stalwart support of her husband after accusations of Bill Clinton's extramarital affair with Gennifer Flowers surfaced. "Hillary Clinton Stands By Her Man" *BBC News* (January 27, 1998). The outlandish performance of the new campaign song (with revised lyrics) by an unidentified singer wearing fishnet stockings can be found on YouTube: http://youtube.com/ watch?v=g7cazQNF4eo (accessed May 8, 2009).

77. Lam, "Little Saigon Mulls Poor Showing by Vietnamese-American Candidates."

78. This is a popular belief in California, particularly in Orange County and San Jose, the two largest Vietnamese communities outside of Vietnam. In other parts of the country, such as Chicago and Houston, the Democratic Party has garnered solid support from Vietnamese immigrants. For example, Hubert Vo won the election for the Texas House of Representatives seat from District 149, defeating incumbent Republican Talmadge Heflin in 2004.

79. Michelle Park Steel, "The New Face of the Grand Old Party," *AsianWeek: The Voice of Asian America*, April 27, 2007, http://AsianWeek.com.

80. My-Thuan Tran, "Rival denounces Rep. Sanchez's comments about Vietnamese," *Los Angeles Times*, September 25, 2010.

81. Tran Quang Hai, "The Westminster Business District Seeks Ways to Widen Appeal," *Los Angeles Times*, August 23, 1998, Orange County edition.

82. The Vietnamese American community lobbied to put Little Saigon on the map as an officially designated "special tourist zone." The freeway signs were finally erected in 1988.

83. Colette Marie McLaughlin and Paul Jesilow, "Conveying a Sense of Community Along Bolsa Avenue: Little Saigon as a Model of Ethnic Commercial Belts," *International Migration* 36, no. 1 (1998): 49–65.

84. Trini Tran, "A Time for Big Decisions in Little Saigon."

85. Arjun Appadurai, *Modernity at Large: Cultural Dimensions of Globalization* (Minneapolis: University of Minnesota Press, 1996).

86. Trini Tran, "A Time for Big Decisions in Little Saigon."

87. Gabriel Elliot, "Bolsa District—Little Saigon," *APA Orange County Planner*, March/April 1996.

88. My-Thuan Tran, "Vote May Produce a Cultural Milestone; Vietnamese American Majority May Serve on Westminster Council" *Los Angeles Times*, October 15, 2008.

89. Madison Nguyen earned a position as a councilmember in San Jose, California, representing District 7 in 2005. Janet Nguyen is county supervisor of the First District of California's Orange County. Nguyen defeated her opponent Trung Nguyen, a peer of the politically powerful Van Tran, for the supervisor position in a close and highly contested race in 2007. While both these women earned their respective places in American politics, the Vietnamese American community has alternately criticized them for not representing their interests.

3. Pageantry and Nostalgia

1. Sarah Banet-Weiser, *The Most Beautiful Girl in the World: Beauty Pageants and National Identity* (Berkeley: University of California Press, 1999); Banet-Weiser, "Crowning Identities: Performing Nationalism, Femininity, and Race in the United States Beauty Pageants" (PhD diss., University of California, San Diego, 1995); Natasha Barnes, "Representing the Nation: Gender, Culture and the State in Anglophone Caribbean Society" (PhD diss., University of Michigan, 1995); and Colleen Ballerino Cohen, Richard R. Wilk, and Beverly Stoeltje, *Beauty Queens on the Global Stage: Gender, Contests, and Power* (New York: Routledge, 1996).

2. Banet-Weiser, *The Most Beautiful Girl in the World*, 125.

3. Judy Wu's examination of a Chinese American beauty pageant, "'Loveliest Daughter of Our Ancient Cathay!': Representations of Ethnic and Gender Identity in the Miss Chinatown U.S.A. Beauty Pageant," *Journal of Social History* 31 (Fall 1997): 5–31.

4. Lisa Lowe argues that Asian American history in the United States "produces cultural forms that are materially and aesthetically at odds with the resolution of the citizen to the nation" (Lowe, *Immigrant Acts: On Asian American Cultural Politics*, Durham, N.C.: Duke University Press, 1996, 6).

5. Most pageants have three rounds of competition during which the contestants must wear one compulsory *ao dai*, one *ao dai* of her choice, and one Western evening gown. The compulsory *ao dai* is usually made for the contestants by a sewing company that sponsors the pageant, whereas the *ao dai* of choice must be purchased by the contestants. According to the *Orange County Register*, the cost of an *ao dai* ranges from $300 to $530 (Hieu Tran Pham, "Eastern Tradition with a Western Twist," *Orange County Register*, January 19, 1997).

6. Nam Hoang Nguyen, e-mail correspondence with author, September 11, 1999.

7. Eric Hobsbawm, "Introduction: Inventing Traditions," in *The Invention of Tradition*, ed. Eric Hobsbawm and Terence Ranger (Cambridge: Cambridge University Press, 1983), 1–14.

8. "Greetings from Organizing Committee," *The 1997 Miss Vietnam Tet Pageant of Northern California*, Huyen Tran Coproducer (VEN Productions, 1997). International Miss Vietnam website, http://www.vietscape.com/hoahau97 (accessed December 17, 2010).

9. Benedict Anderson, *Imagined Communities: Reflections on the Origin and Spread of Nationalism* (London: Verso, 1993). What is interesting about this "imagined community" is that it does not have a state. Vietnamese nationalism is based on a politics of exile that is extremely anticommunist and prodemocracy.

10. The largest anticommunist rally that marked the Vietnamese American community's emergence into the American media spotlight was the Hi-Tek Video protest where the Vietnamese community of Little Saigon, California, came out in droves to demonstrate against a video store owner who posted a picture of Ho Chi Minh and hung the flag of the Socialist Republic of Vietnam in public view.

11. Van Ngan, "Traditional Vietnamese Male Attire," Vietnamese Culture: A 1970's Perspective *Vietnam Bulletin* 6 (February 8, 1971), http://www.destinationvietnam.com/aboutvn/culture/tranthong/tranthong06.htm (accessed April 1998). When President Diem was overthrown in 1963, the national dress was so closely identified with his administration that it sank with him into oblivion.

12. Lan Vu, "The *Ao Dai* Evolution," *Vietnow* (May/June 1996): 51.

13. Ngan, "Traditional Vietnamese Male Attire." Using the *ao dai* as cultural and political resistance against the communists has become more complicated because the *ao dai* has made a resurgence in the Socialist Republic of Vietnam. By the late 1980s, the *ao dai* had regained popularity among young women in Vietnam. It is mainly seen worn by young women in the business sector. It regained its permanent role as the national dress of Vietnam after Vietnam Airlines flight attendant Truong Quynh Mai won the prize for "Best Traditional Costume" at the Miss World Pageant in Tokyo in 1995.

14. The popularity of the *ao dai* has generated interest from within the community and has gained cultural and historical significance in American museums. In 2007, the San Jose Museum curated an exhibit complete with history, displays, etc.

15. "Background," 1997 International Miss Vietnam Pageant website.

16. "IMVP Philosophy," 1997 International Miss Vietnam Pageant website.

17. "IMVP Philosophy," 1997 International Miss Vietnam Pageant website.

18. AT&T donated $500 to the 1995 *Hoa Hau Ao Dai* Pageant in Long Beach, California. Because American corporate sponsorship brings funds and prestige to pageants, Vietnamese Americans also benefit. Nevertheless, they cannot always depend on sponsorship from mainstream America because the funds are much more difficult to obtain and require advanced planning of up to a year. Most community events, including the *ao dai* pageant, are planned between four to eight months in advance.

19. Arjun Appadurai, *Modernity at Large: Cultural Dimensions of Globalization* (Minneapolis: University of Minnesota Press, 1996); Roger Rouse, "Thinking through Transnationalism: Notes on the Cultural Politics of Class Relations in the Contemporary United States," *Public Culture* 7 (1995): 353–402.

20. Now some production companies have made the videos available for sale by mail order through the Internet. Though the marketing of these videos is prohibited by the communist government in Vietnam, they still circulate through the black market.

21. Rita Felski, *The Gender of Modernity* (Cambridge: Harvard University Press, 1995). Felski explains that "nostalgia emerges as a recurring and guiding theme in the self-constitution of the modern; the redemptive maternal body constitutes the ahistorical other and the other of history against which modern identity is defined" (38).

22. It is impossible to know which regions the contestants actually come from or identifies with most unless they are allowed to speak with tonal linguistic inflections that often reveal a person's general regional identity. Moreover, historical records indicate that it is numerically impossible for all the regions to be equally represented because an overwhelming majority of immigrants migrated from the South. Only a small number of immigrants in the United States were from the North or the Middle regions. Finally, regional identities are never fixed. For example, it is very possible for a Northerner to migrate to the South as a child, to be raised in the South by parents who speak the Northern dialect, and, as a result, to speak both dialects. See Sucheng Chan, *Asian Americans: An Interpretive History* (Boston: Twayne Publishers, 1991), chapter 8.

23. Benedict Anderson, *Imagined Communities*; Partha Chatterjee, *The Nation and Its Fragments: Colonial and Postcolonial Histories* (Princeton, N.J.: Princeton University Press, 1993); and Lydia Liu, "The Female Body and Nationalist Discourse: The Field of Life and Death Revisited," in *Scattered Hegemonies: Postmodernity and Transnational Feminist Practices*, ed. Inderpal Grewal and Caren Kaplan (Minneapolis: University of Minnesota Press, 1994), 37–62.

24. I thank Caroll Smith-Rosenberg for her keen observation here.

25. Jesse W. Nash, *Vietnamese Values: Confucian, Catholic, American* (PhD diss., Tulane University, 1987), 252.

26. Diem Trang, contestant in the 1996 Miss Tet Vietnam Northern California Pageant. Vietscape website. VEN Entertainment. http://www.vietscape.com/

27. Extra funds left over from the pageant are meant to be donated to charity organizations. This pageant focused on refugee orphans, but others assisted at-risk youth and cultural preservation projects such as Vietnamese language school.

28. Nash, *Vietnamese Values*, 255.

29. Ibid.

30. De Tran, "Miss Saigon: Vietnam Is Miles and Years Away, but Its Tradition Hasn't Been Lost on a Beauty Queen in San Jose," *San Jose Mercury News*, May 30, 1992, C1, C8.

31. Rajagopalan Radhakrishnan, *Diasporic Mediations: Between Home and Location* (Minneapolis: University of Minnesota Press, 1996). What I mean by "hyphenated identity" is that both sides of the "hyphen" are emphasized rather than just privileging one over another. Beauty contestants are expected to negotiate their identity so that they retain both the Vietnamese and the American sides of their identities.

32. Debates about cosmetic surgery abound, particularly among feminist scholars who believe that cosmetic surgery can be prowoman or antiwoman. Susan Bordo offers harsh criticism of cosmetic surgery, while Kathy Davis, Virgina Blum, and Victoria Pitts-Taylor argue that transforming the body allows women to find happiness in themselves. Susan Bordo, *Unbearable Weight: Feminism, Western Culture, and the Body* (Berkeley: University of California Press, 2004); Virginia L. Blum, *Flesh Wounds: The Culture of Cosmetic Surgery* (Berkeley: University of California Press, 2003); and Victoria Pitts-Taylor, *Surgery Junkies: Wellness and Pathology in Cosmetic Culture* (New Brunswick, N.J.: Rutgers University Press, 2007).

33. Eugenia Kaw, "Opening Faces: The Politics of Cosmetic Surgery and Asian American Women," in *In Our Own Words: Readings on the Psychology of Women and Gender*, eds. Mary E. Crawford and Rhoda Kesler Under (New York: McGraw-Hill, 1997), 55–73.

34. Wendy Chapkis, *Beauty Secrets: Women and the Politics of Appearance* (Boston: South End Press, 1986); Kathy Peiss, "Making Faces: The Cosmetics Industry and the Cultural Construction of Gender, 1890–1930," *Genders* 7 (Spring 1990): 143–69. Peiss's discussion of race and color as it was projected by the cosmetics industry and beauty culturalists was most useful to me. I am inclined to think that, in the case of the Vietnamese community, plastic surgeons have become the new "beauty culturalists."

35. David Palumbo-Liu, *Asian/American: Historical Crossings of a Racial Frontier* (Stanford, Calif.: Stanford University Press, 1999), 98.

36. Sander Gilman, Elizabeth Haiken, and others have explored the erasure of ethnic features in public figures such as Fanny Brice and Michael Jackson.

37. The scholarship that informed this piece includes Judy Wu, "'Loveliest Daughter of Our Ancient Cathay!': Representations of Ethnic and Gender Identity in the Miss Chinatown U.S.A. Beauty Pageant," *Journal of Social History* 31 (Fall 1997): 5–31; Cohen, *Beauty Queens on the Global Stage*; Banet-Weiser, *The Most Beautiful Girl in the World*. More recent scholarship on beauty pageants in Asian American communities includes Lon Kurashige, *Japanese American Celebration and Conflict: A History of Ethnic Identity and Festival, 1934–1990* (Berkeley: University of California Press, 2002); Martin F. Manalansan IV, *Global Divas: Filipino Gay Men in the Diaspora* (Durham, N.C.: Duke University Press, 2003); Rebecca Chiyoko King-O'Riain, *Pure Beauty: Judging Race in Japanese American Beauty Pageants* (Minneapolis: University of Minnesota Press, 2006); Christine Reiko Yano, *Crowning the Nice Girl: Gender, Ethnicity, and Culture in Hawai'i's Cherry Blossom Festival* (Honolulu: University of Hawaii Press, 2006).

38. The pressure to look "beautiful" has forced many Vietnamese immigrant women, rich and poor, to go to any lengths to undergo plastic surgery. This includes filing fraudulent medical claims for cosmetic surgeries as medically necessary. According to David R. Olmos, "Investigators believe the scheme already involved several hundred patients, and possibly more. Nearly all are women and roughly 70% are Vietnamese Americans undergoing cosmetic surgery." ("Plastic Surgery Insurance Fraud Scheme Alleged," *Los Angeles Times*, October 26, 1997, A1).

39. Laura Mulvey, "Visual Pleasure and Narrative Cinema," *Screen* 16, no. 3 (Autumn 1975): 6–18.

4. Consuming Transcendent Media

1. *Paris by Night* used videocassette technology at the beginning but has grown to reflect the changing technology by converting some of their products to DVD. While the older videos remain available as videocassettes, *Paris by Night* began to exclusively produce their shows in DVD format in 2004. A different, less expensive technology, video compact discs (VCDs), also exists, but most VCDs are pirated and circulate primarily in Asia.

2. The attempts made by the communist government to regulate and censor music in Vietnam have failed miserably. Hence, it is semilegal to buy and own music, videos, CDs, and karaoke laser discs produced by Vietnamese in the diaspora in Vietnam. Moreover, because no copyright laws are enforced internationally, producers do not profit from the sale of these illegal copies. For further discussion of the Vietnamese musical diaspora, see Ashley Carruthers, "National Identity, Diasporic Anxiety, and Music Video Culture in Vietnam," in *House of Glass: Culture, Modernity, and the State in Southeast Asia*, ed. Yao Souchao (Pasir Panjang, Singapore: Institute of Southeast Asian Studies, 2000), 114–49; and "Vietnamese Singers Who Produce Western-Style Pop," report by Gerry Hadden, National Public Radio, *Morning Edition*, January 18, 2000.

3. Thuy Nga Online, http://www.thuyngaonline.com (accessed April 20, 2009). Before DVD technology became the mainstay of Vietnamese homes, live variety performances were released concurrently on VHS and DVD. Although the company now releases them solely on DVD, I will refer to them as videos throughout this chapter.

4. Adelaida Reyes Schramm, "From Refugee to Immigrant: The Music of Vietnamese in the New York and New Jersey Metropolitan Area," in *New Perspectives on Vietnamese Music: Six Essays*, ed. Phong T. Nguyen (New Haven, Conn.: Yale Center for International and Area Studies and the Association for Vietnamese Music Research, 1992). According to Reyes Schramm, who conducted field work in refugee camps in Bataan and Palawan, the Philippines, as soon as Vietnamese refugees regained their freedom of expression, they experimented with music that included "love songs, religious songs, and songs that express personal feelings that were not directed toward country, parents, Communism and Uncle Ho" (95).

5. Bruce C. Klopfenstein, "The Diffusion of the VCR in the United States," in *The VCR Age: Home Video and Mass Communication*, ed. Mark R. Levy (Newbury Park, Calif.: Sage Publications, 1989), 21–39.

6. Dona Kolar-Panov, "Video and the Diasporic Imagination of Selfhood: A Case Study of the Croatians in Australia," *Cultural Studies* 10, no. 2 (1996): 288–314.

7. See Kolar-Panov, "Video and the Diasporic Imagination of Selfhood: A Case Study of the Croatians in Australia; and Schein Louisa, "Forged Transnationality and Oppositional Cosmopolitanism" in *Transnationalism from Below*, ed. Michael Peter Smith and Luis Eduardo Guarnizo (New Brunswick, N.J.: Transaction Publishers, 1998); Jo Ann Koltyk, "Telling Narratives through Home Videos: Hmong Refugees and Self-Documentation of Life in the Old and New Country," *Journal of American Folklore* 106, no. 422 (Fall 1993): 435–49.

8. Jesse W. Nash, "Confucius and the VCR: Vietnamese Values Find a Haven in the Electronic Age," *Natural History* 97, no. 5 (May 1988): 28–31.

9. Stuart Cunningham and Tina Nguyen, "Popular Media of the Vietnamese Diaspora," in *Floating Lives: The Media and Asian Diasporas*, ed. Stuart Cunningham and John Sinclair (St. Lucia, Queensland, Australia: University of Queensland Press, 2000), 91–135.

10. Sydney Truong, "*Paris by Night*: Phenom or Phizz?" *Vietnow* (March/April 1996): 56–59.

11. One of the strategies of Vietnamese businesses establishments throughout the diaspora is to continue to use the brand names of renowned companies and businesses so that they can play on the nostalgic sensibilities of customers who long for things associated with the days before the fall of Saigon.

12. Information gathered from "Tenth Anniversary Celebration," *Paris by Night* 24, VHS (Westminster, Calif.: Thuy Nga Productions, 1994).

13. Nhi Lieu, "Overlapping Diasporas: Chinese Money, Little Saigon, and the Struggle to Define Vietnamese Identity in the United States" (unpublished paper, University of Michigan, 1999).

14. Mark Chalon Smith, "The Big Mix: Little Saigon's Video Kicks," *Los Angeles Times*, February 5, 1989.

15. Cunningham and Nguyen, "Popular Media of the Vietnamese Diaspora."

16. "Gia Biet Saigon [Farewell Saigon]," *Paris by Night* 10, VHS (Westminster, Calif.: Thuy Nga Productions, 1986); "Tenth Anniversary," *Paris by Night* 24 (Westminster, Calif.: Thuy Nga Productions, 1995); and "20 Nam Nhin Lai [20 Years Looking Back]," *Paris by Night* 32, VHS, directed by Richard Valverde (Westminster, Calif.: Thuy Nga Productions, 1995). All these videos contain actual footage of war and the violence of exile in clips that feature a strong American presence in Vietnam as well as the American withdrawal from the fallen capital of Saigon.

17. Cunningham and Nguyen, "Popular Media of the Vietnamese Diaspora," 119.

18. Judith Colburn, "Terror in Saigontown, U.S.A.," *Mother Jones*, Feb/March 1983.

19. The glamorous self-indulgent politics of individualism undoubtedly influenced Vietnamese immigrants and refugees as it celebrated capitalism and the freedom to buy. Deborah Silverman, *Selling Culture: Bloomingdale's, Diana Vreeland, and the New Aristocracy of Taste in Reagan's America* (New York: Pantheon Books, 1986).

20. My use of the word *recent* is relative here because there are delays in the translation and production process.

21. According to the "Vietnamese Singers Who Produce Western-Style Pop" report by Gerry Hadden, National Public Radio, *Morning Edition*, (January 18, 2000), 2.5 million Vietnamese worldwide consume music produced in the diaspora.

22. Ylan Q. Mui, "Culture on Rewind: Vietnamese Video Series Links a Far-Flung People to their Past," *Washington Post*, July 12, 2001.

23. William T. Liu, Mary Ann Lamanna, and Alice K. Murata, *Transition to Nowhere: Vietnamese Refugees in America* (Nashville, Tenn.: Charter House, 1979); James Freeman, *Hearts of Sorrow: Vietnamese-American Lives* (Stanford, Calif.: Stanford University Press, 1989); and Adelaida Reyes, *Songs of the Caged, Songs of the Free: Music and the Vietnamese Refugee Experience* (Philadelphia: Temple University Press, 1999).

24. James Rutledge, *The Vietnamese Experience in America* (Bloomington: Indiana University Press, 1992), 45.

25. What constitutes "authentic Vietnamese culture" is in constant debate. I do not believe that an "authentic Vietnamese culture" exists. Rather, Vietnamese culture is constantly *authenticated* by the Vietnamese in different social and historical contexts and for very specific political purposes. See Hien Duc Do, "A Space of Their Own: Vietnamese Music Legends in America" (lecture, University of Michigan, November 2, 1998).

26. "Mother," *Paris by Night* 40, VHS (Westminster, Calif.: Thuy Nga Productions, 1997).

27. This "controversy" received uneven media attention in different parts of diaspora. Because it coincided with the time of Princess Diana's death, one journalist claims that mainstream media channels may have overlooked it. K. Oanh Ha, "Some Seeing Red over Videos," the *Orange County Register*, December 27, 1997.

28. Cunningham and Nguyen, "Popular Media of the Vietnamese Diaspora," 121–24.

29. Ibid.

30. The "younger generation" is a viewer anywhere between the ages of five and thirty-five. These fans of *Paris by Night* tend to be foreign-born immigrants, but many American-born Vietnamese also enjoy the videos for their cultural value. According to one young Vietnamese American woman, "I like to learn Vietnamese language by listening to the music." Julie Pham, interview with author, Irvine, Calif., (July 7, 1999).

31. De Tran, "Songwriters Return to Love," *San Jose Mercury News*, December 20, 1993: "One of the problems this has created is that Vietnamese songwriters often do

not receive the royalties they deserve. Some songwriters claim that it is difficult to make a living under such practices but others argue that their music would not live on if singers do not perform their songs."

32. Theodor Adorno, "On Popular Music," portions reprinted in *A Critical and Cultural Theory Reader*, ed. Antony Easthope and Kate McGowan (1941; repr., Toronto: University of Toronto Press, 1992), 211–23.

33. Dorinne Kondo, *About Face: Performing Race in Fashion and Theatre* (New York: Routledge, 1997), 16. Other scholars who have written about the politics of pleasure include Janice Radway, *Reading the Romance: Women, Patriarchy, and Popular Literature* (Chapel Hill: University of North Carolina Press, 1984); and Tania Modleski, *Loving with a Vengeance: Mass-produced Fantasies for Women* (Hamden, Conn.: Archon Books, 1982).

34. In cities all over the United States, community-based nonprofit organizations that assist Vietnamese Americans often invite Vietnamese performers based in California to perform at fundraisers. In both Southern and Northern California, community leaders and aspiring Vietnamese American politicians joined with Vietnamese singers for a get-out-the-vote campaign that would register Vietnamese citizens to vote. Modeled after MTV's "Rock the Vote" campaign, these free concerts registered thousands of Vietnamese Americans, mainly youth, to be part of the political process.

35. This has happened to a number of performers, including seasoned professionals like Huong Lan, who made the "mistake" of returning to Vietnam.

36. A show in Chicago suffered from low attendance because of protests against two popular *vong co* opera singers from Vietnam, causing the organizer a net loss of approximately $30,000. Tam Van Nguyen, Community Economic Development Coordinator, Vietnamese Association of Illinois, interview with author, August 2002.

37. Naficy, *The Making of Exile Cultures: Iranian Television in Los Angeles* (Minneapolis: University of Minnesota Press, 1993), 147.

38. Reyes, *Songs of the Caged, Songs of the Free*.

39. Carruthers, "National Identity, Diasporic Anxiety, and Music Video Culture in Vietnam."

40. Hamid Naficy, "The Poetics and Practice of Iranian Nostalgia in Exile," *Diaspora* 1, no. 3 (1991): 295. Naficy's work on exilic media has offered much insight on homeland fetishization.

41. Here poaching seems to be on the side of cultural producers who are not part of the American culture industry. Nevertheless, poaching can occur by both cultural makers and fans themselves. See Michel de Certeau, *The Practice of Everyday Life*, trans. Steven Rendall (Berkeley: University of California Press, 1984); John Fiske, *Understanding Popular Culture* (Boston: Unwin Hyman, 1989); and Henry Jenkins, *Textual Poachers: Television Fans and Participatory Culture* (New York: Routledge, 1992).

42. I would like to thank Son Lieu for his keen observations and numerous helpful suggestions in analyzing music and cinematic imagery.

43. "Fifteenth Anniversary Celebration," *Paris by Night* 46, VHS, directed by Michael Watt (Westminster, Calif.: Thuy Nga Productions, 1998).

44. "Fun Facts for the Film Buff on *West Side Story*," http://www.alt.tcm.turner.com/essentials/2002/trivia-westside.html/ (accessed July 25, 2002); and James Berardinelli, review of *West Side Story*, http://www.movie-reviews@collossus.net/w/westside.net/ (accessed July 25, 2002).

45. Nguyen Cao Ky Duyen, telephone conversation with Viet Horizons, radio broadcast, April 14, 2001, http://www.viethorizons.com/audio/04142001_rec.rm/ (accessed April 2003).

46. "Fifteenth Anniversary Celebration," *Paris by Night* 46, VHS, directed by Michael Watt (Westminster, Calif.: Thuy Nga Productions, 1998).

47. Anh Do, "Dazzling a Crowd: Vietnamese Singers Put Own Stamp on U.S. Tunes," the *Orange County Register*, November 19, 1991.

48. "Nhu Quynh's Family, Husband, and Children," *Vietfun Daily Entertainment Update*, http://www.vietvui.net/nhu-quynhs-family-husband-and-children/393/ (accessed May 1, 2009).

49. The use of the term *yellowface* borrows from the work on blackface minstrelsy and subsequent studies on yellowface performance. Eric Lott, *Love and Theft: Blackface Minstrelsy and the American Working Class* (New York: Oxford University Press, 1995); Michael Rogin, *Blackface, White Noise: Jewish Immigrants in the Hollywood Melting Pot* (Berkeley: University of California Press, 1996); Joseph Won, "Yellowface Minstrelsy: Asian Martial Arts and the American Popular Imaginary" (PhD diss., University of Michigan, 1996).

50. "Biography," Dalena's Music Portal, http://www.dalenanet.com/biography.asp. (accessed May 1, 2009).

51. *Cover Girl: A Gift from God*, directed by Nguyen Tan Hoang (San Francisco: Kimchi Chige Productions, 2000).

52. Shanda Sawyer's website, http://www.shandasawyer.com (accessed April 25, 2009).

53. These ideas were sparked by Janet Davis's rich and compelling study of the railroad circus in turn-of-the-century America: Davis, *The Circus Age: Culture and Society under the American Big Top* (Chapel Hill: University of North Carolina Press, 2002). Davis's concept of a contested terrain is useful for thinking about popular culture's role in challenging dominant ideologies of race, gender, sexuality, and the American nation.

54. *Paris by Night* videos are also one of the premier venues to learn about innovative products from Asia. Before Americans even heard of the Hawaii Chair, for example, Vietnamese audiences of diasporic videos had already seen the infomercial. The Hawaii Chair represents one of those preposterous examples whereby one can lose inches off one's waistline while sitting on an electric spinning chair that rotates around like the hula.

55. Ky Duyen House website, http://www.kyduyenshop.com/(accessed October 2, 2009).

56. For *Paris by Night* audiences as well as for the beauty pageant fans, as I discussed in the previous chapter, the *ao dai* projects a particular image of beauty that evokes nostalgia for the homeland. The symbolic meaning behind the *ao dai* has also inspired the fashion shows featured in many *Paris by Night* videos. The person responsible for some of these *ao dai* designs is none other than Thuy Nga herself. Using fabrics from famous couture designers such as Yves Saint Laurent, Christian Dior, Paco Rabanne, and Nina Ricci, Thuy Nga uses Western high fashion and blends it with notions of tradition and modernity to create a diasporic Vietnamese "high" culture.

57. Neal Gabler, *Life the Movie: How Entertainment Conquered Reality* (New York: Alfred A. Knopf, 1999).

58. Web survey respondent from Virginia, "Thinh," October 29, 2000.

59. Web survey respondent "Uyen," October 31, 2000; Web survey respondent "Linh," January 18, 2001; and Web survey respondent from Pittsburgh, Penn., anonymous, February 21, 2001.

60. Web survey respondent "Long Thanh," May 6, 2001.

61. Web survey respondent "Ryan," November 17, 2000.

62. "Linh."

63. "Twentieth Anniversary Celebration," *Paris By Night* 71 (Westminster, Calif.: Thuy Nga Productions, 2003). During the video, awards were given out to songwriters and other renowned artists.

64. According to an ad on Craigslist entitled, "10/28–11/3: Seeking contestants Mrs. All Nations Universal, and More . . . (Houston/Galveston)" the Mrs. All Nations Universal Pageant is "The only International competition to Salute The married lady, who will represent her state or country. The competition is to be held October/ November 2009 in Houston, Texas. The competition is based on interview, written essay, creative Scrapbook and formal attire. Stage experience not required. Mrs. All Nations Universal. Was created to promote today's our Married ladies. Will have a wonderful experience. The new Mrs. All Nations Universal. WINNER in addition to a wonderful collection of gifts and Prizes She will represent all our Mrs. All Nations Universal. Ladies around the World" (http://houston.craigslist.org/eve/1012225715.html [accessed April 25, 2009]).

65. Web survey respondent,"Lan," February 15, 2002.

66. Web survey respondent, "Thuan," September 12, 2001.

67. Web survey respondent, "Tricia", August 7, 2001.

68. Sander L. Gilman, *Making the Body Beautiful: A Cultural History of Aesthetic Surgery* (Princeton, N.J.: Princeton University Press, 1999); and Joanne L. Rondilla and Paul R. Spickard, *Is Lighter Better?: Skin-Tone Discrimination among Asian Americans* (Lamham, Md.: Rowman and Littlefield, 2007).

69. David Palumbo-Liu, *Asian/American: Historical Crossings of a Racial Frontier* (Stanford, CA: Stanford University Press, 1999), 95.

70. Gilman, *Making the Body Beautiful*, 22.

71. Stuart Hall, "Notes on Deconstructing the 'Popular,'" in *People's History and Socialist Theory*, ed. Raphael Samuel (London: Taylor & Francis, 1981), 227–41.

72. "Thoi Trang va Am Nhac [Fashion and Music]," *Paris by Night* 57, VHS, directed by Kent Weed (Westminster, Calif.: Thuy Nga Productions, 2001).

73. One particular organization has been highly influential in challenging the representations rendered in *Paris by Night* videos: the Vietnamese American Arts and Letters Association (http://www.vaala.org/). VAALA consists of a collective of artists, filmmakers, spoken-word performers, authors, composers, designers, and musicians that have actively worked to create, perform, and render the Vietnamese American experience through art. Nevertheless, as a nonprofit, localized, creative, and independent arts organization in Southern California, it does not have the sway and overwhelming support that for-profit entertainment companies have.

Conclusion

1. Richard Marosi, "Vietnam's Music Invasion" *Los Angeles Times*, August 8, 2000.

2. I thank Lok Siu, Grace Wang, and two anonymous readers from the University of Minnesota Press, for their suggestions to meditate on the future of diasporas for this community. Lok C.D. Siu's book *Memories of a Future Home: Diasporic Citizenship of Chinese Panama* (Stanford, Calif.: Stanford University Press, 2005) has also been a useful guide for me to think through these larger ideas about diaspora and the homeland state.

3. For Vietnamese audiences and adoring fans, the shows provide a chance to be close to celebrities and idols of the diaspora and watch them perform live. In the course of my research, I attended four live concerts, three of which were held at the famed Aragon Ballroom, a renowned venue in Chicago's Uptown neighborhood often used by mainstream American music acts. When the Vietnamese community is unable to reserve the Aragon, the concerts are staged at the Chicago Amory Park, an indoor facility resembling a large gymnasium that hosts other community events such as the annual Tet festival.

4. Vietnamese performers earn from $500 to $2,000 per show depending on their popularity.

5. Peter Vu, interview with the author, September 1, 2002, Aragon Ballroom, Chicago, Ill.

6. Ngoc Huynh, interview with the author, September 1, 2002, Aragon Ballroom, Chicago, Ill.

7. Tam Van Nguyen, interview with the author, May 12, 2003, Chicago, Ill.

8. Patricia Nguyen, interview with the author, May 12, 2003, Chicago, Ill.

9. Beth E. Kolko, Lisa Nakamura, and Gilbert Rodman, ed., *Race in Cyberspace* (°: Routledge, 2000). Lisa Nakamura, *Cybertypes: Race, Ethnicity, and Identity on the Internet* (New York: Routledge, 2002); and Lisa Nakamura, *Digitizing Race: Visual Cultures of the Internet* (Minneapolis: University of Minnesota Press, 2007).

10. Nakamura, *Digitizing Race*, 11.

11. Web survey respondent, "Marlene," December 3, 2002.

12. Dhavan V. Shah, Nojin Kwak, and R. Lance Holbert, "'Connecting' and 'Disconnecting' with Civic Life: Patterns of Internet Use and the Production of Social Capital," *Political Communication* 18 (2001): 141–62.

13. Web survey respondent from New York, "Phuong," November 17, 2001.

14. Web survey respondent, anonymous, October 19, 2001; and Web survey respondent, anonymous, November 21, 2001.

15. Web survey respondent from Australia, "Nha Trang," October 15, 2001.

16. Web survey respondent from San Francisco, "Sonny," October 30, 2000.

17. Web survey respondent from Toronto, "Ky Hien," October 20, 2000.

18. "Phuong."

19. Web survey respondent "Thuy Linh," November 21, 2000.

20. Web survey respondent "Long Thanh," May 6, 2001.

21. Web survey respondent, anonymous, October 16, 2001.

22. Web survey respondent from New Jersey, "Thi," March 30, 2001.

23. Arjun Appadurai's various "-scapes" are useful in helping me frame these flows. Arjun Appadurai, *Modernity at Large: Cultural Dimensions of Globalization* (Minneapolis: University of Minnesota Press, 1996).

24. New studies show that Vietnam has become quite receptive to cultural production in Asia, particularly from Korea: Viet Nguyen and Viet Le Nguyen, "Ghostly Stories, Haunted Memories: South Korea and Viet Nam," paper presented at the annual meeting of the American Studies Association, Washington, D.C., 2009; and Viet Le, "Pop Tarts: Intersections of Historical Trauma, Contemporary Pop, and Art in Korea, Vietnam, and America," paper presented at the annual meeting of the American Studies Association, Washington, D.C., 2009.

25. In addition to music, Vietnamese film production also attracted a new audience offering a number of different genres from traditional opera to modern situational comedy. Vietnamese films diversified the entertainment menu for Vietnamese immigrants, offering plots and storylines compatible with what audiences perceived as Vietnamese culture.

26. Philip Taylor, *Fragments of the Present: Searching for Modernity in Vietnam's South* (Honolulu: University of Hawai'i Press, 2001), 26. This music was not new per se, but rather it consisted of rearrangements and rerecordings of musical creations during the wartime era of the 1950s and 1960s.

27. Ibid., 25.

28. Like Taylor, Kieu Linh Caroline Valverde also explores the complex nature of transnational music, yet she gestures toward a more conciliatory, collaborative end product. See Kieu Linh Caroline Valverde, "Making Transnational Vietnamese Music: Sounds of Home and Resistance," in *East Main Street: Asian American Popular Culture*, ed., Shilpa Davé, LeiLani Nishime, and Tasha G. Oren (New York: New York University Press, 2005).

29. Sunaina Maira, *Desis in the House: Indian American Youth Culture in New York City* (Philadelphia: Temple University Press, 2002).

30. U.S. Department of State, http://www.usinfo.state.gov (accessed May 27, 2005); and British Broadcasting Corporation, "Vietnam Gets Morale Boost," June 20, 2005, http://news.bbc.co.uk/1/hi/world/asia-pacific/4104272.stm (accessed October 6, 2008).

31. Aihwa Ong, *Neoliberalism as Exception: Mutations in Citizenship and Sovereignty* (Berkeley: University of California Press, 2006).

32. Phi Ngo, interview with author, Baldwin Park, Calif. (August 21, 1999); David Truong and his wife, Jennifer Trinh, interview with author, Baldwin Park, Calif. (August 2, 1999).

33. Elaine Tyler May, *Homeward Bound: American Families in the Cold War Era* (New York: Basic Books, 1988, 2008). Also see George Lipsitz's illuminating essays in *American Studies in a Moment of Danger* (Minneapolis: University of Minnesota Press, 2001).

34. Duong Van Mai Elliott, (Minneapolis: University of Minnesota Press, 2001) *The Sacred Willow: Four Generations in the Life of a Vietnamese Family* (New York: Oxford University Press, 1999).

35. Andrew Heinze, *Adapting to Abundance: Jewish Immigrants, Mass Consumption, and the Search for American Identity* (New York: Columbia University Press, 1990); Elizabeth Chin, *Purchasing Power* (Minneapolis: University of Minnesota Press); and Lisa Sun-Hee Park, *Consumer Citizenship: Children of Asian Immigrant Entrepreneurs* (Stanford: Stanford University Press, 2005).

Index

Nhi T. Lieu is assistant professor of American studies at the University of Texas at Austin.